THE SANGAMO FRONTIER

THE SANGAMO FRONTIER

History and Archaeology in the Shadow of Lincoln

ROBERT MAZRIM

THE UNIVERSITY OF CHICAGO PRESS

Chicago and London

Robert Mazrim is director of the Sangamo Archaeological Center in Elkhart, Illinois, and also serves as the historical resources specialist for the Illinois Transportation Archaeological Research Program at the University of Illinois at Urbana-Champaign.

The University of Chicago Press, Chicago 60637
The University of Chicago Press, Ltd., London
© 2007 by The University of Chicago
All rights reserved. Published 2007
Printed in the United States of America

16 15 14 13 12 11 10 09 08 07   1 2 3 4 5
ISBN-13: 978-0-226-51424-6 (cloth)
ISBN-10: 0-226-51424-2 (cloth)
ISBN-13: 978-0-226-51425-3 (paper)
ISBN-10: 0-226-51425-0 (paper)

Library of Congress Cataloging-in-Publication Data

Mazrim, Robert.
The Sangamo frontier : history and archaeology in the shadow of Lincoln / Robert Mazrim.
    p.   cm.
Includes bibliographical references and index.
ISBN 0-226-51424-2 (cloth : alk. paper) — ISBN 0-226-51425-0 (pbk. : alk. paper)
1. Springfield Region (Ill.)—Antiquities. 2. Historic sites—Illinois—Springfield Region. 3. Excavations (Archaeology)—Illinois—Springfield Region.
4. Archaeology and history—Illinois—Springfield Region. 5. Lincoln, Abraham, 1809–1865—Homes and haunts—Illinois—Springfield Region. 6. Frontier and pioneer life—Illinois—Springfield Region. 7. Springfield Region (Ill.)—History—19th century. 8. Springfield Region (Ill.)—History, Local. 9. Sangamon River Valley (Ill.)—History, Local. I. Title.
F549.S7M39 2007
977.3'56—dc22

2006018787

∞

The paper used in this publication meets the minimum requirements of the American National Standard for Information Sciences—Permanence of Paper for Printed Library Materials, ANSI Z39.48-1992.

for Frank Robert Mazrim
1908–1985

Contents

Acknowledgments

One of the more interesting aspects of the discipline of archaeology is its ability to bring together people from a variety of backgrounds and perspectives. The studies and excavations described in this book were conducted over a fifteen-year period, and relied on the efforts and support of a number of individuals.

In the late 1970s, John Walthall, chief archaeologist at the Illinois Department of Transportation, introduced historic resources to the massive transportation-based archaeological surveys. Nearly thirty years later, that program continues to provide a constant stream of information regarding the frontier period in Illinois, much of which is present in the overviews found in this book. John has also provided me with a number of resources over the last fifteen years, and my perspectives on early nineteenth-century material culture owe much to our frequent collaborations.

As director of the Illinois Transportation Archaeological Research Program, Thomas Emerson was responsible for our work at the Old Village locale at Peoria in 2001, but perhaps more important, he has also managed to build a research-based environment in the difficult world of cultural resource management. That environment has both directly and indirectly fostered much of my work regarding frontier Illinois, and Tom's program at the University of Illinois will no doubt inspire new authors and studies in the future.

As the director of the contract archaeology program at the Center for American Archeology, Kenneth Farnsworth encouraged and supported a number of settlement and transportation-related studies, which were crucial in building an understanding of early land use in central Illinois. Ken opened a door for me nearly twenty years ago, has generously provided many hours of assistance in the field, and has served as a patient editor for much of my work in recent years.

Dennis Naglich, my excavation partner during three years of work at New Salem, has brought his skills as a field archaeologist to a number of my underfunded projects. During our work at Peoria, Duane Esarey, formerly of the Dickson Mounds Museum, graciously contributed his research into the French history of the Illinois River Valley, and we have shared many hours of inspiring research and good conversation ever since. Curtis Mann, manager of the Sangamon Valley Collection at Lincoln Library, has shared his research into the social history of early central Illinois on numerous occasions, and has brought his experience, enthusiasm, and friendship to many of the projects described in this book.

Richard Taylor of the Illinois Historic Preservation Agency brought me to New Salem in 1994, and still encourages me to see the people behind the artifacts. Dick's perspectives have been a valued addition to the work described below. David Hedrick, site manager of Lincoln's New Salem State Historic Site, not only made our excavations there possible and very pleasant, but also continues to support a framework for its integration into an important interpretive program. Thomas Schwartz of the Abraham Lincoln Presidential Library has initiated new projects that promise to further synthesize the archaeological information concerning Lincoln's central Illinois home with that of the written record.

Terrance Martin of the Illinois State Museum conducted the faunal analysis for several of the studies described below. Thomas Wood of the University of Illinois, Springfield, patiently assisted in the navigation of numerous county records. On many occasions, Gillette Ransom has contributed her efforts and boundless enthusiasm to our museum at Elkhart. The Chimento, Green, Isringhausen, O'Brien, Sullivan, Pasquesi, and Ransom families have served as conscientious stewards of important archaeological sites in the region. Robert Devens of the University of Chicago Press not only provided the impetus for this publication, but also contributed a number of important insights that helped shape the book. Finally, Cynthia, Frank, and Ruthann have provided just about everything else along the way.

Introduction

Journey to Sangamo

You have lived in the old house as long as you can remember. Each room has been permanently mapped in your head and is filled with more memory than furnishings. All corners are familiar, and each object has a story. With each passing year, you become less aware of the details of your surroundings, and the place becomes a comfortable blur.

Gradually, however, you find yourself looking at some of the rooms differently. You begin to spend more time in the basement—in areas that you had taken for granted for years. Not all at once, but over a few months, you begin to realize that there are rooms down there that you never knew existed; there are doors obscured from view by furniture so familiar that you looked right past them. One room, two, and possibly several more.

Inside these rooms are books. Some are written in languages that you recognize, and others appear foreign. Some water damage, some worm-holes, and missing pages. You begin to read the stories. As strange as the texts appear, these stories are about places that you recognize as familiar and close by—up the road, or behind the place you used to ride your bike as a kid. There are even a few stories about the yard behind the house.

Those hidden rooms, those strange books, and those surprising and slightly surreal stories, are what archaeology has given to me. Archaeology is a science that relies on objectivity and a controlled examination of data. But once one acquires these things—kind of like the rules of

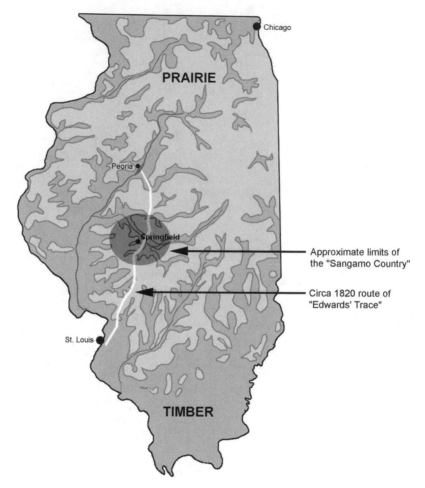

FIG. 0.1 Location of the Sangamo Country frontier and route of Edwards' Trace.

grammar in a foreign tongue—one acquires a strange set of tools that can be used for much more than just composing a technical report. They can also open up new points of view and new ways of seeing.

This book is about the recollections and debris of a particular place at a particular time. The place is a roughly 1500-square-mile area in what we now call central Illinois (figure 0.1). The time was a roughly twenty-year period in the early nineteenth century. The Sangamo Country, named after a shallow river that cut through the prairies, underwent a great change as a young American culture poured itself into an aboriginal wilderness. The change was sudden, and for a short time this place was the center of attention for many of those interested in living on the edge of the western American settlements.

The Sangamo Country was first colonized by American farmers and merchants between two wars—the War of 1812 and the Black Hawk War. In this region, both wars were essentially conflicts between colonial Euro-Americans (who had begun looking around Illinois during the Revolutionary War) and certain tribes of Native Americans, who had themselves only recently arrived. The landscape that both groups walked across, however, was littered by the debris of a century of French occupation, and by that of 100 centuries of many other Native American groups, most of whom we will never name. Twenty years before the Civil War, the area had been tamed. What was once a particular place with a particular history became connected and blended with other places and histories, to become simply another county in America's Midwest.

The archaeological excavations described in this book (as well as the histories that have been pieced together from the written record) help to better define a place and a time; they also allow us to see past the veneer of a familiar history and a modern landscape. When I began digging here—both in the ground and in the old papers—I did so to see through to a time when this placed howled from the crash of the frontier. One of the goals of this book is to remind us that this place (like many places) was once much different. Not only different from what lies before modern eyes, but also different from what we've come to expect from our traditional notions of American history. Archaeology has a peculiar ability to enhance and also to challenge the written word, to uncover the little aspects of daily life long since passed. It also returns an authentic ghostliness to a landscape so flattened by the plow and by pavement.

Central Illinois Now, Sangamo Then

As you drive north out of St. Louis on Interstate Highway 55, the Gateway Arch towers overhead. The gracefully modern gesture set in front of the western sky memorializes the trans-Mississippi expansion of American settlement, which essentially began in St. Louis. Below, the chocolate-brown Mississippi River, swollen from the water dumped into its channel at the mouth of the Missouri River twelve miles to the north, flows toward New Orleans. Occasionally a barge or two rides the current southward, with containers full of corn, soybeans, or limestone gravel.

Immediately across the river in Illinois looms a tangle of overpasses and exit ramps. Traffic is fast and congested. From the road, semi-trucks block the view of the traffic ahead, as well as the blighted, post-industrial landscape of East St. Louis located immediately below the elevated expressway.

The Illinois shoreline across from St. Louis forms the edge of an un-usually large floodplain, stretching ten miles to the east. Topographically, the landscape is like a hand print in the sand: the palm is the floodplain and the fingers are the various rivers and creeks that flow toward the Mississippi at the wrist. Beyond the tips of the fingers are the uplands.

A few miles northeast, the remnants of the industrial landscape grad-ually give way to marshes that surround floodplain creeks that were long ago straightened, moved, or just filled in. Near the center of this modi-fied landscape sits a massive, grass-covered hill on one side of the inter-state. The great lump is a landfill, created by enormous quantities of gar-bage generated by thousands of households many miles away—millions of buried chicken bones, plastic wrappers, shampoo bottles. Beyond the landfill, there are more marshes and the traffic thins out a bit.

Within sight of the bluff line in the northeast is another large hill, on the opposite side of the road. Known as Monks Mound, this hill may also contain some incidental garbage, but garbage that is more than 700 years old. The largest prehistoric earthwork in North America, Monks Mound towers 100 feet above a massive archaeological site that was a thousand years ago a sacred city, populated by as many as 20,000 people. Now, gas stations and old residential neighborhoods have gouged the edges of the site. At its core, however, stands the mound, and a patch of manicured lawn that is now a state historical site.

As the highway reaches the edge of the floodplain, it rises up into the forested bluff line, continuing northeast across a rolling terrain, inscribed by small creek valleys and ravines. Twenty-five miles from the river, the view opens up, and the landscape flattens again. Gradually, architecture succumbs to cornfields. In August, the fields create a sea of green, com-posed of a strangely perfect covering of corn or soybeans, each plant the same height and color. The crops are only occasionally interrupted by a few weeds or a fence line; it is hard to imagine who is going to use so much food. In November, the sealike plain is brown and barren, com-posed of naked, plowed soil, covered with the stubble of broken corn stalks. In the distance, tree lines mark the occasional creek valley. Along these small, shallow creeks are the thin forests of modern central Illi-nois, consisting primarily of young trees less than 100 years old.

Like much of the central Illinois uplands, this landscape is dotted with the shaded yards of two-story frame farmhouses. Usually painted white and about seventy-five to one hundred years old, some of the dwellings appear worn out or antique remnants of another time that has become history. For the world described in the following pages, however, such houses would be fancy, modern, and novel signs of the future.

If you were leaving St. Louis in 1819, the westward expansion that would eventually be memorialized by the arch was still in its infancy. The entire town fit within the shadow that would be cast by the arch 150 years later. Activity west of town was still largely based on the fur trade. St. Louis essentially marked the western edge of civilization. If you did not live there, you had probably visited town to buy something, as the muddy riverbank was dotted with wooden warehouses and retail stores. The town was busy with commerce conducted both in English and French.

There was no bridge across the water. Instead, the river was crossed by several flat, poorly made wooden ferries. Traveling on horseback, both you and your horse were charged for the ride. By the time you reached the Illinois shore, the sounds of the busy town were barely audible.

As you left the beach, it was not difficult to find your way east—there were several well-worn trails that meandered around the shallow, backwater lakes and through the tall grasses of the floodplain. The plain on the east side of the river was known as the American Bottom, a name coined by the French when the Spanish controlled the west side of the river, and the Americans the east.

On your ride across the floodplain, you would soon encounter a great mound that had been abandoned for 500 years. It was tree-covered, but clearly a relic of an ancient time. A group of Trappist monks had settled nearby ten years earlier, resulting in the unusual name Monk's Mound. Nearby, lay fragments of stone tools and large pieces of clay pottery in the freshly plowed soil. You would have recognized them as old, but you would have had no idea just how old they really were.

Approaching the forested bluffs, you might have noticed that the number of trails had diminished, but the one that you followed was well worn and easy to follow. You might remember the ferry operator referring to the route as Edwards' Trace—a reference to territorial governor Ninian Edwards. As you crossed out beyond the edge of the bluff and followed the trail as it hugged a timberline, you would have begun to feel the creeping sensation of leaving everything behind.

The uplands were known for their impressive expanses of prairie. If you were originally from Kentucky or Pennsylvania, you would have never seen anything like this. Oceans of head-high grasses, highlighted with patches of tiny, unusual flowers, blowing and swaying in the slightest breeze. Your revelry in the beauty of this scene would soon be tempered by the painful bite of several green-headed flies and by the realization that if you lost sight of the trail or the tree line on your left, you would be lost for days. The bright afternoon sun would soon become unwelcome.

In an hour or so, the trace would have dipped from the uplands down into a forested creek valley, where you would soon be greeted by a dark canopy of ancient oaks, walnuts, and hickories. The forest floor was free of brush and easy to navigate. A mile or so into the forest flowed a small creek—waist deep and fifteen or twenty feet wide—that had been visited for millennia. Down on your knees, you and your horse would drink.

———

Today, and about an hour and a half from St. Louis near mile marker eighty-five lies the outskirts the Springfield metropolitan area. The city of Springfield is the capital of Illinois, with a population of about 115,000. Downtown are the many state government offices and an imposing capitol building constructed just after the Civil War. Five blocks to the northeast stands an earlier, smaller capitol building, crafted of local limestone long before the war.

Tourists frequently mill about that old capitol, and even more visitors stream in and out of an old clapboarded house, surrounded by a suspiciously well-swept urban neighborhood. Most of the million or so people who visit the Springfield community each year do so for one reason: to hear stories and see places associated with a single individual who moved to the area about thirty years before the Civil War. The former home of a martyred president, the Springfield area is known as the Land of Lincoln. His old house has become a national park, and his name has become iconic.

Just north of town, out past the airport, flows a shallow, slow-moving river (figure 0.2). The Sangamon River is one of the larger tributaries of the Illinois River, stretching seventy miles east into the once prairie-covered uplands of central Illinois. Today, the river drains several thousand square miles of corn and soybean fields. That water empties into

FIG. 0.2 The Sangamon River.

the Illinois River, then Mississippi River, and finally ends up in the Gulf of Mexico at New Orleans. On a steep bluff crest overlooking the Sangamon, and about fifteen miles northwest of Springfield, is New Salem, a place designed to look like the past. Its cluster of log houses are replicas, built on top of an archaeological site that was also once home to the former president. Constructed before Lincoln's clapboarded house and the stone capitol building in Springfield, New Salem's log houses, log stores, and log mills were abandoned before the birth of our great-great-grandparents. Rebuilt in the 1930s, the replica log village serves as a reminder.

Today, it is almost impossible to look beyond the highways, mown lawns, strip malls, and the many miles of fields broken by machines each spring to understand that this place was once so remote. Nearly 200 years ago, this region underwent an enormous change, from an ancient landscape ever so slightly altered by the ebb and flow of ten thousand years of aboriginal culture, to the beginnings of a landscape completely rearranged by the offspring of ideas born in Europe 500 years earlier. We use the word *frontier* to describe this transition, but that all-too-common word is no longer able to convey the distant, strange complexity of the beginnings of us here. What was once the Sangamo—an embryo of the things we understand as our life in Illinois today—is lost.

Just three years after the first American farmer built a little house made of logs (in lands that he really had no right to occupy) the change was underway and unstoppable. Dozens of similar little houses were perched just inside the timber, surrounded by new clearings, stumps, and wood piles. Nearly two centuries later, all has been straightened, bridged, or plowed under. All but the tiniest, darkest corners have been long since illuminated. Like most places, the landscape has been tamed, and it is increasingly difficult to see the many previous lives of this place. Now and then, however, something punctures this veneer, reminding us of the antiquity of some things, and the extinction of others. Some bits and pieces—their garbage and our artifacts—become ambassadors.

The descendants of European colonists who became "Americans" with the coming of the Revolutionary War arrived in what we call Illinois over 200 years ago. They found ancient forests and vast prairies that had been home to many others before them. The Americans brought with them old ways, new ideas, and thousands of objects made in far away cities. Most of this book will be concerned with the buried remnants of this complex luggage. Ideas, traditions, and provisions were used to craft new homes, which for a brief time were untethered from both their ancient roots and their new democratic inspirations. By their very setting, in the forested margins of an ancient prairie about to change forever, these were remarkable things.

In large part, the structure of this book mimics the way that a historical archaeologist considers and assembles information when first approaching an archaeological site in Illinois. It is a journey that often starts in a library, leads to a hole in the ground, and ends in a laboratory. In part 1, we begin with an introduction to the arrival of the Americans in Illinois, an arrival that was announced by the sounding of a bell along the Mississippi River in the summer of 1778. That bell also signaled the start of the American frontier period in this region.

A century later, residents of Illinois began actively digging the ground in order to understand those who had lived here before them, thus introducing archaeological practice to the area. The earliest of these efforts centered on the excavation of ancient remains associated with prehistoric Native American inhabitants of Illinois. Not long after the beginning of the twentieth century, however, Illinoisans of European descent became interested in the archaeological record of their own ancestors. Residents of central Illinois especially wished to better understand and portray the frontier lives of Abraham Lincoln and his neighbors.

The modern process of archaeology often begins with a wide-angle view of both the archival history of a region and an overview of what is already known of its archaeological record, which here is provided in part 2. We begin with the cultures that occupied the landscape before the summer of 1778, including a century of French occupation and over 10,000 years of Native American occupation. We then move on to look at the first Euro-American inhabitants of the region and the ways that they settled the landscape they would later call the state of Illinois.

Part 3 introduces the background information—archival and archaeological—that historic archaeologists draw upon to interpret the remains of a particular site. This section of the book introduces readers to frontier-era homes and farms, and to the types of goods used by families of this period.

With background information in hand, we are able to focus more tightly, both regionally and chronologically. In part 4, our slow zoom descends into a more detailed history of early nineteenth-century Sangamo Country. Part 5 features tours of the archaeological sites themselves, and represents the "discovery" part of the process. These places, all within the limits of the Sangamo Country and all abandoned long before the Civil War, include homes, stores, taverns, and a pottery shop. Each of these sites was also part of the frontier community that Abraham Lincoln found when he moved to the region in the summer of 1831. In fact, he visited several of them. His presence, or the shadow that he later cast, often preserved their memory, ensured their survival, and prompted the visits of archaeologists nearly two centuries later.

PART ONE

Americans, Frontiers, and Archaeology

The Making of an American Frontier

They say it began with the ringing of a bell, down by the Mississippi River in a little town whose residents spoke French. It was early July, and it was probably hot. The river may have been a bit low, and the wheat would have filled the fields, waiting for rain. In the town of Kaskaskia, there were several hundred villagers whose parents and grandparents had built the little town around a mission chapel seventy-five years earlier. The mission had grown into a large, weather-worn church, inside which hung a big bell cast in France decades earlier. On the evening of July 4, 1778, it was ringing again. The Americans had arrived.

In the late winter of 1778, two years into the American Revolution, Lieutenant Colonel George Rogers Clark (under the guidance of Patrick Henry and Thomas Jefferson) began planning an attack on a British post in the far western Illinois Country. It was Clark's brother William who, with Meriwether Lewis, would ascend the Missouri River twenty-six years later, ultimately making the West that was Illinois in 1778 into the Midwest that it is today. From Virginia, Clark raised a company of about 175 men who were to advance toward the Illinois Country, each with the promise of a land grant of 300 acres in the far western region, upon their success of capturing the British post at the old French town of Kaskaskia.

The village of Kaskaskia was already a historic one by the time of the American Revolution, although most colonial Americans living on the eastern seaboard knew nothing about it. The French founded Kaskaskia in 1703 as a mission and fur trading post. At that time, Illinois was still considered part of Canada by the French government. The village had grown quickly into a stable colonial community, in many ways resembling villages in France built centuries earlier. The French speaking residents of the village encountered by Clark were second and third generation residents of Illinois. Most were descendants of French Canadian fur traders, many of whom had married Native American women.

Ten years prior to Clark's arrival, the population of the village had grown to about 900 (figure 1.1). In addition to those who farmed and traded furs, there were merchants, carpenters, masons, blacksmiths, tailors, bakers, physicians, and many slaves living and working in a village that consisted of three principal east-west streets, and four or five small side streets. At the center of the village stood a large church, built about twenty-five years earlier, on the site of a least two others. In its bell tower hung a bell that had been cast in La Rochelle, France in 1741. The big church with its arched ceiling, white marble altar, carved reliquaries, and large painting of the Immaculate Conception was the only structure of its kind for hundreds of miles. It was also a little slice of old Europe, surrounded by a wilderness none of us can know today.

In the spring of 1778, Clark and his men descended the Ohio River from Fort Pitt (modern Pittsburgh) until they reached the Illinois shore at the site of an abandoned French fort known as Fort Massac. Here, they climbed the bluffs into the forests of southern Illinois and began a 120-mile overland march to Kaskaskia, which was situated in the Mississippi valley. The trail was a poor one, and the company was nearly lost in an open prairie on the third day of their march. The men ran out of provisions on the fourth day, and on the night of the sixth—July 4th— they descended into the Mississippi valley, on the opposite side of a small river (also called Kaskaskia) from the French village. They quietly captured a small French farmhouse and prepared to advance on the British post.

As a result of France's loss of the Seven Years War in 1763, French Illinois had fallen to British control, although the British military did not actually arrive at Kaskaskia until 1765. Aside from a new administrative presence and new uniforms at the fort, little had changed at Kaskaskia; the place was still very French in its customs, religion, language, and history. The residents of Kaskaskia and other nearby villages were not particularly loyal to their British occupiers, but they also were known to fear the Americans, whom they regarded as desperadoes.

Clark's men crossed the Kaskaskia River in the darkness, surrounded the small village, and captured the British post without firing a shot.

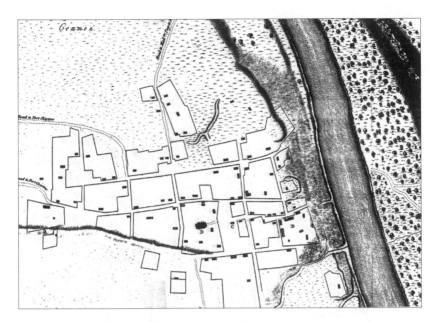

FIG. 1.1 Eighteenth-century plan of the village of Kaskaskia.

The British governor is said to have been in bed when Clark's men entered his quarters. Thus the Americans captured the village of Kaskaskia. Clark surprised the alarmed villagers with a simple offer: in exchange for an oath of fidelity, the French residents of Illinois would receive the same freedoms and privileges enjoyed by the Americans who now occupied their village. Their land and personal property would remain theirs, and most importantly, the activities of the Catholic churches in the colony would not be disturbed. On the night of July 4, someone entered the old church in the center of Kaskaskia and rung the church bell. The sound of that bell literally signaled the beginning of the American frontier period in Illinois.

Gradually, the old village began to be populated with American families—primarily Virginians of Scotch-Irish or English descent. Kaskaskia would serve as the seat of government as Illinois became an American county, and then an American territory. The location of the village, however, was a precarious one. The town had been established on low ground situated between the Kaskaskia and the Mississippi rivers, immediately south of a bend in the Mississippi. During the mid-nineteenth century, several floods began carving a new channel behind the village,

FIG. 1.2 The French church bell from Kaskaskia; the First State House at Kaskaskia collapsing into the Mississippi; and what was once downtown Kaskaskia as it appears today.

and into the mouth of the Kaskaskia. The subsequent erosion and widening of the new Mississippi River channel carried away most of the town in a matter of a few years. People moved away, some of the bodies in the old cemeteries were exhumed. The rest was left to the river, and the surviving stone, brick, and log houses tumbled into the water.

Modern Kaskaskia, relocated just downstream from the muddy beach that was once the original village, looks like most late nineteenth-century communities in rural Illinois. The brick church in the new village, however, is a direct descendant of the little mission established on the banks of the Kaskaskia in 1703. Few visitors manage to find the place, as it far from the beaten path of tourism. In a tiny museum at the edge of town rests the bell from the old church at Kaskaskia (figure 1.2). Enshrined in a little white room, the big metallic thing rests quietly, the enormity of its history almost completely muted.

The "Frontier"

While our picture of the "Old West" usually consists of gold rushes, wagon trains, and 1870s saloons beneath the shadow of the Rocky Mountains, it was the settlements along the Mississippi that defined the West for Americans following the Revolutionary War. When Lewis and Clark launched their expedition up the Missouri River in 1804, they embarked from the shores of an old French colony perched at the edge of territorial America. The Mississippi River was more than some water to cross, and was also more than a boundary removed by the Louisiana Purchase. It was the western edge of the West. As the Corps of Discovery began to push that line back, behind it swelled the frontier.

"Frontier" is one of those overused terms that tends to lose its meaning, conjuring stereotypes drawn from grade-school filmstrips and bad television. This is unfortunate, as the term refers to a remarkably complex and intriguing cultural phenomena. The frontier generally signaled a transition, when a particular society expanded its boundaries into what was considered to be a "wild" landscape. The ways in which that society began to transplant itself offer insights into its ideals, priorities, and its vision of itself and its future. Complicating matters was the fact that these landscapes were usually already occupied by another culture, which did not see the landscape as wild at all, and which had already called the place home.

From a historiographic point of view, our modern concepts of the American frontier are a little over a century old. Very near the end of the nineteenth century, Frederick Jackson Turner (a student and later a professor at University of Wisconsin), stressed the importance of a better understanding of the process by which Americans colonized successive wilderness regions of the continent. At the time, the last western frontiers in America had closed only two decades earlier.

In the forests of North America (regarded as blank canvases with no history), Turner and some of his students pictured a harsh, unyielding environment that stripped newly arrived pioneers of many of their ancestral traditions, as well as the accouterments of a dawning industrial revolution. The result, they patriotically argued, were societies and institutions that were new and distinctly "American." Such simplistic and romantic notions of the frontier were in part products of the Victorian era, and they also took their place in a long line of histories written by colonial powers.

In fact, what Americans of the late eighteenth century regarded as the western wilderness had a long and complex human history, stretching back 12,000 years before the arrival of Europeans. To many of those who moved west from the original colonies, however, the ancient aboriginal history of the place (not to mention the Native American societies that were still occupying the West) was basically part of the scenery. It was also actually quite evident (even in Turner's time) that the cultural traditions of the immigrants who moved west were hardly "stripped away" by the environment in which they built their log houses. Many facets of the cultural identity of the inhabitants of the western frontiers—where and how they set up housekeeping, what they ate, what they wore, or even the songs they sang after dark—echoed the traditions of their forefathers in southern England, Ireland, Germany, or Norway.

The term *frontier* was not an invention of historians—it was used by the very people who were living there. In most cases, the term appears to have been a geographical one. In early nineteenth-century Illinois, for instance, the frontier simply referred to the most advanced settlements situated on the edge of a wilderness occupied by Native Americans. Often, the word was used in conjunction with an attempt to describe the vulnerability of particular settlements to Indian attack. As the perception of that vulnerability faded, so did the use of the term. During the early nineteenth century, the United States Census Bureau also used the term to measure the density of new settlements. A region occupied by no more than two Euro-Americans per square mile was a frontier.[1] The Native Americans were not counted.

For our purposes, the term *frontier* is both a geographical and temporal one, used to refer to a brief period of transition (figure 1.3). During this period, Americans transformed what they recognized as a wilderness into a series of interconnected communities with organized social, political, and economic boundaries, as well as a working system of trade and internal improvements. In Illinois, an early nineteenth-century frontier community was characterized by settlements located at the edge of unsurveyed government or Indian-controlled lands. Within these frontiers were dispersed clusters of settlements oriented with respect to natural resources and topography (as opposed to land surveys or sociopolitical districts). These settlements were serviced by only embryonic systems of local government, reliable transportation, and surplus-based agricultural economies.

What would become the state of Illinois in 1818 underwent the transition that we call the American frontier between 1778, the year of Clark's capture of Kaskaskia, and about 1840. The transition did not oc-

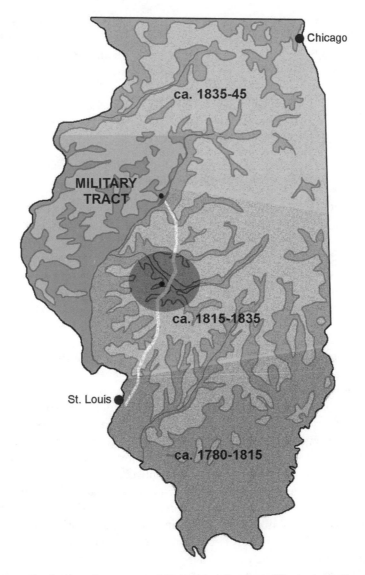

FIG. 1.3 South-to-north movement of the American frontier in Illinois, circa 1780–1845.

cur all at once, or uniformly across the state. The frontier moved over time, and within Illinois that movement was basically a northerly one. By 1810, the American settlements had surrounded the old French communities along the Mississippi River. By 1820, they had reached well into the central portion of the state, transforming the forests that cut through the vast upland prairies there. By 1840 in the northern part of the state, what had been Indian country ten years earlier was beginning to look much like the older communities to the south. Plows cut into old forest soils, new roads wound along timberlines, and bridges, mills, and the smoke from new chimneys appeared on the horizon. A landscape that had looked basically the same for millennia was about to change forever. Twenty years before the Civil War, we were everywhere, and the frontier was pushed further west.

The 1800s

Most modern Americans probably regard the nineteenth century as one era—the black and white time before electric lights, refrigerators, penicillin, automobiles, radios, and television. In fact, there were many eras of great change between the artificial bracket of 1800 to 1900.

The early years of that century are also much further back than most of us realize. From our viewpoint today, the tales handed down from our grandmother's grandmother still do not reach the frontier period in Illinois. The bulk of the items we recognize as antiques in the local antique store actually postdate the Civil War, and reflect technologies, fashions, and traditions that would have represented the future to a resident of 1830 America.

This is not to say that 1830 was as primitive as we are often led to believe. Throughout the eighteenth century, the middle classes had been offered an increasingly wider range of refined goods, technologies, and comforts that had once been the province of only the most wealthy. By the time the English colonies had been transformed into the first American states, many elements of what we would consider a reasonably modern life were familiar to families of even limited means. The beginnings of the factory system and an ever-increasing international trade introduced a new era of mass production and mass consumption. The result would change forever many ancient folkways, and give birth to the modern consumer.

The frontier period in Illinois coincided with the introduction of many new things, and the fading of many old ways. Mass production served to make an increasing variety of goods cheaper and less likely to be made at home or by a local craftsman. Pottery was imported from England, printed cloth from New England, cast iron vessels and tools from Pittsburgh. Window glass, bottled foods, and new medicines became cheaper and easier to get. At the end of the frontier period in Illinois, inventions such as the match, the steel plow, and the percussion cap reached deeply into everyday life. In a matter of a single generation, open-hearth cooking, practiced by humans for millennia, was largely re-placed by cooking stoves. Even the concept of time would change shortly after the close of the frontier in Illinois, with the coming of the railroads and the need to synchronize our clocks.

In other words, there has been a certain level of extinction since 1840, and there exists a significant gulf between then and now. That gulf, and those extinctions, are what drives much of archaeology, and makes the excavation of a 200-year-old house site not fundamentally different than the excavation of a 1000-year-old house site. The year 1840 lay at the end of an ancient road, and the beginning of the world with which we are familiar today. The colonization of the Sangamo Country occurred during this remarkable time.

Gaps in the Record

There are the libraries above ground, and there are those down below. Above ground is the world of the written record—of histories that were intentionally and self-consciously recorded. Below, the archeological record offers another form of history—an unintentional and often for-gotten one.

Paperwork from the early nineteenth century is reasonably abun-dant, although archival records from rural frontier communities of the period are less so. Much of our information regarding the structure of those communities is based on the kinds of primary documents that tend to appear upon the establishment of a new local government, such as court, deed, or census records. But this material usually does not reflect the content and character of the daily lives of those who were living in the new western settlements. Beyond the probate inventory (which listed the contents of a dead man's home) or the occasional long letter written to a relative living elsewhere, seeing into the physical uni-verse of the early nineteenth-century frontier is difficult. Because the frontier period of Illinois closed around 1840, we also cannot have a single photograph taken during this period.

In any given period, what is written down reflects only a certain por-tion of the realities of the time, and those writings also reflect a partic-ular vantage point. This holds especially true for the descriptions of the western settlements of the first half of the nineteenth century. Literacy on the Illinois frontier was spotty, and most of what was written down involved business accounts, court cases, and newspaper articles about lo-cal or national politics. Most of those who were actually living in the new frontiers were not particularly interested in recording what they saw—they were simply living their lives, much like today.

In some instances, recent arrivals to the western frontier would write detailed descriptions of their new homes for family members back east. Some of these letters were saved and published by their descendants later in the nineteenth century, when the stories of the old frontier were becoming more meaningful. In most cases, however, this correspondence was limited to a particular segment of the population—educated individuals from urban communities in the mid-Atlantic or New England states, or the "Yankees." It was also this segment of the population that was more likely to keep journals that described their new lives and homes. Like their letters, these journals were often published years later by their family, or were sometimes published as "guides" for would-be immigrants to the West.

Educated people from more urbanized environments, however, were the minority of the population in Illinois before 1840, and their views were often quite different from that of the majority of the frontier residents who had immigrated from the rural Upland South (Kentucky, Tennessee, Georgia, and the Carolinas). As a general rule, upland southerners were less literate than their occasional Yankee neighbors were, and this is partly why we have fewer descriptions from their point of view. Perhaps just as important was the fact that for the upland southerner living in Illinois, the new frontier did not really warrant describing. The settling of unknown lands had been practiced for several generations, and detailed accounts of log cabin construction and hog butchering practices would have hardly been entertaining to the sisters or grandmothers left in Tennessee. Moving west was second nature, and the "frontier" was simply home.

Many of the detailed period descriptions of the early nineteenth-century frontier were written by those who did not live there—and did not wish to. Accounts of travels through the new West were a popular form of literature during the early nineteenth century. While some of these claimed to serve as guides written for the benefit of new immigrants, most were simply travel literature, written by well-educated residents of the urban east (and a fair number of traveling English gentlemen). These accounts often dramatized the difference between rural, western lifestyles and those found in the older or more urban communities in the east. Such contrasts made good reading, and were aimed not at readers living in log cabins, but the book-buying public in the cities.

The writings of William Faux provide a good example of highly biased but richly detailed descriptions of the western frontier, as told by someone who really did not belong out there. Faux, an English gentleman farmer and traveler, visited the midwestern frontier in 1819. During his journey, he described groups of people heading west as "very wild looking and Indian like." The cabins that he stopped at along the way were described as "wretched," or likened to "miserable holes." Their inhabitants were usually represented as dirty and half naked. Faux clearly saw the West as something very different than what he was accustomed to: "This morning Mr. Ingle, on descending a ladder from his cock-loft bed-room, into which sun, moon and stars peep and all the winds and storms of heaven blow upon us, was left suspended by his arms to the chamber floor, while the ladder fell under him. Such are the miserable shifts to which people here submit without grumbling."[2]

Faux and some of his contemporaries seem to have found the entire landscape oppressive. Faux didn't like the noise *or* the quiet he found in the West, which at the time included Ohio, Indiana, and Illinois. He complained that the "everlasting sound of falling trees, which being undermined by the fires, are falling around every half hour, night and day, [producing] a sound loud and jarring as the discharge of ordinance, and is a relief to the dreary silence of these wilds, only broken by the axe, the gun or the howling of wild beasts." Thomas Hamilton described the Mississippi valley as one of "solemn gloom."

The pictures these authors painted of the new western settlements quickly became fixed in the imaginations of those who did not live on the frontier, wherever it was at any given time. That picture was also enhanced years later, by the very words of those who had actually practiced frontier living. For example, Clarissa Hobbs described her journey across central Illinois in 1824: "The woods on each side beset with Indians and wild beasts, my grandchildren, don't you think it took a fearless great grandfather and a brave great grandmother to encounter these perils of the wilderness? . . . civilization had reached this part of Illinois. It was a vast wilderness of Indians and wolves."[3]

Perhaps unbeknownst to Clarissa Hobbs's grandchildren, however, was the fact that there were actually plenty of American settlements in central Illinois by 1824, and the Native American presence had been driven to near extinction in that part of the state by the mid 1820s. The "vast wilderness of Indians and wolves" of central Illinois was, in fact, described by many visitors to the area during the 1820s as a proverbial land of milk and honey. In contrast to Hobbs's recollections are William Green's cautionary words to Abraham Lincoln's biographer William

Herndon, who was researching life at the frontier village of New Salem in central Illinois. Greene simply stated "I think you rather over draw the picturesque."[4]

The last quarter of the nineteenth century saw an explosion of published county histories in the Midwest, each with dramatic firsthand accounts of the hardships of the early years of settlement in a given area. The fact that these publications appeared in such great numbers during this time probably reflects the point at which those who were old enough to remember the frontier now recognized it as a way of being that had truly disappeared. In 1880, the publishers of a history of Sangamon County tried to explain: "One can hardly conceive how great a change has taken place in so short of time. In no respects are the habits and manners of the people similar to those of sixty years ago. The clothing, dwellings, the diet, the social customs, have undergone a total revolution, as though a new race had taken possession of the land."[5]

Clearly, the old settler societies and the publication of their stories attempted to articulate the gulf between the modern world of 1885 and that of 1830. But to do so, they often chose somewhat misleading language that tended to emphasize or even glorify their hardships. The stories glossed over the astonishing ability of American culture to rapidly transform, tame, and make comfortable millions of acres of aboriginal forest.

What were are left with, if we take the themes of these accounts at face value, are lurid accounts of the primitive, dangerous (but potentially lucrative) conditions of the West by nonresidents interested in selling books, coupled with pitiful accounts of the hardships and privations of frontier living by those who were telling good stories to their grandchildren.

Many of the passages in those publications actually betray such oversimplified and dramatized notions of wildness and hardship, however. Eliza Farnham, who was born in New York and who moved to Illinois in 1836,[6] observed that the homes of the original settlers of central Illinois were generally cleaner and more comfortable than people back east were led to believe. Another traveler, Charles Hoffman, found a "choice collection of books" in the corner of a log cabin that was "not at all different from the usual dwelling of the frontier settlers." He also noted that a "degree of general cultivation" was not necessarily uncommon on the frontier, but that it simply stuck out as odd or displaced. Thomas Hamilton contradicted many writers who observed a lack of goods, provisions, and niceties of life. He described the West as "the chosen abode of plenty," where provisions were so cheap that "no one ever seems to dream of economy."[7]

Some writers also observed that the wilderness way of life was not necessarily bound to practicality. Christiana Tillson, who settled central in Illinois around 1820, told a remarkable story about a visit to a home whose fireplace was equipped with only one andiron—the missing half of the pair having been replaced with a stone. Such an arrangement sounds like an example of quaint frontier practicality, but the story continues with the owner entering the house:

> he finally came in bringing a stone, which he threw down with an oath, saying he had had his eye on that rock for some time, and thought it would be a match for the one in the fireplace. He commenced pulling out the andiron, swearing at the fire for being too hot. His wife looked on tremblingly, and asked why he was not willing to have the andiron remain, as it was "a heap better than the stone." With another string of oaths, he jerked out the poor andiron, and taking it to the door, threw it as far as he could into the yard.[8]

William Faux had his patience tried by the less-than-practical frugality of his Ohio hosts, who placed an iron pot holding their supper directly into the fire, instead of hanging it over the flames using a simple pot hook. Suddenly, the meat and sauce "all took fire," and the meal was ruined. Apparently, his host refused to purchase pothooks from a local blacksmith, because those imported from Pittsburgh were cheaper. Meanwhile, the meal was consigned to the flames.

The motivation behind the move into a new frontier community was not always as simple as the desire to better one's life, at least financially. The reader can practically see Faux shaking his head in disbelief when he described a family who had recently cleared forty acres of timbered land (no small feat), harvested two crops in eighteen months, only to put the place up for sale because they wished to move "farther from the road." The English immigrants Morris Birkbeck and George Flower (who established a settlement in southeastern Illinois in the late 1810s), often remarked in their writings about the transient nature of the initial settlers of the Illinois frontier, and how brand new improvements (new cabins, herd of cattle, and freshly cleared and plowed fields) were readily offered for sale to new arrivals.

The deed records of such transactions, at least in central Illinois, suggest that selling out so quickly did not necessarily produce much of a profit margin for these first settlers. Instead, as Birkbeck and Flowers were keenly aware, it was a deep-rooted sense of wanderlust that seemed to push many settlers into the next frontier very shortly after their own efforts had created a semblance of "civilization." Gershom Flagg, who moved to Illinois from Vermont in 1818, summed up the phenomena: "the whole movement seems to be to the westward . . . and when they get there they go on beyond the West ward."[9]

The pioneer settler was also not necessarily a model of fortitude. Rebecca Burlend's own account of her immigration to Illinois in 1831 was intended to illustrate her family's frontier hardships, but also betrays an utter lack of preparation for what lay ahead. Her family obtained passage on a steamboat from St. Louis (a rather modern luxury—many families walked), which ascended the Illinois River and dropped them off on the shores of rural Pike County. Night had fallen, and to the family's chagrin they found no "formal landing place," no "luggage yard," and no one nearby to tell them how to get where they were going: "in a few minutes we saw ourselves stranding by the brink of the river, bordered by dark wood, with no one near us to tell us where we might procure accommodation or find harbour. . . . It was in the middle of November, and already very frosty. My husband and I looked at each other until we burst into tears, and our children observing our disquietude, began to cry bitterly."[10]

This is not to belittle the difficulties facing the first American settlers of the early nineteenth-century West. Those were, of course, many. But such hardships and dangers were for the most part well understood by those whose fathers and grandfathers had been moving west since before the American Revolution. Life on the frontier was one of subscription to an oft-repeated and reasonably predictable pattern of colonization. It was perhaps only after the passing of the postcolonial era, the coming of the early industrial age fostered by the Civil War, and the arrival of high Victorian culture, that log cabin living began to take on a more alien and distant quality for those telling and listening to the stories of pioneer settlement.

There is also a subtext in many of the descriptions of the early nineteenth-century West that represents a more subtle and astute observation about a fundamentally important aspect of frontier life during the period. By the 1830s, the newest western settlements had been visited by outsiders for decades, as each new community crept further across the continent. A reoccurring theme in the observations made by many visitors (and perhaps part of the attraction of visiting the new settlements), was the notion of obtaining a glimpse back in time. Or as the author O. E. Rolvaag phrased it, to return "to the very beginning of things."[11]

William Darby (a traveler from New York) remarked that he had encountered within a space of 300 miles, "human beings from the most civilized to the most savage," who recalled to him the "primitive times of history." Faux warned of the dangers of "retrograding" in lands "quite out of society." George Flower proved him right, when he was nearly attacked by a "savage dog" whose owner sat nearby, naked, and "quietly fanning himself with a branch of tree." Another traveler asked for a chamber pot, only to be handed a kitchen kettle. That decidedly unhealthy practice, in its own little way, represented an undoing of centuries of evolution of specialized ceramic vessels for specialized tasks.[12]

Chistiana Tillson described a Presbyterian minister working in the western settlements who found himself struggling to read his favorite Burns poems from within a world of hewn wood, all the while falling into "log cabin dialect" and "log cabin notions of things." George Flower added a touch of the surreal when he described a bed built of posts driven into the dirt floor of a small cabin: "said posts, driven into the ground by an axe, were sprouting buds, branches, and leaves." George Spears, an early settler of central Illinois who had immigrated from the Upland South in the 1820s, admitted years later that he had seen "things done and said in those days that looked very strange to me coming out of a civilized country."[13]

In certain respects, these observations were correct. The lifeways practiced in the western settlements of the early nineteenth century did indeed reflect a return to earlier times. The wide range of craftsmen found in the older eastern communities was replaced by only the most utilitarian blacksmiths, coopers, cabinetmakers, and potters. The well-established education systems of the urban communities in the east were virtually nonexistent in fledgling frontier communities. Markets for farm produce were prohibitively distant, causing a return to subsistence-level production during the first years of settlement. Cash economies were largely superseded by the ancient practice of barter—at least when it came to the purchase of basic goods and services. Perhaps nowhere was the resemblance to ancient lifeways more immediately apparent than in the nature of the frontier dwelling itself. Three hundred years of evolution toward segregated, specialized work and living spaces (often housed in spacious frame or brick dwellings) had plunged into the poorly lit, one or two room, neomedieval cabin, again centered on the hearth.

Yet as will be seen in the following pages, the frontier was not composed simply of things from the past—it was also well stocked with new comforts and fashions. Residents of rural 1825 Illinois could purchase the latest printed Staffordshire tea sets within a year of their introduction to the middle classes of London, but they boiled water over the open flames of fireplaces made of mud and logs. This contrast of ancient and modern ways—played out across an aboriginal landscape still echoing from 100 years of French occupation and 10,000 years of Native American presence—makes this twenty-year moment of the "frontier" such a remarkable and strange time in American history. Sangamo was just one of those moments in time.

CHAPTER TWO

The Arrival of Archaeology
and the Shadow of Lincoln

How travelers and immigrants interpreted what they encountered in the West varied. Regardless of how appalled or enchanted they were by what they found on the frontier, what they took time to write about in their journals was not usually the prosaic, but the novel. Meanwhile, the newspapers recorded the big events, and the lawyers recorded the deeds. Thus, we are left with few written records that include descriptions of the fundamental elements of everyday life. That written record, however, has never really provided a complete picture of culture, society, or the daily life of the individual. How accurately and detailed would our very modern records depict our individual daily lives, interests, habits, concerns, and traditions today? On the other hand, think of how many of these things are reflected in the debris that we place into the garbage can each week. It is the prosaic that is first uncovered by the trowel.

Shortly after their bell-ringing celebration in the summer of 1778, the Americans at Kaskaskia received a bill from a local merchant for twenty bottles of rum "for a refreshment after their taking possession of the Illinois Country."[1] With that bill begins the creation of the archaeological record of the American frontier of Illinois, and somewhere in the Mississippi valley lay the remains of those mundane but very historic rum bottles.

From that day forward, Americans came to Illinois, bought things from stores, and dutifully emptied or broke many of them. Goods became garbage and were discarded into an open hole, a ravine, or a river-bank. Two hundreds years later, their garbage is our artifact.

The Beginnings of Archaeology in Illinois

People have been digging up the garbage of other people for a long time. The first American settlers of Illinois quickly encountered the pre-historic remains of the 12,000 years of aboriginal culture that had pre-ceded them. These consisted primarily of chipped stone tools and clay pottery fragments found in the freshly plowed soil. Representing thou-sands upon thousands of tiny reflections of extinct technologies, tradi-tions, and beliefs, the enormity of these remains was basically lost on us until very recently.

By the late 1800s, antiquarians were actively digging into two-thousand-year-old cemeteries, searching for clay pots and stone tools buried by a variety of ancient cultures that they lumped together as "the mound builders." Some of these early explorers opened private muse-ums, or published their discoveries concerning these "lost races." By the beginning of the twentieth century, a new kind of folklore had been cre-ated from things found in the ground, deepening Illinoisans' sense of antiquity toward the place they called home: "In our trenches in the mounds on the bank of our great River, we are simply searching for a bit of history. Our heroes have no name. The Mound-Builder kings, if such there were, have gone down into the tomb enveloped in the silence of oblivion."[2]

In Illinois, one of the earliest bridges between nineteenth-century antiquarianism and modern archaeological science was constructed on a farm overlooking the confluence of the Spoon and Illinois Rivers in Fulton County. At the turn of the century, the Charles Dickson family discovered an ancient cemetery on the property while building a new home. Much like the antiquarians of the nineteenth century, they re-covered a wide range of grave offerings from the cemetery (including clay pots, stone tools, shell ornaments, and stone pipes), which they dis-played in their home.

As early as 1915, however, one of Charles's sons, Marion (and pos-sibly his brother Ernest) began digging into other areas of the farm. In-stead of simply opening the graves and removing the intact artifacts, however, Marion carefully excavated at least some of the skeletons he encountered, leaving the remains exposed *in situ*, or in their original po-sition. Why he did this is unclear, but such careful excavation of skele-tal remains is necessary if one is truly interested in examining the remains themselves, rather than simply retrieving grave goods. One of the basic principals of modern archaeology—the controlled excavation of culturally disturbed soil—may have been practiced on the Dickson farm as early as the fall of 1915, based on photographs kept by the family.[3]

Marion's nephew, Don Dickson, took an interest in these excavations during the 1920s. Noticing the worldwide interest in things archaeological that followed Howard Carver's discovery of the tomb of Tutankhamen in 1922, Don conducted his own excavations on the farm, and sheltered the exposed skeletal remains (which dated to about 1100 AD) under a tent (figure 2.1). Further, the Dicksons invited their neighbors and the local public to visit the ancient cemetery. The tent was soon replaced by a permanent building, which the Dicksons opened as a private museum in 1927. Before the Depression, the exposed cemetery was visited by tens of thousands of tourists each year. The family sold the site to the State of Illinois in 1945, and the original excavations were maintained until 1992. That year, protests by several Native American groups resulted in the closure of the burial exhibit, which is now covered by an elevated floor and a new multimedia exhibit.

The regional archaeological programs created within university anthropology departments were, in part, inspired by the Dicksons' finds, and the University of Chicago began excavating mortuary sites near the Dickson farm in the late 1920s.[4] Early scientific archaeological excavations focused primarily on prehistoric remains. Historic archaeology is a more recent discipline, and examines the remains of cultures living on the landscape since the time of written records—or about 1670 in Illinois. The first historic archaeological studies focused on contact-era Native American sites, or French-period sites such as fortifications.

Most early historical excavations were conducted for a single purpose—the reconstruction of a historically significant place. Archaeological techniques were employed to establish the locations of buildings, and to approximate their size and method of construction. Artifacts encountered along the way were either discarded or saved as novel relics illustrating narratives based solely on the archival record. Today, the discipline attempts to look at all aspects of archaeological evidence—disturbances in the ground, remnants of architecture, and the artifacts left behind by the site's former occupants—to create not only a picture of a building that once stood there, but the behavior of the people who spent time inside, and the culture of which they were a part.

Today, most of the archaeology that makes the newspapers in the Midwest is salvage archaeology. A series of federal and state laws are designed to ensure the identification and assessment of archaeological sites

FIG. 2.1 Excavations from the 1920s and displays at the Dickson family farm.

in the path of federally funded or permitted construction projects. These laws gave birth to the modern cultural resource management programs that are responsible for most of the archaeology in the Midwest today.

Unfortunately, as is the case with most such programs, the system is far from perfect. Due to vagaries of the laws, lax enforcement of those laws (particularly in urban areas), and frequent underfunding, plenty of significant archaeological sites that are legally eligible for archaeological study and salvage are destroyed by development each year. Further, most forms of private development do not fall under the preservation acts designed to protect archaeological remains. This is probably as it should be, otherwise modern construction would screech to a halt, and salvage archaeology would become a bureaucratic juggernaut. The result, however, is the utter destruction of hundreds of archaeological sites for every one that is professionally investigated.

In the early 1990s, I visited several construction sites where I watched helplessly as dozens of pre–Civil War archaeological features, and tens of thousands of artifacts, were exposed by bulldozers. Some were technically protected by the law; others were not. They all saw the same fate, however, as they were carted away to landfills. In an effort to address sites that fall outside of federally funded salvage or study, I began assembling a loose-knit group of professional and avocational archaeologists (as well as willing backhoe operators and other well-wishers), who would donate their time to salvage sites threatened by development. This ultimately led to the establishment of the Sangamo Archaeological Center, a privately-funded organization whose mission is to study and salvage pre–Civil War historic sites and artifacts, and to make the results of those studies available to the general public. The center operates the Under the Prairie Frontier Archaeological Museum, and curates one of the largest collections of pre–Civil War artifact assemblages in the Midwest. But the battle is uphill. Most of the excavations discussed below (both research and salvage based), were entirely unfunded and conducted on a volunteer basis, or were partially funded through private sponsors.[5] Of course, there is still plenty to do once the artifacts are out of the ground, and the publication of the studies, the display of the materials, and the long-term care of the artifacts and debris is an ongoing struggle.

Archaeology 101

The archaeological process examines human behavior through the study of what people have done to the ground, and what they have left in the ground. Archaeologists follow abandonment, destruction, and decay. Without some form of extinction or loss, there is no need for us. We try to tell stores that were never written down on paper, or to offer a different perspective on the tales and events found in the libraries and archives.

While archaeology has seen its share of treasure, usually found buried in the tombs of great leaders, archaeological excavations more commonly encounter the little things of daily life—whenever that life was lived. These details can be applied to broader cultural or social topics, such as international trade, changes in a particular technology, or the way people approached the various problems associated with making a living. The tools and methods used in this discipline can point to remarkably fleeting constructions: a campfire that burned for three hours five hundred years ago, or a single post that stood behind a barn for three months in 1822.

The experience of an archaeological excavation changes from site to site. Some projects focus on sites that are rich in artifacts, subsurface features, and information; these tell much about a particular place, time, or way of life. Others produce just enough information to be frustrating, speaking in broken sentences at best. Moment to moment, work on an archaeological site most often involves routine and procedure, punctuated only occasionally by what feels like a discovery. For the most part, one spends days, weeks, or months (depending on the budget) assembling tiny fragments of information. When stitched together, these sometimes create a momentary glimpse into the past. This glimpse will always be fleeting and incomplete, but the ability to peer into the past in any manner is a remarkable thing.

In the field, the archaeological process allows us to excavate and record culturally disturbed soil (and its contents) to reconstruct on paper what is removed by the shovel and trowel, and also to preserve the context of the artifact groupings found in that soil. This controlled excavation allows us to see, through changes in soil color and artifact content, sequences of events that altered the ground surface and the soil beneath it (figure 2.2).

In order to read the imprints of cultural activities left in the soil, one must first understand what undisturbed soil looks like. In the Midwestern uplands, a typical soil profile begins with a layer of dark, organic topsoil, usually ten to sixteen inches thick. Below this is a much more compact and less organic subsoil. In most of Illinois, the subsoil consists of a yellow sticky clay. While the organic topsoil has developed over the last ten thousand years (while people have been living in North America), the clay subsoil predates the arrival of humans in North America, and therefore will not contain artifacts unless it was disturbed from above.

Unless a site has been impacted by erosion or plowing, the ground surface that is visible today is basically the same surface that was visible in 1830—with the possible addition of a few inches of humus created by the decay of grasses and leaves. So, on a 170-year-old site, one will encounter 170-year-old artifacts immediately below the grass. If that site

FIG. 2.2 Controlled excavation allows for the distinction between undisturbed and culturally disturbed soils. The dark stain is a filled pit dating to the 1830s, surrounded by lighter colored, undisturbed subsoil.

is plowed, then those artifacts will be visible on the ground surface, but will have been moved and broken by the action of the plow.

Until very recently, Americans disposed most of their household garbage very near the house. On a rural, pre–Civil War farmstead, food remains, broken dishes, and broken bottles were usually swept up inside the house and deposited into rubbish piles outside or scattered directly on the ground surface. Concentrations of debris generated by the occupants of a site are sometimes referred to as "middens." Such discrete samples of domestic debris have the potential to reveal much about the diet and habits of a site's occupants.

At a site occupied for a long period of time, the topsoil can be gradually thickened by organic and inorganic garbage tossed onto the ground surface, as well as by the decay of grasses, leaves, or animal manure. The result can be a thin "layer cake" of soil and garbage that can offer a chronological look at changes in the habits of those living on the site (figure 2.3). In most cases, however, that thin, layered topsoil has long since been disturbed, either by the occupants themselves, by erosion, or by plowing—which has impacted the majority of rural archaeological sites in Illinois.

Human activity often disturbs the topsoil or subsoil. The disturbance

FIG. 2.3 An example of soil development associated with human activity. Here, the ground surface of 1790 is approximately eighteen inches below the modern surface.

FIG. 2.4 Examples of archaeological features common on early nineteenth-century rural sites: post holes (top), a log cabin footing (middle), and crop storage pit (bottom).

can be unintentional (created by heavy foot traffic or erosion caused by clearing away vegetation), or intentional, such as the digging of a hole or the building of a foundation. Soils disturbed by human activity can be read like a book. The simple act of the digging a post hole (or cutting through the topsoil and puncturing the subsoil below) will leave a scar in the subsoil for centuries. Often, such a hole becomes filled with a mixture of soils, as well as garbage, leaving behind a colorful footprint of the activity that occurred there. Any such cultural disturbance in the topsoil or subsoil is called a *feature* (figure 2.4). A feature may consist of a small posthole, a shallow pit, a stone-lined well, a brick-lined cellar, or a modern concrete slab.

If we could find Clark's rum bottles from 1778, they would certainly become important visual relics of the first Americans to arrive in Illinois. Aside from their historic character, however, most archaeologists wouldn't really know what to do with them by themselves. Single items have a very limited vocabulary, compared to the groups of artifacts that are related in some way. Better than twenty broken bottles from the party would be the entire pile of garbage of which they were once part. In the end, then, the archaeology of Clark's soldiers would hinge in large part on our ability to reconstruct their shopping habits.

Archaeologists do not generally find single objects floating in the soil—they find groups of objects that are interrelated (figure 2.5). We call those artifact groupings "assemblages." An artifact assemblage reveals the relationships among its individual elements, as created by a common context. This may be the fact that all of the artifacts in a particular grouping were discarded into an open pit over a period of three weeks, or from the back door of the kitchen onto the ground surface for twenty years. The best assemblages are those with well-defined temporal or functional brackets—two years' worth of kitchen trash from Mrs. Smith's house, for instance, or five years' worth of blacksmithing debris from Mr. Young's shop. The assemblages are chapters in a book, or sometimes they are the entire book.

Our twenty-first century lives have now become completely surrounded by objects that have little to do with the principal elements of survival and making a living. Before 1840, there were also plenty of nonessential goods, even in rural areas, but most household objects still revolved around food: the musket balls, knives, and hoes used in its harvest, the clay pots used for its storage, the iron pots used for its preparation, or the refined earthenware plates used for its service. Tea cups, table knives, dry mustard bottles, whisky flasks, and smoking pipes—all of these are elements of food, and the technological and social aspects of its consumption.

The emphasis of food-related artifacts within the archaeological record is heightened by the fact that many of the nonfood-related objects, such as clothing, furniture, and even the architecture itself, consisted almost entirely of organic materials, which after having been broken and discarded, were burned for fuel or quickly decomposed into the soil. By contrast, the aluminum, molded plastic, and synthetic fibers in our mattresses, kitchen chairs, shoes, and electronic devices will last a very long time in the ground. As we generally don't generally bury our garbage in the backyard anymore, however, future archaeologists will have little to examine on a single household basis. Centuries into our future, a home-

FIG. 2.5 Artifacts are recovered from collection units by screening the soil through wire mesh.

site from 1830s will be far more articulate to archaeologists that a home-site from 2030.

Archaeology at Old Salem Hill

Thanks largely to Abraham Lincoln, some of the earliest historical archaeology in the country was conducted in central Illinois. Shortly after Lincoln's death in 1865, people began visiting a lonely bluff-top pasture overlooking the Sangamon River, known to the locals as Old Salem Hill. The bluff had been the site of a short-lived commercial village called New Salem, inhabited during the 1830s by 100 to 200 people. One of those residents had been Lincoln, who lived there between 1831 and 1837.

Sixty years after its abandonment, its remains became a shrine—not only as an early home to Lincoln, but as *the* place that saw his transformation from a backwoods laborer into one of the world's great leaders. During the first decades of the twentieth century, the archaeological imprints left behind on Old Salem Hill were used to conjure a vision of a primitive past that soon seeped into the consciousness of millions of

Americans. The site of this little frontier village is now the busiest state historic site in Illinois, visited by over a half million people annually. Many of the icons and stereotypes of the American log cabin frontier were born on this little hill overlooking the Sangamon River.

Local residents remembered that people began climbing up the steep slope of Old Salem Hill about ten years after Lincoln's death, or about thirty years after the town had been abandoned. In the 1890s, a chautauqua was established across the river. The Old Salem Cumberland Presbyterian Chautauqua (like many such places in Victorian America) was part resort, part religious retreat, and part cultural festival. Some participants built summer homes on the grounds, while others pitched tents. A parade of speakers and entertainers provided inspirational entertainment for the visitors. Included in each summer's activities were pilgrimages to Old Salem Hill.

Across the river were the ruins of an old milldam, and atop the steep bluff, a narrow, oddly-shaped field was peppered with slight depressions. Those depressions were archaeological features, and they were the main attraction for the historically conscious Victorians who climbed Old Salem Hill. The most important of these features was also the closest to the river. Perched at the edge of the high bluff overlooking the water was a swale in the ground surface about fifteen feet in diameter. This was the eroded remnant of an earthen-walled cellar, once located beneath a log store building in the village of New Salem. After the building had been dismantled, the old cellar had been allowed to fill in naturally, resulting in the overgrown depression that greeted visitors to the site decades later.

At this spot in the summer of 1831, a twenty-two-year-old Abraham Lincoln got a job. He was hired to run a small dry goods store, then owned by an entrepreneur named Denton Offutt. Earlier that year, Offutt had hired Lincoln and his stepbrother to build a flatboat and ship a cargo of hogs and produce to New Orleans. Lincoln had spent the early spring at another small town located a few miles up river (Sangamo Town) building the boat. After his two month trip to New Orleans, he returned to clerk at Offutt's new store at New Salem. Very little is known about the nature of Lincoln's job, and it has been traditionally assumed that his role was simply as temporary hired help.[6]

Offutt's business failed in less than a year, and Lincoln, as the story went, found other things to do. Less than ten years later the entire town (save for a single residence occupied by the new owner of the sawmill) had vanished from the hill. The mill owner's house was abandoned around the Civil War, and by the 1890s, the place was a quiet field. The depression that marked Offutt's store—and the site of Lincoln's first job in the area—had become the principal attraction on the hill. In the center of the depression grew three trees—a sycamore, an elm, and a sweet locust. Growing close together, the three trees appeared to grow from a common root. The Victorians, thinking about the martyred president, saw symbolism—the North, the South, and Lincoln in between, uniting. Someone even climbed up the central tree and carved a portrait of Lincoln into the living wood.[7] The "Three Graces" was an early and significant Lincoln shrine, and it was essentially an overgrown archaeological feature (figure 2.6).

The Old Salem Chautauqua began to fade after the turn of the century. The popularity of Old Salem Hill, however, persisted. The wood carver had to retouch his portrait now and then, and eventually, someone posted a sign forbidding the taking of relics from what was a dying tree. Visits to Old Salem were still very much pilgrimages, and the place was regarded by many as almost a holy one.

A plan for an actual resurrection of the village of New Salem began around the turn of the century. It would require the rebuilding of primitive log houses where they had stood in the 1830s to provide for a more graphic illustration of Lincoln's humble beginnings. Former residents of the village, now in their seventies and eighties, were asked to recall the layout of town, which they had seen only briefly as children. Drawings and maps were made from old memories, and in 1906 William Randolph Hearst purchased the property, so as to protect it from development.

During the 1910s, a remnant of the Chautauqua Association, the Old Salem Lincoln League, began to execute the plans for rebuilding New Salem. As the few recollections of the layout of the village did little to anchor it to the empty landscape, the Lincoln League turned to the archaeological record. Each of the depressions visible on the ground surface, together with few scattered piles of soft mud brick and the occasional filled well, were direct connections to the town that had now existed in memory seven times longer that it had existed on the hill. In the spring of 1918, the Lincoln League brought shovels to Old Salem and began digging into the depressions. In doing so, they conducted some the first historical archaeological excavations in America, predating those at Williamsburg, Virginia.

The goals of these early efforts were very simple—to locate each structure and to approximate its shape and size. Unlike modern archaeology, the efforts of the Lincoln League (like many early excavations across the country) were more akin to simple architectural detective work. We have very little information about what the Lincoln League

FIG. 2.6 The partially filled cellar at the site of the Offutt Store on Old Salem Hill, with the "Three Graces" growing from its center, circa 1890.

found that summer. A few of the artifacts they unearthed were later placed into a new museum on the property. Only two photographs exist of the actual excavations, which were conducted at another Lincoln-related site within the limits of the village (known today as the Second Berry-Lincoln Store). One of these photographs depicts an open field,

FIG. 2.7 One of the few photographs surviving from the excavations conducted by the Lincoln League on Old Salem Hill in 1918. This is a view of the corner of a cellar feature associated with the Second Berry-Lincoln Store.

with two piles of backdirt marking the locations of their work. The other records a partially emptied cellar feature, which would have been located beneath the floor of the old store (figure 2.7). Seventy-seven years later, I would find myself photographing my own excavations, just behind that cellar.

It was the memory of Lincoln that brought shovels to Old Salem Hill in 1918, as well as 1995. Our work would have had no place were it not for the fact that the site had been preserved as a shrine to this particular individual. In fact, the archaeological site of New Salem has not been the only beneficiary of that memory. Much of what we know about the central Illinois frontier is a result of the Victorians' interest in Lincoln's early days. Lincoln's tenure in this area served as a shellac, inadvertently preserving a plethora of facts, stories, details, original documents, and archaeological sites that would have very likely perished had it not been for the fervent interest in Lincoln's life that began shortly after his assassination.

Most of what we know about two of the first three towns to be platted in the Sangamo County is based on recollections, reminiscences, and early histories that were inspired by Lincoln's life in these places. The frontier-era history of the third—the capitol city of Springfield—has until very recently been poorly understood, in part due to the fact that Lincoln *didn't* move there until after that period in history.

Immediately after his death, his former friends, business partners, colleagues, neighbors, and remote acquaintances began recollecting details about Lincoln's early life. Historians descended on the surrounding central Illinois communities, searching for stories about Lincoln's primitive youth, and the frontier community of which he had been a part. As reward for their answers, Lincoln's old neighbors, and the children of his old neighbors, were given a place in the pantheon of characters in what was an increasingly apocryphal tale of the origins of greatness. More historians would arrive to ask a new round of questions, and the stories told by children and grandchildren became more and more rigid. By the 1920s, the tale of New Salem—its origins, its residents, and Lincoln's activities there—were tied up in a neat, oft-told package. By the 1950s, they were practically cast in stone. Meanwhile, more archaeological remains lay in the ground, waiting.

PART TWO

Illinois in History

CHAPTER THREE

Before the Americans

There is a story, first told by an unknown French writer sometime in the late 1600s or early 1700s, about an event that occurred in central Illinois during the spring of 1680. Earlier that winter, the noted French explorer Robert Cavelier Sieur de La Salle had a small company of men construct a small, stockaded fort (remembered later as Fort Crevecoeur — or "broken heart") on a little hillock five hundred feet from the shore of a lake that the Peoria tribe of the Illinois Indians called Pimitoui. From this base, exploratory parties were sent to the Mississippi valley, and up the Illinois River, while La Salle left to replenish their supplies. In La Salle's absence, the men stationed at the little fort promptly looted its equipment, and deserted back into the northern woods of the Great Lakes. When one of La Salle's officers, Henry de Tonti, returned to the fort in the spring, he is said to have found a message: *Nous sommes tous des sauvages* (we are all savages). Thus, that autumn, Illinois' first substantial European edifice began to crumble and enter the archaeological record.

The first European settlers of what would become Illinois were French. Illinois was, in fact, French. Most Illinoisans today don't fully realize that this region was once a French colony that was *part of France:* French language, French government, French customs, French recipes bubbling in French pots. About fifty years officially, closer to a century unofficially. The French frontier began with a handful of mission chapels and small forts for the fur trade, built alongside several Indian villages during the last decades of the seventeenth century. Towns and farm fields came next. By the 1740s, French Illinois was feeding New Orleans, and second-generation residents of European descent were living in houses that needed repair. During the 1750s a distant war was fought against the British, and in 1763, the end of the Seven Years' War marked the end of so many plans in Illinois.

Those Who Greeted the Europeans

Long before they settled here, French priests and fur traders of the upper Great Lakes and Canada knew this region as "the land of the Illinois." The Illinois were a group of tribes (the Peoria, Kaskaskia, Cahokia, Tamaroa, and Michigamea[1]) that shared the same language and similar customs. They occupied present day Illinois, eastern Missouri, southern Iowa and northeastern Arkansas (figure 3.1). The French had heard of the Illinois at least as early as the 1630s, when several of the Illinois tribes were living along the Mississippi, and perhaps the upper Illinois River valley.

The Illinois themselves were immigrants, probably arriving from the east around 1600. Before 1600, lay another twelve thousand years of aboriginal nations, tribes, and cultures, settling and ultimately leaving what we now know as Illinois. The enormity of such a past is difficult to comprehend and describe. Most of us think back only two or three centuries when we picture the American past. This must be multiplied by forty to reach the beginning of these stories. Many assume that the stone arrow points found in the cultivated fields once belonged to the same "Indians" encountered by the likes of Captain John Smith or George Custer, but time is much deeper here. In fact, a Native American born in 1750 would have found a grooved stone ax or corner notched knife blade nearly as arcane as we do today—and rightly so, as it had been laying on the ground for thousands of years before its discovery.

Because of the great cultural tidal wave of the fur trade (which reached the western Great Lakes from the northeast in the early 1600s), European knives, axes, and glass beads arrived in the Illinois Country well before the first Europeans. Although they probably had little or no direct contact with French traders before the second half of the seventeenth century, the Illinois obtained these goods (in exchange for furs and enslaved members of other tribes) from their neighbors to the north and east soon after the beginning of that century.[2]

The gradual arrival of the first trade goods that trickled into Illinois signaled an extraordinary change. This had been a world composed only of reshaped elements of the forest—carved wood, tanned hide, burnt

Capitaine de la Nation
des Illinois, il est armé de sa pipe, et de son dard.

FIG. 3.1 A seventeenth-century depiction of a member of the Illinois nation.

clay, shaped stone, and the ancient customs that lay behind each of these things. Then, from some canoes, or wrapped in hides and carried on someone's back, the things of distant European cities arrived—forged iron, blown glass, and gunpowder. Brass kettles and iron blades altered forever the meaning of the old clay pots and stone tools that had been made for millennia. Ancient designs and stories soon began to change.

The earliest known meeting between the French and the Illinois is believed to have taken place 300 miles north of present-day Illinois, at a tiny mission on the southern shore of Lake Superior. In 1665, the French built a small mission known as Saint Esprit at the back of Chequamegon Bay on Lake Superior. The bay was a point of rendezvous for a number of Native American tribes, many of whom resisted the missionary's teachings. During the late 1660s, missionaries at Saint Esprit met members of the Illinois, who had come to trade in the area. In 1669, Father Jacques Marquette arrived at Chequamegon where he too learned of the "Illinois Country."

Two years later, Marquette accompanied Louis Joliet on a trip to explore the Mississippi, hoping to find that it flowed to the west and emptied into the Pacific Ocean. When they entered the river from the mouth of the Wisconsin in 1673, they were probably not the first Europeans to do so, but they were probably the first to write an account of their trip. Marquette and Joliet found a large Illinois village on the Des Moines River, near its junction with the Mississippi. That archaeological site was only recently discovered, and will probably paint one of the better pictures of the lives of the Illinois during the seventeenth century.[3]

The explorers followed the Mississippi as far south as Arkansas, and returned north after they realized that the river kept flowing south into the Gulf of Mexico. When they arrived at the mouth of the Illinois River, they ascended it, instead of following the Mississippi back north. One hundred and fifty miles up the Illinois, they encountered a large lake created by the widening of the river. The lake was known as Pimitoui by the Illinois, and would later be known as Peoria, after the band of the Illinois that moved to the banks of the lake.

Seventy-five miles further up river, Marquette's party found a large summer village occupied by the Kaskaskia band of the Illinois. They stopped only briefly in the village before returning to the north. Marquette returned in the spring of 1675, however, when he established the Mission of the Immaculate Conception. The little chapel, probably built of sapling poles and bark, may have been the first European structure in Illinois. It was Marquette's arrival in 1673 that marked the abrupt transition between 12,000 years of "prehistory" and the time of written history in Illinois.

Probably much like it had many times in prehistory, the Native American cultural landscape shifted dramatically during the mid eighteenth century. Shortly after the turn of the century, the Kaskaskia moved their summer villages to the broad Mississippi floodplain in southwestern Illinois, near the mouth of a river that would soon be named after them. Meanwhile, the Sauk and Fox moved to the Rock River valley from Wisconsin around 1740, and were still living on Rock Island (where the Rock River empties into the Mississippi) during the 1830s.

Also during the 1740s, the Potawatomi "displaced" the Peoria Illinois (through constant small-scale warfare) from the Illinois valley, and by the 1770s, dominated the Peoria Lake area. The Kickapoo, who had been hunting the prairies of northeastern Illinois for years (from their principal villages in the upper Wabash Valley), moved into the prairies of central and northeastern Illinois by the late 1700s. Years of warfare had dramatically reduced the population of the Illinois by the late 1700s, and the combined population of the nation, after which Illinois had been named, was approximately 2000 by the time Clark's men arrived at Kaskaskia. There had been as many as 10,000 members of the Illinois a century earlier.[4]

A French Colony

The account of Marquette's journey opened the Illinois region to explorers and fur traders, as had been the process in the upper Great Lakes for many years. Most of the earliest French missionary and fur trading activity in Illinois took place around Marquette's mission and Peoria Lake. La Salle built a second fort on a limestone cliff on the opposite side of the river from Marquette's mission in 1682, and La Salle's lieutenant Henri de Tonti built another fort along Peoria Lake in 1691. A new mission was also constructed nearby, but neither the fort nor the mission at Peoria lasted long; the lake was largely abandoned by the French priests and the military around 1710.[5]

La Salle's short-lived Fort Crevecoeur was already remembered as historic by the French by the mid 1700s. Its location was marked on maps of North America long after its demise. The Peoria area, however, remained primarily a Native American settlement during the first half of the eighteenth century. During this time, French traders conducted business and married native women at seasonal Indian villages located on both sides of the lake. Its strategic location half way between Lake Michigan and the Mississippi River (as well as the wild game offered by the lake itself), kept Peoria Lake a busy place for those involved in the fur trade.

The French government also had an interest in encouraging actual settlement of the Illinois Country. Occupation of the region by priests and transient fur traders was a start, but stable, year-round agricultural villages resembling those in French Canada or rural France were the foundations of a colonial community. True domestic settlement of Illinois by the French began during the first decade of the eighteenth century, but it began 200 miles south of Peoria, along the east bank of the Mississippi (figure 3.2).

The French ultimately relocated their missionary and fur trading interests to two new locales along the Mississippi, first settled by the Cahokia and Tamaroa bands of the Illinois. Missions were established in the fertile floodplain at what would be called Cahokia in 1699, and Kaskaskia in 1703. These were followed by the seasonal homes of French traders and their Indian wives, and later, by French families who emigrated from Canada.

———

The vast floodplain later known as the American Bottom is located within what was (and still is) a great hub of transportation created by the nearby junctions of the Mississippi, Missouri, and Ohio rivers. This, combined with the presence of their fur trading Native American partners and a very fertile alluvial soil, made the region an ideal location for the focus of the French colonization of the upper Mississippi valley. The French were not the first to figure this out; their villages were located very near the ruins of massive temple mound complexes of the prehistoric Mississippian cultures, which had flourished in the American Bottom 600 years earlier.

The cultural center of what would become the French colonial community in Illinois was the village of Kaskaskia. Nearby, the French government constructed Fort de Chartres in 1720, and a new village known as New Chartres gradually surrounded the fort. Fort de Chartres was rebuilt and enlarged in 1726, and again in 1755. The 1755 fort was built of stone, and would have been one of the more impressive structures in the Mississippi valley at the time (figure 3.3). The nearby villages of Prairie du Rocher and St. Phillipe appeared in the 1720s, and the village of Cahokia (which was technically the oldest settlement, dating to the

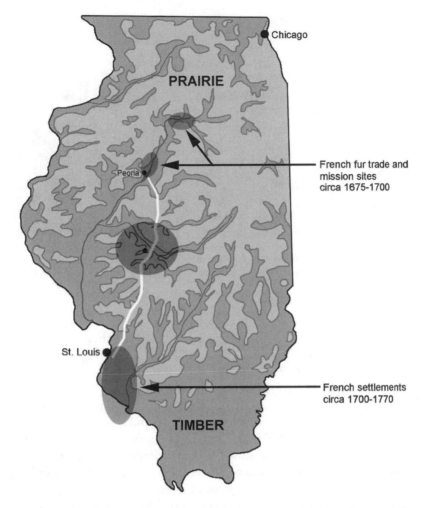

FIG. 3.2 Principal seventeenth- and eighteenth-century French locales, shown with the later limits of the Sangamo Country.

1699 construction of a mission there) served as the northernmost outpost of this French colonial community.

Approximately 200 French were living in the Illinois Country in 1728, and by the mid-1730s, their new wheat and cornfields were feeding not only the community in Illinois, but much of New Orleans as well. Meanwhile, thousands of bales of fur were harvested throughout the Midwest and shipped to Europe via New Orleans or Montreal. The

FIG. 3.3 The ruins of the circa 1754 powder magazine at Fort de Chartres as it appeared around 1900. Later restored, the building is now considered the oldest European structure in Illinois.

French population of the Illinois Country had grown to over 2000 by the mid-1750s. Although the colony was not particularly valuable to the French government, it had become a stable and comfortable homeland for the French residents of Illinois in less than fifty years.

Most residents of the French communities in Illinois lived in small villages composed of residential lots, long lots, and commons. On a residential lot stood a main dwelling (figure 3.4), and a series of outbuildings, including barns, stables, hen houses, and sometimes slave quarters. Behind this residential lot usually lay a long narrow strip of arable lands, which could also be used for wood lots or orchards. Such "long lots" are perhaps the most distinctive feature of maps of French villages in the Illinois Country. In many cases, a cluster of adjacent long lots were often enclosed by a single, massive fence of upright posts to keep farm animals from the field crops inside. The animals themselves were often kept together on a separate commons for pasturing, or were allowed to wander the streets and surrounding lands.[6]

Conflicts between the English colonies and the French government began with a struggle to control the Ohio Valley during the early 1750s. In the summer of 1754, French and Indian troops from Fort de Chartres assisted in the battle against Colonel George Washington's troops at Fort Necessity.[7] The year 1756 marked the beginning of the Seven Years' War (or the French and Indian War) between England and France. The remote Illinois Country was not considered particularly important to ei-

FIG. 3.4 The circa 1790 Martin-Boismenue House in Prairie du Pont, Illinois, is a rare example of an intact, traditional French dwelling of vertical log construction.

ther government at the time. When French Canada fell to the English in 1760, however, it became clear that things would soon change along the Mississippi. French Louisiana, including the Illinois colony on the east bank of the Mississippi, was transferred to the English in the Treaty of Paris in 1763, although British soldiers did not actually arrive to occupy the colony until 1765.

Following the British control of the villages in Illinois, many French villagers fled across the river, to lands then controlled by Spain. The French population of Illinois fell considerably. The British soldiers took control of Fort de Chartres, but the big stone fort had been constructed too close to the Mississippi shoreline, and it soon began to crumble into the river. It was abandoned in 1772. Meanwhile, the town of St. Louis (founded by merchants from New Orleans in 1764) soon rose to become the new center of the fur trade, conducted by French and Native Americans on Spanish soil. St. Louis would dominate trade in the Midwest for nearly a century.

Very little archaeology has been conducted at the sites of the eighteenth century French communities. Most of the early excavations at French sites have focused on rebuilding forts. Less than ten eighteenth-century French houses have been examined archaeologically in Illinois,

FIG. 3.5 This late eighteenth- or early nineteenth-century spirits bottle neck (with preserved cork still in place) was found at the site of the Gateway Arch at St. Louis, and is one
of the few artifacts known to have survived the construction of the memorial grounds.

and two of the French towns—Cahokia and Prairie du Rocher—are
still occupied today, with French names on some of the mailboxes.

The heart of the old French town of St. Louis became the scene of
one of the greatest archaeological tragedies to occur in the Midwest. In
the 1960s, the construction of the Gateway Arch—a monument to
westward expansion—almost entirely destroyed the site of eighteenth
century St. Louis, from which that expansion began. Although the archaeological remains of the eighteenth and early nineteenth century village had already been impacted by late nineteenth century warehouses,
the intact footprints of dozens of pre-1830 structures, and thousands
of colonial and frontier era artifacts, were bulldozed and carted away
to landfills (figure 3.5). The archaeological record was then replaced
by a subterranean museum with, ironically, very few period artifacts to
display.[8]

A French Outpost and an Old Road

The old fur trading center at Peoria would see some changes as a result of the arrival of the British as well. Probably because the area was regarded as remote even by Illinois Country standards, several French families settled on the west bank of the lake during the 1760s and 1770s. The locale would have offered the temporary opportunity to return to the old ways, in a community still populated primarily by Native Americans, and effectively out of reach of the small and poorly equipped British garrison at Fort de Chartres.

By the late 1760s, a cluster of French houses and new farm fields had been constructed near the ruins of a small trading post built a little more than ten years earlier. Never formally laid out, and occupied by a small number of intermarried French and Native Americans, this little village would become known as the "old French village" by the end of the 1700s. In 1763 a British merchant mentioned a French fort "of very little importance" at Epic (Peoria) that was manned by an officer and five men. In 1764, Commandant St. Ange at Fort de Chartres mentioned the theft of horses and slaves from French residents at Peoria. In 1777, British officials dismissed the French settlers along the Illinois River as "only a few Canadians who do not litigate because they own nothing."[9]

A second, more formal French village was established less than two miles downstream by a French Canadian named Maillet in 1778. The New Village, or La Ville de Maillet soon drained most of the population from the Old Village. By the end of the 1700s, it was said to have contained about fifty buildings, including a windmill, a winepress, several trading houses, and a church.[10]

The American Fur Company established a small post at the New Village in 1806, although the year-round population of the settlement remained small. By the early nineteenth century, the community was described as populated by "Indian traders, hunters, and voyagers," who had formed "a link of connection between the French residing on the waters of the Great Lakes and the Mississippi river."[11] It was the road to Peoria that would soon bring the first Americans into the Sangamo Country, seventy-five miles to the south.

––––––

Most of the movement between the American Bottom and Peoria occurred on the water—up and down the Illinois and Mississippi rivers. Canoes and bateaux of the seventeenth and eighteenth century were capable of transporting tons of cargo, and the lack of rapids and the slow currents of these rivers presented few problems for upstream travel. Further, throughout most of human history in North America, most people spent much of their time in the river valleys, where game, water, and rich soils were abundant.

People have always followed trails as well. Overland alternatives to riverine transportation would have been useful in times of drought, flooding, and unstable ice cover of the Illinois River. Also, a north-south line drawn between the American Bottom and Peoria communities shows that such a route would have been considerably shorter than following the riverbank on foot, when river conditions made canoe travel difficult or impossible.

The specifics regarding overland transportation before the early 1800s in Illinois are not well documented, however. Only recently have we begun to recognize the importance of such trails in the formation of early American settlements, and in particular, the importance of a single trail that formed a link between the old French villages in the American Bottom and the fur trading communities at Peoria Lake.

Before his death in 1907, Springfield historian Zimri Enos began writing an article about an "old Indian trail" that passed immediately east of Springfield (figure 3.6). He remembered faint trace of the trail from his childhood in the 1830s. Former Illinois governor and early pioneer John Reynolds had provided the best period description of the trail, when he wrote of its use in a campaign against the Kickapoo and Potawatomi during the War of 1812. It was from this campaign that the trail became known as Edwards' Trace after Territorial Governor Ninian Edwards, who led the militia up the old road. In the late nineteenth century, Enos was able to plot its course from Edwardsville (on the northern edge of the American Bottom) to just north of Springfield. He knew, as Reynolds and others had remembered, that the trail ultimately found its way to Peoria. Finally, in 1986, historian John Mack Faraghei reminded us of the importance of the road, along which the first settler of Sangamon County (Robert Pulliam) had built a cabin in 1817.[12]

In the late 1980s, I began to look at the land purchase and county court records of Sangamon County, and I found that the trail crossed through the heart of the earliest settlements associated with the Sangamo Country.[13] The fledging county government also recognized that the road's improvement was one of the first orders of business upon the creation of Sangamon County. Clearly, the old Indian trail not only predated American settlement of the region, but it actually helped shape that settlement.

FIG. 3.6 Views of ground-surface remnants of Edwards' Trace in central Illinois, near Lake Springfield (top, shaded) as it appeared in 1990, and at Elkhart Hill (bottom) as it appeared circa 1950.

In 1813, Ninian Edwards remarked that the French were using the road to drive cattle, and that Peoria was, in fact, not the end of the road. The trail continued northward, where it connected to another late eighteenth-century French community—the village of Prairie du Chien in present-day southwestern Wisconsin.[14] Like Peoria, Prairie du Chien was an old Native American rendezvous that was "domesticated" by French families after the British took control of the original communities. So, as the French villages at Peoria and Prairie du Chien grew during the last quarter of the eighteenth century, the old trail became an important link between those remote communities and the principal trading center of St. Louis.

There are even earlier accounts of travel on the road northward from the old French villages. In 1756 Jean-Bernard Bossu traveled from Cahokia to Peoria "through a beautiful, large prairie twenty five leagues long." On his journey, some Indian companions "used sticks to kill little birds, which they call strawberry bills." In the fall of 1721, a party of 400 French soldiers and Peoria Indians marched overland from Fort de Chartres to Peoria Lake in an effort to attack the Fox Indians located there. When they found that the Fox had fled, the troops returned south and arrived at Fort de Chartres exhausted from "a badly planned excursion into the Illinois prairie."[15]

The earliest reference to the use of Edwards' Trace that I have been able to locate dates to 1711—less than ten years after the founding of Kaskaskia. In the spring of that year Father Marest, a priest from the mission at Kaskaskia, undertook a journey north to Michilimackinac (in present-day northern Michigan). Marest described a slow and cautious trip during which his companions encountered signs of "war parties," and which soon made his feet very sore.[16]

Since the early 1990s, we have also begun to notice that several prehistoric sites found in the central Illinois uplands, which were previously considered odd and out of place due to their upland setting, are in fact located along the Edwards' Trace corridor. During certain periods of prehistory, intensive settlement of the uplands was somewhat unusual, with most settlement occurring in the major river valleys. Special mortuary or ritual sites too, are usually found close to the rivers and the centers of settlement.

Along the trace however, several intensive habitation sites, substantial cemeteries, and special ritual sites have been found, and their discovery came as a real surprise. Such sites include seemingly isolated Early Woodland and Mississippian villages in strictly upland settings, a unique and elaborate Late Archaic mortuary site, and an extensive village and mound complex dating to the Middle Woodland period that is located twenty-five miles further into the uplands than the nearest similar site.[17]

While our understanding of prehistoric settlement patterns in the uplands is still in its infancy (compared to what we know about the river valleys), there is circumstantial evidence that there was a band of activity across central Illinois that resembled activity normally found in the river valleys. It is almost as if the Edwards' Trail corridor was the equivalent of a river channel, passing across the upland prairies, with these sites situated on either shore. While much more survey of the uplands beyond the Edwards' Trace corridor is needed, it certainly seems possible that the general route followed by Father Marest in 1711 is not 300 years old, but 3000. And that old way crossed through the heart of the Sangamo Country.

CHAPTER FOUR

The Americans

In the fall of 1778, after their mission to capture Illinois was complete, Clark's men returned home to Virginia. They told their neighbors and their in-laws of what they had seen, and over the winter some decided to pack up their families and return west. These families would become the first Americans to settle Illinois. There was by no means a tidal wave of immigration—that would come later. Between 1779 and 1786, fewer than seventy American families actually settled in the region.[1] But this was the beginning.

In 1787 the lands bordered on the west by the Mississippi River, on the east by Pennsylvania, on the north by the lower Great Lakes, and on the south by the Ohio River were recognized as the Northwest Territory of the United States. Three years later, the county of St. Clair was created within the territory, encompassing the old French and new American settlements along the east bank of the Mississippi. In 1800, the Indiana Territory was established, and then in 1809, the Illinois Territory was created from its western half. The French village of Kaskaskia, over a century old at that time, became the new territorial seat of government.

The first American settlers of Illinois set up housekeeping in what still looked and felt like a French place. The antiquity of the region was immediately obvious to most. John Reynolds (who arrived as a child and would later become governor of Illinois) compared the strangeness of his first glimpse of the village of Kaskaskia—and the surrounding "quasi civilization"—to the effect of a view of another planet. The old church at Kaskaskia was a marvel to the Americans, and the "huge old pile," with its "storm-beaten casements" and "quaint, old fashioned spire" was described as if it was centuries, rather than decades, old. Even as late as 1810 Robert Robinson, a clerk at the land office at Kaskaskia, complained that he could not process claims for land by local residents, as most of the paper records and were in French, and so many of the locals spoke no English.[2]

A New West

When the Americans first arrived, they chose sites for the farmsteads that were located within or very near the old French settlements between Kaskaskia and Cahokia. The arrival of the first American frontiersmen to the Illinois Country was evidently not a pretty one (figure 4.1). As early as 1779, French residents of Kaskaskia complained that American soldiers were stealing cattle and supplies, and had begun to sell liquor to the local Native Americans. Even their fellow countrymen described the behavior of the first American colonists as ripe with drunkenness and violence, particularly when compared to the "extremely

FIG. 4.1 An English artist's conception of Americans in the Midwest, drawn during the late 1820s.

agreeable" manners of the French. At St. Louis, for example, Frederick Bates was intimidated by local Americans who were well armed with pistols, knives, and rifles, and by the actions of one "Bravo-Erratic" who had gouged out the eyes of another recent arrival.[3]

The ways in which the Americans chose to settle the landscape was very different than those of the French. For nearly a century, the French residents of the Illinois Country had settled in small, nucleated villages in the floodplain along the Mississippi River. Villagers lived in close proximity to one another, and each family farmed long strips of land immediately adjacent to the village, much as their grandfathers had in rural France. The result was a series of tightly knit communities (both physically and socially), surrounded by land that was left as it always had been.

Soon after their arrival from Virginia and Kentucky, the American settlers scouted out large tracts of land in the uplands overlooking the old French villages. These farmers had little interest in establishing residential villages, and instead desired plenty of distance from their neighbors. Most families selected what would become 160 to 320 acre parcels of timbered high ground on which to construct a few cabins for the extended family. The result of what one nineteenth-century historian proudly defined as "true Saxon instinct of ownership" was a diffuse distribution of the population: large tracts of land "claimed" by (and thus, accessible to) only a few. Of course, this method of settlement gave little room to the local Native Americans, whose seasonal patterns of land use had coexisted with the French nucleated communities for decades.

The creation of new frontiers in Illinois followed an oft-repeated pattern of migration that, by the early nineteenth century, had been practiced by rural Americans for generations. A family's move to an emerging frontier region usually began with an exploratory trip made by one or two members of the extended family. Fathers or young adult sons would scout out a region during the fall or early winter. Once an attractive locale was found, and if the family lived out of state, the scouts would begin to improve the parcel of ground, camping there for the winter while clearing trees and building a temporary shelter. In the spring, the scouts would return to collect their family and sometimes their neighbors. They then led a wagon train to the new homestead in time to begin planting crops. These extended family clans were often quite large, made up of several heads-of-households, accompanied by wives, children, brothers, cousins, and neighbors.

In Illinois, the first American settlements consisted of loose concentrations of farms occupied by members of the same extended family, and settlements were separated by several miles. These clusters of family farms often developed informal place names, such as Turkey Hill, Shiloh, Ridge Prairie, or Goshen. The shape, size, and boundaries of these settlements seems to have been based on the size of the families that created them, as well as the topography of the area.

The first American settlers in a frontier region chose ground, built homes, and plowed fields on lands that they did not and could not own. Part of the intrinsic nature of the frontier was the fact that the land had yet to be surveyed, mapped, and offered for sale by the United States government. Technically, the first residents of the frontier were trespassing, although such settlement was usually encouraged. The practice of "squatting" (or improving and occupying government wilderness land prior to its availability for sale) had a long history in the colonization of the Northwest Territory and was an integral part of the colonial process during the early nineteenth century.

The cultural landscape of the American frontier in Illinois was dominated by one cultural group—the upland southerners—or former residents of the hill country of Kentucky, Tennessee, western Virginia, northern Georgia and Alabama, and the Carolinas. These families of Scotch-Irish descent shared a traditionally rural lifestyle based on small scale, subsistence-based agriculture supplemented by wild game hunting and animal herding. Mobility and a fierce sense of independence and self-sufficiency were also important aspects of upland southern culture. Such traits were ideal and natural to the colonization of a new wilderness landscape. Early accounts usually agree that it was "backwoodsmen" from the south who first ventured into the western wilderness, living a transitory lifestyle as they moved in advance of actual permanent settlement.[4]

Settlers from the South were soon followed, in smaller numbers, by immigrants from the New England states. With a cultural heritage tied to the lowlands of southern Britain, these immigrants generally led more urbanized, educated, and commercially based lifestyles. Yankee pioneers are usually remembered as land speculators, town planners, and merchants. Of course, plenty of upland southerners operated stores and plenty Yankees practiced simple, small-scale farming. Broadly speaking, however, the two immigrant groups followed traditional lifestyles whose contrasts were often noted by visitors to the west. A sense of "us and them" remained strong between the two groups during the first half of the nineteenth century, and was vividly expressed during the Civil War.

The "Germs of Civilization"

By 1800, the focal point of immigration to the Illinois Country was St. Louis, where new settlers would first arrive, purchase provisions, and learn more about the surrounding lands. The small French trading town had become the economic center of the upper Mississippi valley, with direct connections to Paris and London via New Orleans, Philadelphia, and Montreal. With an economy built on the fur trade, St. Louis provided the markets and material necessary for laying the foundation of a new American civilization in the Illinois wilderness. For over sixty years, most of the goods sold in the frontier communities of Illinois and Missouri passed through warehouses perched along the bank of Mississippi at St. Louis. In this way, the wholesale merchants of St. Louis and their purchasing practices greatly influenced the character of the material culture of the Illinois frontier during the first decades of the century.

At the time of the Louisiana Purchase in 1804, there were nearly 3000 people living in and around the town of St. Louis on the west side of the Mississippi River. The character of the old French town began to change soon after the transfer of the territory. Between 1804 and 1816, 80 percent of the families moving into town were American. By the end of the first decade of the nineteenth century, St. Louis was still the fur trade center for the lingering French population, but was also the principal market for the imported and eastern American goods that were sought by the new American population of the Illinois Country.[5]

Immigration to the region increased greatly after the close of the War of 1812 in 1815. Attracted by the postwar population boom, many new American merchants rushed into St. Louis (figure 4.2). In 1816, the town plat was expanded for the first time since its founding in 1764, adding about thirty new blocks to the town. In 1817, the first steamboat docked at Saint Louis, signaling the beginning of much more efficient access to eastern industries and wholesale markets. In 1820, the population of the little town of St. Louis was bulging at 4598. By 1821, there were at least forty-six mercantile houses located in the town, more than half of which had been established after 1817.[6]

Across the river in Illinois, the first American commercial services appeared in the extended family settlements in the uplands. Before the appearance of actual towns, certain members of a given community would offer their specialized skills as a service to the community. This usually consisted of small-scale blacksmith shops, horse-powered mills, and coopering or carpentry shops. Such activities were usually conducted on the craftsman's farm when he was not in the fields. Families

FIG. 4.2 An engraving of St. Louis as it appeared from the river around 1815.

living along well-traveled trails often opened their homes to visitors. These informal "taverns" offered meals and a place to spend the night. George Flower described a new tavern and blacksmith shop in southeastern Illinois as "germs of civilization."[7]

New towns began to appear in the uplands during the 1810s, and particularly after the end of the War of 1812. Most were formally surveyed and platted for a landowner or speculative partnership. Many frontier era towns in Illinois grew up around a water-powered mill, situated on a river or secondary creek (figure 4.3). Saw and gristmills were vitally important to the early frontier economy, as they transformed the bulky corn crop into grain, thus creating a value-added commodity more lucrative to transport to distant markets such as St. Louis or New Orleans. Mills also created another important local commodity—sawn lumber— that was used in the flooring, siding, and trim of log and frame dwellings. Lumber was also necessary for the construction of flatboats used to carry farm produce to downstream markets.

Those waiting for their grain or lumber at the mill immediately became potential customers for other services, and mills were usually soon followed by distilleries, taverns, and dry goods stores. These provided the core of the commercial services found in frontier era towns. For this reason, many towns were platted around or adjacent to mill seats, for the express purpose of selling lots to merchants or craftsmen. In this way, frontier-era towns in Illinois were more akin to modern strip malls than residential communities. Many shopkeepers or craftsmen actually owned farms and permanent residences outside of the limits of town, and stayed in town only part time. It was not until new towns

FIG. 4.3 The Bale family flour mill at the foot of Old Salem Hill, as it appeared around 1870. Enlarged during the mid-nineteenth century, the original sawmill and gristmill was constructed in 1829 by John Camron and James Rutledge, and anchored the town of New Salem.

grew and stabilized that residential lots became an important part of their fabric.

If mills were the commercial centers of early towns, then taverns were their social centers (figure 4.4). A tavern in rural early nineteenth century America was not what we think of as a tavern or bar today. Instead, the tavern was more of a small boarding house, where travelers could spend the night, and purchase evening and morning meals. Taverns also served as temporary housing for local residents, as well as social centers in small commercial villages. In most cases, these structures differed little from a typical house, except that most were probably two-story. One or two rooms upstairs and one down were used for sleeping, while the main ground floor room of the tavern consisted of the kitchen and dining area. Often, the first frame or brick structure to be constructed in a frontier community was a tavern. Eliza Farnham, who moved to central Illinois in the 1830s, left behind a richly detailed description of a village tavern:

> The apartment was redolent of tobacco smoke and the fumes of brandy. In one corner was a little triangular box containing sundry bottles, glasses, cigar boxes, etc. In the opposite one a flight of stairs leading to the room above. The company . . . seemed to consist principally of villagers. They

FIG. 4.4 A nineteenth-century depiction of diners at a tavern. Such a scene would have been common in the Sangamo Country during the 1820s and 1830s.

were complimenting each other in various potations of brandy, whisky, and other similar beverages, betting on horses and candidates for country offices, and discussing a notable wolf hunt that had recently taken place, at which a fine horse had broken a leg. A few were rationally talking over different methods of agriculture adopted in the neighborhood, and speculating of the profitable results of each[8]

Farnham's distaste for liquor consumption obscures her narrative of the tavern as a social center, and perhaps because she visited during the day, as a place to find a bed for the night.

Along with taverns and mills, dry goods stores formed the nuclei of small commercial centers that served as "towns" during the earliest years of frontier colonization of Illinois. William Faux was told that merchandizing was the most profitable pursuit on the western frontier, "and the liberal professions the last and worst." Serving as the mercantile connection to the nearest urban entrepôt (usually St. Louis), such stores stocked a wide and eclectic variety of durable goods and nonlocal foodstuffs. In the country, the core inventory included foodstuffs such as sugar, coffee, tea, salt, and whisky. In the cities, dry goods wholesalers often created prepackaged crates designed specifically for merchants of "the country trade." These packages contained a variety of middling essential and nonessential goods, which had become traditionally popular in rural communities.[9]

A typical frontier community dry goods store probably consisted of a single front room fitted with rough plank counters and shelves, and a back room storage area. Large cellars were also important for the storage of valuable goods (such as whiskey) or foodstuffs such as coffee, sugar and tobacco. It was from small, rural dry goods stores that most settlers purchased cloth from New England, Staffordshire table and tea-wares, regionally made crockery, cast iron vessels from the Upper Ohio Valley, hats and shoes made in the nearest city, as well as household utensils, tools, and hardware. Foodstuffs such tobacco, sugar, coffee, tea, and salt were perhaps the most important part of most storekeepers' inventories. Small retail stores also sold locally made or imported liquors, either by the barrel, the bottle, or the individual serving. The latter usually required a tavern license from the county, however.

While some trade at the country store was conducted with hard currency, most of the purchases made in rural, frontier communities were based on credit and barter.[10] The same held true at the mills and other businesses. Tavern keepers may have conducted the biggest trade in specie. At the stores, however, customers could, and usually did, exchange a variety of farm produce for imported wares. The storekeeper then liquidated this stock at the nearest commercial center, such as St. Louis.

Perhaps more similar to the rural tavern or bar of today was the grocery of the early nineteenth-century frontier. The distinction between a grocery and a dry goods store is difficult to make today, but they were clearly seen as different forms of business during this period. While they probably offered a range of goods and foodstuffs, groceries were most remembered for the selling of alcohol—even though standard dry goods stores and taverns also sold liquor by the serving. It was at a grocery, however, that young men assembled for the express purpose of drinking, and it was generally the grocery that was blamed for fostering bad behavior in the neighborhood.

Again, Eliza Farnham left a rich account of a grocery located near her home in Tremont, Illinois (situated along Edwards' Trace):

> our next door on the left was a grocery—a groggery would be a truer name. . . .
>
> Many a day's tranquillity and a many a night's rest did this horrid place destroy . . . their sickening shouts and groans reached one everywhere.

Sometimes these diabolical orgies lasted two or three days and nights without pause, and then a time of comparative quiet followed.

But here they assembled, two or three miserable lost spirits from the eastern states, and as many Kentuckians of the lowest class; and here, hand in hand, they led each other to ruin [11]

Upon the outset of the War of 1812, the county of Madison was created within the Illinois Territory, encompassing the wilderness lands immediately north of the American settlements (as well as the future Sangamo Country), and stretching northward to Canada. By 1815, one of the northernmost towns on the new Illinois frontier was the new town of Edwardsville. The village was probably platted with the idea of accommodating a new land office, which was needed for the survey and sale of the still largely unoccupied lands to the north. That office opened in 1816, and thus the town was assured visitors. Reflecting the land office-related activity, Gershom Flagg observed that by 1819, there were "enough lawyers to sink the place." [12]

Over the next several years, the little land office sent surveying parties into the vast wilderness that lay immediately to the north—including the lands surrounding the Sangamon Valley. At the same time, Edwardsville, platted directly along Edwards' Trace, would serve as a jumping-off point for those headed north to prospect for new lands. In 1819, Hooper Warren established the *Edwardsville Spectator*, which would become the first newspaper to serve the frontier communities in central Illinois. In 1826, Warren followed the tide of immigration northward, and reestablished his printing office at Springfield, renaming the paper the *Sangamo Spectator*.

PART THREE

Archaeology of the Frontier

CHAPTER FIVE

At Home, 1800–1840

While Illinois was known for its prairies, they were not particularly attractive to farmers arriving in the region before 1840. The beauty of the prairies impressed all visitors and new arrivals, but most understood that the beauty was deceptive. For the American farmer, these were hostile places. The head-high grasses were difficult to navigate, and offered no cover from the sun. They were host to biting flies and snakes, and low wet areas that could bog a horse down to its knees. Below, the root systems of the prairie grasses were ancient and remarkably durable, and would not be effectively broken by the plow for years to come.

The seasonal prairie fires were a source of wonder for newcomers, and many marveled at their beauty as well as their hazard. Settlers in the American Bottom would climb to the peaks of ancient burial mounds to watch the fires burn on the horizon. Gershom Flagg observed that the fires could burn across the landscape as fast as a horse could run. It was also the annual fires that burned away new tree growth, and kept the timberline along the creeks and rivers stable for centuries. Visitors also remarked on the barren landscape left behind after a fire: "I can conceive nothing more desolate than the appearance of that boundless plain. The fires had traversed it in the autumn as far as the eye could reach . . . the black and charred surface was all that met our vision." [1]

Unlike the French and Native Americans before them, the Americans also avoided low areas, believing standing water to be the source of bad air (or "miasmas") thought to cause common illnesses such as bilious fever or the ague. New immigrants warned family members in the east of the "sickly season" (during the hot and humid months of July and August) when mysterious fogs brought illness from "a green poison looking scum" on stagnant waters.² In fact, it wasn't the fog, it was the mosquitoes in the fog that brought malaria, crippling new communities during the late summer and early fall.

The first American farmers in Illinois usually chose level, well-drained ground situated just inside the forest, with access to both a nearby creek and the open prairie. The forest, of course, offered the wood necessary for fuel and construction, and provided ground that was easier to cultivate than the root-bound soils of the open prairie. The nearby prairies, however, offered grazing lands for animals, and the edges of the prairies themselves formed lines of navigation in what were still poorly understood lands.

An average farm situated on an eighty-acre parcel probably had about ten to twenty acres in cultivation during the 1810s. This grew to twenty to forty acres during the 1820s and '30s, depending on how long the family had been there, and how much help they had in the fields. The cultivated ground was usually divided into several fields, located on the periphery of the timber, and enclosed with a split rail fence to keep the hogs and cattle out of the crops. Corn was the dominant crop in the fields, supplemented by vegetable gardens close to the house, and usually by a stand of fruit trees. Livestock was allowed to free range during the frontier period, and there were few enclosed pastures in early Illinois.

The farming practices of frontier Illinois were dominated by the traditions of the Upland South. Families from the southern hill country practiced small-scale, subsistence based agriculture that was composed primarily of pork and corn products and supplemented by wild game. Travelers' accounts, daybooks, and diaries all speak of a diet overwhelmingly dominated by pork. Many travelers wearily recalled having been served bacon morning, noon, and night on the western frontier. Pork was easily preserved through salting and smoking, and thus provided a reliable foodstuff. Lard was also nearly as important as the meat obtained from the butchered animals, and used in so many aspects of upland southern cooking.

Beef cattle, on the other hand, appear to have been few on frontier-era upland farmsteads. Likewise, dairying traditions were very minimal amongst transplanted southerners, particularly when compared to those from the mid-Atlantic or New England states. Cheese making was rare in households of southern descent, and lard usually replaced butter for frying, browning, or baking. A few cows were kept on hand for milk and occasional slaughter. Families from the east, however, probably kept more cattle, and practiced small-scale dairy production such as butter making.

Chickens were an important part of the local diet, and would have been underfoot at most farmsteads, as well as in town. Most accounts suggest that chicken was usually fried in the lard rendered from the slaughter of pigs. The most common wild game in the Illinois diet was venison, wild turkey, and river fish, as well as small mammals such as squirrels and rabbits. From period accounts, it appears that both southerners and those from New England supplemented their diets with these foods. From an archaeological perspective, however, it seems that those supplements were quickly eclipsed by domesticated animals in the diets of both ethnic groups.

From the fields, the most important crop in the upland southern diet was corn. Corn meal had been used in bread making in their homes for generations, and in frontier Illinois, wheat bread was uncommon. This contrasted sharply with the French farms of the eighteenth century, where wheat was an important staple and export crop. The dominance of corn meal also contrasted the dietary heritage of those from New England. However, it does not appear that immigrants from the east brought intensive wheat production with them to Illinois during the frontier period. This was probably due to a lack of infrastructure to support the production and sale of wheat flour, which did not become common until after the close of the frontier period in most Illinois communities. Corn also produced another important southern food staple — grain alcohol. Still houses were common in frontier communities, and whisky was served with meals, as well as a recreational beverage. In 1823, Gershom Flagg reported a field of corn "not of our common sort," but grown from seed brought from the Mandan Indians living in the northern plains, along the upper Missouri River.[3]

Families from the east did not match their southern neighbors' enthusiasm for whisky either, but there is also little evidence of beer making in frontier era communities. A brewer was working in the English settlement of Wanborough in the early 1820s,[4] but it was German immigrants (who arrived in large numbers during the 1830s) who would establish the first significant breweries in central Illinois. There is both archival and archaeological evidence that southerners and easterners consumed small amounts of French wine out in the country as well.

Gardens produced a variety of vegetables, many of which could be held over for use during the winter months. While sugar was available at the local stores, honey was perhaps the most common sweetener during the early years of the frontier, particularly on upland southern farmsteads. In fact, some of the earliest expeditions in the Sangamo Country were led in search of honey. Peter Hill, whose family moved into central Illinois in the 1810s, recalled rubbing honey "on anything we wanted."[5] Vinegar was used in pickling meats and certain vegetables. Both coffee and tea were consumed, and local storekeepers imported both. Period accounts suggest that coffee was more prevalent than tea on the western frontier, and those from the east took the preparation and consumption of afternoon tea more seriously.

With the corn in the fields, apples on the trees, and pigs foraging in the woods, life on the upland southern farm was reasonably quiet for much of the year, particularly in the eyes of those from New England. Gershom Flagg remarked in a letter back home that "the people of this territory . . . do the least work I believe of any people in the world."[6]

Houses

In Illinois, a building from the 1820s is a rare and wonderful thing. Much of the architecture of the frontier was (by the very nature of its setting) fleeting, temporary, or poorly built. As the Americans pushed out into the uplands north of the old French villages, most of the buildings they built first were of horizontal log construction—log cabins. This is not because they did not know how to build frame or brick houses; rather, horizontal log architecture simply came first on the frontier. A log building was easy to build, and required only trees, mud, some stone, and a few days of hard work.

Horizontal log construction is thought to have been introduced by German immigrants in Pennsylvania, although Scotch-Irish immigrants further to the south immediately adopted this form of quick and simple architecture. As most residents of the western frontier moved several times in one generation, such dwellings were simply the most appropriate shelter for this form of colonial lifestyle (figure 5.1).

Most log houses built in central Illinois during the 1820s and 1830s were regarded as temporary by their builders. If a family found themselves in an area that did not suit them (or more commonly a place that was considered a temporary stop), then a log house was a practical, minimal investment. From this perspective, one can compare the log cabin of 1820 to the trailer home of 1980.

If a family decided to remain in a community as it passed through its initial era of settlement and began to stabilize, the cabin was usually replaced by a frame house. In Illinois, a lot of log cabins were replaced

FIG. 5.1 Early nineteenth-century log dwellings in central Illinois that survived into the late nineteenth century (top) and late twentieth century (middle, bottom). Note the door, sealed window, and frame additions to the middle example, and the central breezeway and fireplace cutout in the lower example.

during the 1830s and 1840s. In some cases, the family would simply build a new house right in front of the old one, using the old cabin for a kitchen or for storage until it finally fell down. In other cases, the log house was enlarged by successive frame additions, tripling or quadrupling the size of the house, and completely obscuring all evidence of its log core (figure 5.2). Better for archaeology is the family that decided to relocate the house well away from the original, leaving behind an archaeological signature of their frontier tenure of the property that would not be impacted by later activities.

Aside from the occasional survivor that provides more specific or idiosyncratic details, we know only the basics about early nineteenth-century log houses in Illinois. Most were constructed before the invention of photography, and were not considered worth documenting once photography arrived. Much of what we now know about dwellings from the early nineteenth century come from period descriptions, often written by visitors from the east who did not live in log houses themselves. By the onset of the Civil War, few were built in Illinois, and by the late nineteenth century, those that remained were becoming novelties.

The construction of a small log dwelling began with the clearing and leveling of a small patch of ground, and the creation of some form of foundation. This could be a continuous foundation of stone or brick, or more commonly, a series of stone or wooden piers. This was followed by the felling of enough mature trees to make forty or fifty logs for the four walls. In central Illinois, these were usually oaks. The logs were either hewn square, or were left round. The flat surfaces of hewn logs, however, fitted more tightly together and presented a more finished appearance. The ends of the logs were then notched and fitted together at the corners of the buildings, making for a very stable structure.

To keep out the weather, the gaps between the logs were chinked with stones or wood scraps and filled with clay. Many log buildings would have been covered in milled or hand-ryed siding, making them more weather tight, and also giving them a more finished appearance. Coated in a few layers of whitewash, these log cabins would have looked much less primitive than we imagine them today. Also contrasting with our modern notions of pioneer life is the fact that many log houses were not necessarily built by their occupants. Period accounts commonly refer to property owners hiring local carpenters to build their houses.

Most log dwellings were essentially small rectangles, measuring at the smallest twelve by fourteen feet, or more commonly sixteen by twenty or eighteen by twenty-two feet. Most were probably one story high, or more accurately, a story and half. The ground floor was usually

FIG. 5.2 Not all log houses looked primitive, as seen in this sided and whitewashed example (top). Below is a circa 1870 rendering of a log dwelling in Sangamon County, modernized during the mid-nineteenth century by frame additions. Note the log outbuilding on the right.

constructed as a single room, which was then often divided into two rooms by a partition of planks. The house was fitted with one or two doorways, and most had at least one or two windows, providing light in what was always a dimly-lit space. We know less of the construction of the window frames originally used in log houses of the 1820s or 1830s in Illinois, simply because they were usually replaced during the mid-nineteenth century. Houses of the period may have been fitted with fixed sash, single-hung, casement, or sliding sash windows. The window-panes themselves, shipped from the upper Ohio Valley by the 1810s, generally measured eight by ten inches.

The attic or loft space, accessed by a ladder, served as a sleeping area or storage area, depending on how many people were living in the building (figure 5.3). Eliza Farnham remembered spending a night in such a loft during July, which "afforded about as rational a prospect of re-pose . . . as the engine room of a steamboat," and was inhabited by "not over a million mosquitoes."[7] Two story log structures were somewhat common, providing more formal sleeping rooms that were accessed by narrow "boxed" or corner stairway. The log core of the home was often enlarged with small frame additions that provided extra bedrooms or more storage. In time, the building could be surrounded on three sides by such additions.

The fireplace was the center of the log home before 1840, as it had been since the Middle Ages in Europe. In Illinois, fireplaces were usu-ally positioned on the gabled end of the building, and in the earliest buildings, chimneys were often constructed of logs—like the rest of the house. Cats' clay chimneys were fireproofed with a coating of clay on the interior of the lower portions of the chimney and firebox. The clay soon baked hard, but eventually loosened and fell into the fire, requiring oc-casional upkeep. While this sounds like architecture borne of hardship, this was not necessarily the case. Brick and stone were available, as was the time and expertise to construct a durable chimney. A log and clay chimney represented a *choice*.

Most of the fireboxes themselves seem to have been made of soft mud brick, although log and mud fireplaces would have also been found in the area, particularly during the early years of settlement. Christiana Tillson remembered having her log chimney replaced with a brick one, a few years after the construction of the house. In front of the fireplace, a brick or stone hearth kept sparks and embers from igniting the floor-ing and provided a work surface for cooking.

Although stoves for heating were known, they were very rare in Illi-nois during the frontier period. Those that were used were probably

FIG. 5.3 A ladder to the second story and trap door to the cellar in a log dwelling in northern Wisconsin. Note the narrow pole handrail and the whitewashed log wall.

found most often in a few stores or other commercial buildings. Christiana Tillson observed a "sheet iron" stove in an office in central Illinois in 1822, and there is archaeological evidence of the use of a stove in a store at the 1830s village of New Salem.[8] In the majority of the dwellings on the frontier, the hearth remained the center of the house as it had been for centuries.

While accounts of dirt floors exist, they are described in such a way as to suggest they were less common than wood flooring of some kind. Even the more crudely constructed cabins probably had floors made of puncheon logs. Milled planks were also abundant in communities served by a sawmill, and would have been used for flooring as well as doors, door trim, and built-in cabinetry. Interior walls were often whitewashed, or coated in a sandy, lime plaster made on site.

Under the floor, and usually in the kitchen area of the house, was a small cellar. Not to be confused with a basement, these were usually small earthen pits, accessed through a trap in the floor. As they were used for keeping foods cool and dry, pit cellars were more similar to a modern refrigerator than a subterranean room. Rebecca Burlend remembered seeing an earthen walled pit cellar that housed "two or three large, hewn tubs, full of lard, and a lump of tobacco."[9] Cellar sizes increased significantly during the close of the frontier period in Illinois, probably in response to more permanent architecture, and the more frequent construction of larger frame buildings.

Particularly in the eyes of those who lived in the cities, the log houses on the western frontier appear to have commonly lacked well-made furnishings. Travelers' accounts speak of "rude shelves" tacked to walls, or corner cupboards "made of clapboards, backwoods fashion." Rebecca Burlend described a "sideboard" made of several boards nailed together and supported by a timber in the wall. Regarding a bed seen in a frontier cabin, Eliza Farnham sniffed "the only thing that indicated the exercise of powers superior to the ingenuity of a beaver, was a wide shelf over it." Christiana Tillson simply gave up describing what she saw in the homes of the West: "If I had the endurance to write all I would like, I would tell of some of the freaks of one-legged bedsteads."[10]

The farmsteads of recently arrived settlers on the Illinois frontier (and particularly those from the Upland South) included few outbuildings. Eliza Farnham remarked that "Their cattle are no better cared for than themselves. No barns or outbuildings, except for a small corn crib, are constructed for years after they settle on a farm."[11] Corn cribs were probably some of the first outbuildings to appear. Because such structures were built entirely above ground, except for stone or wooden piers,

FIG. 5.4 A yard area similar to those of early nineteenth-century rural Illinois, surrounded by a combination split-rail and post-and-rail fence. Bean poles are barely visible in foreground, and plank-edged garden beds are to the left. The small structure on the left is probably a privy or outhouse.

they are usually invisible archaeologically. If the early frontier farmstead had a barn, it was often used for storing hay and sheltering a horse or two—hogs and cattle were allowed to free range. There is some archival and archaeological evidence of smokehouses, used for curing pork. These too, however, only minimally disturbed the subsoil, and are often hard to see archaeologically, save for a patch of burned earth.

Farnham attributed the absence of such structures to "the defective state of the mechanic arts," but also, and perhaps more accurately, to the "unsettled feeling experienced by these strange lovers of the freedom of frontier life."[12] Generally, the appearance of special-function, permanent structures and larger, multipurpose barns, appeared after the close of the frontier period in the late 1830s, reflecting the stabilization of the communities of which they were a part.

The yard surrounding the house had little in common with the lawns of the late nineteenth or twentieth century (figure 5.4). The spaces behind and around the house (and particularly those nearest the kitchen door) were heavily trodden work places. Eliza Farnham described the area surrounding a well as a "great theater of action for the mother and children."[13] Instead of a lawn, one must imagine stacks of wood, a rain barrel, some empty barrels, a pile of hearth ash and another pile of broken glass. Imagine also a well-worn path to and around the well, an open pit, and chickens always underfoot. As fleeting as most daily activities out behind the house were, they often disturbed the subsoil and thus left behind an archaeological imprint. Such activities usually escaped notice or comment by period writers, rendering them visible to us today only through the study of the archaeological record.

CHAPTER SIX

Under the House, Behind the House

Picture a vast, rolling terrain overlooking a small ravine and shallow creek. It is summertime, and it is hot and humid in southern Illinois. For most of human history, this piece of rolling terrain has been tree-covered. Paths through the woods lead to the water. There are deer, wild turkeys, small campfires, and some tents fashioned from hides and sapling poles. Then the American farmers arrive, and steel plows follow closely behind. In one or two generations, an old forest succumbs to cabins, hearth fires, and plowed fields. By the late twentieth century, the hills surrounding the little creek are mostly devoid of trees, replaced by the homogenous landscape of modern agriculture. Here and there is a small patch of mown grass surrounding an old farmstead, with a big barn or a new garage. In the fields, someone picks up a chipped stone projectile point or a fragment of a wine bottle.

When I arrived in the early 1990s at this spot, situated along Silver Creek in the uplands east of the American Bottom, everything was gone. The trees, the houses, the barns—even the topsoil itself. The nearby Scott Air Force Base was about to expand, and its federal funding had required an archaeological survey.[1] The sites of dozens of prehistoric campsites and villages, a few ancient cemeteries, and several American farmsteads were discovered in less than a year. Now it was time to excavate them, and the size of the project was enormous. Backhoes and belly loaders were busy scraping the topsoil off of hundreds of acres of land,

and dozens of archaeologists were clustered in little groups across the landscape, recording hundreds of pit features below the surface.

By midsummer, the project area resembled a desert of dry yellow clay, blowing across small crews of archaeologists huddled over 1200-hundred-year-old pits, 900-hundred-year-old house basins, and occasionally, some of the earliest American-era features that had yet been examined in Illinois. In most cases, each of these eras occupied the same bluff top, and the number of ancient pits and artifacts found far outnumbered those from the time of written history. Small groups of excavators moved from one pit to the next, dutifully drawing them in plan, cutting them into two halves, excavating one half, drawing the cross section, and then removing the second half—artifacts in bags, forms filled out, and then on to the next pit.

Simply walking across the Scott Air Force project area offered a crash course in the human history of Illinois. Amidst all of the features and artifacts, however, what impressed me the most was the sheer lack of contrast between ancient prehistory and history. The occasional historic pit cellar, once located beneath the floor of an American cabin in 1815, looked nearly identical to pits dug 1000 years earlier by cultures we cannot even name. With the nineteenth century came a bit more geometry to the holes in the ground, but they were still holes in the ground. Pits in the earth for keeping food. At the bottom of one, a chipped stone scraper. At the bottom of another, a printed tea cup.

Under the House

What was once visible on the ground surface two hundred years ago and what is visible beneath that same surface today are two very different things. In many instances, archaeology can say only a few basic things about a building that stood on a site—its size, shape, method of construction, and maybe a little bit about how it was finished or trimmed. Often, as in the case of a log cabin built on the ground surface, very little is left to see below ground. Archaeology is very effective at illuminating little activities that occurred in and around the house, however. A broken dinner plate swept out the back door will inevitably tell a tale, and the simple act of digging a hole and filling it back in it will be visible to archaeologists for centuries.

On an historical archaeological site, there are features in the ground and there are artifacts in and around the features. Very often they have little to do with each other, but each is related to a building or an activity that was once part of someone's life. The archaeological signature of a late nineteenth-century farmstead can be pretty complex—often consisting of multiple brick foundations, deep cellars, cisterns, wells, privies, outbuilding and barn footings, buried animal carcasses, and hundreds of postholes. Sites dating exclusively to the early nineteenth century in rural Illinois, however, generally produce only a small number of features, which are often reasonably predictable in their design and function. These usually include a small pit cellar, a brick-lined well, an earthen or plaster-lined cistern, one or two pits used to store root crops in the winter, a shallow privy vault, and maybe two or three shallow pits used to butcher hogs.

At the heart of the site of a frontier farmstead is the cellar feature. These are the bellies of the log houses. The use of the term *cellar*, however, is somewhat misleading, as frontier-era cellars were often only three feet deep and four feet wide—kind of like a refrigerator on its side, which is what they really were (figure 6.1). True subterranean spaces large enough to climb down into and move around in were uncommon in rural households before the 1830s in Illinois.[2] The construction of larger cellars during the mid-1830s in central Illinois probably followed an increased sense of stability after the close of the frontier period.

Before the late 1830s, subfloor pit cellars usually consisted of small, rectangular excavations less than four feet deep and eight feet long. The pits were probably left unlined or sometimes paneled with planks or logs. Access to these facilities was gained through a trap in the floor above, although the user would have simply reached into the hole, or squatted inside below the trap entrance. Most pit cellars were probably located beneath the kitchen of the house—if the house was large enough to actually have a kitchen separated from the rest of the dwelling. At some early sites, these pits were so shallow and broad that they really served primarily as a prepared clay surface beneath the floor.

The purpose of such cellars was to store and keep cool small amounts of foods kept in barrels, crockery pots, or sacks. If they were positioned away from the edge of the building and partitioned from the rest of the crawlspace below the house, such pits would have offered a secure, dry place to keep food. If the cabin was poorly designed, however, the pits would have been a sticky mess after a hard rain, and would have been subjected to nighttime raids by raccoons and possums. For instance, William Oliver described an overnight stay in such a dwelling, where he was forced to shout and stamp on the floor to frighten away a creature making "chirrups and half-stifled squeaks beneath the floor."[3]

The cellars beneath rural, commercial structures of the period were usually broader and slightly deeper, but still had only five feet of head-

FIG. 6.1 A subfloor pit cellar (New Salem, circa 1830) with half of its fill removed. The object on the left is a modern utility line.

room at best. Many were earthen walled, with just a few planks lying on the clay floor. Some stores or taverns, however, were equipped with stone lined cellars that, while shallow, more closely resembled a subterranean room.

Other archaeological features can reveal where a cabin or house once stood. Chimneys made of brick or cats' clay were often seated on a brick or limestone foundation. These are commonly encountered at the base of the topsoil, and can point to the former location of a kitchen hearth. Even if the dwelling had no subfloor cellar, it was usually elevated a foot or two off of the ground surface by piers or a crude foundation. If those piers were deep enough to disturb the clay subsoil, their former presence can be seen even if the site has been plowed and the foundation stones long ago removed. Finally, the crawlspace below an elevated house also provided a good place for dogs or other animals to escape the summer sun. The burrowing that followed often resulted in irregular depressions in the subsoil, indirectly reflecting the location of a dwelling.

Behind the House

Inhabitants of rural nineteenth century Illinois dug holes in the ground for a variety of reasons. Activities related to building construction, food processing, and food storage resulted in cellars, exterior crop storage pits, scalding and butchering pits, privy vaults, and water barrel footings or unlined cisterns. Many of these types of facilities, because they lack obvious geometric designs, are often misinterpreted as trash pits. In fact, there has yet to be a strong argument made for the existence of pits dug expressly for the primary disposal of garbage on an early to mid nineteenth-century site in Illinois.[4]

Complimenting the subfloor pit cellar was the exterior crop storage facility, which was usually located behind or near the house. These pits were precursors to the more modern root or storm cellar that became familiar in rural backyards during the early twentieth century. Frontier-era exterior crop storage pits are usually egg-shaped in plan, with walls that are more gradually sloped than pits found below the house itself. The ovoid plan may reflect the lack of the geometry of an associated ground surface structure, and the ramped walls are probably the result of foot traffic coming and going from the center of the pit.

Such pits were used to store and preserve (or "hole up") farm produce, such as potatoes, apples, cabbages, turnips, squash, or pumpkins during the early winter months (figure 6.2). The shallow pits helped better insulate the crops from frost, and were covered with heaps of earth, straw and branches, or ephemeral wooden structures. When needed, the covering would be pulled back slightly, to retrieve a few vegetables, and then covered over again. The inevitable decomposition of a percentage of these crops may have made storing them under the floor of the house less desirable. Instead, these pits are often found situated near other outdoor features such as wells, or located on the periphery of the site, some-

BUILDING A ROOT HEAP.

COVERING HEAP WITH EARTH.

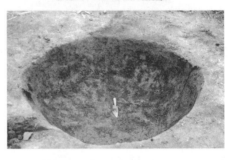

FIG. 6.2 Late nineteenth-century illustrations of the coverings of crop storage pits, and an archaeological example from Menard County, Illinois (circa 1825).

times near fence lines. Residents of southern Illinois continued to use such pits for potatoes, apples, and cabbages well into the early twentieth century.[5]

People have always needed water. In rural settings, some families simply retrieved that water from a nearby spring or creek. Wells, however, were common to even the earliest settlements. Differing little from those used centuries before and decades later, wells of the frontier period in Illinois ranged in depth from ten to forty feet, were usually lined with brick or stone, and drew water from the water table below the surface (figure 6.3). In some cases, the location of a well was clearly based on its proximity to a kitchen door. In other cases (when they are found far from the house itself) the choice of a well site may have been based on someone's understanding of the water table, either from the topography or by "witching" water with divining rods. As always, the most amazing thing about a three-foot wide by thirty-foot deep hole is that

FIG. 6.3 Wells are often the last component of a frontier-era site to be visible on the ground surface. This example in Menard County is lined with soft mud brick, and is thought to have been constructed around 1829. It was still used as a water source into the mid-1970s.

someone dug it with a shovel, and managed to crawl out again. We find that in the country wells were rarely replaced,[6] and thus were not filled with trash during the occupation of the site.

An important and common supplement to the well was the cistern. While the deep well tapped into ground water, the cistern collected rainwater. Located near a building (usually the house), these more shallow excavations caught rainwater that was diverted from the roof via a gutter. Having run off the surface of dusty roofing, the water could have become slightly dirty, and was often used for washing or watering animals rather than drinking. The earliest cisterns in Illinois were often simply unlined shafts in the clay subsoil. In sandy soils, the shafts were sometimes lined with planks. Both of these methods also tended to cloud the water with soil. In some cases, a coating of plaster was applied directly to the clay walls of the facility. By the mid nineteenth century, most cisterns were actually lined with brick and plaster, which made them cleaner and more stable.

The lack of indoor plumbing resulted in another common feature type—the outhouse or privy. Still common in rural settings well into the mid twentieth century, the privy was the preplumbing form of the toilet; it consisted of a hole in the ground to collect human waste and was covered by a small structure fitted with a bench for sitting. The nature of the structure covering a privy varied, but most outhouses consisted of very small, insubstantial shelters.

The vaults below also varied in size, method of construction and depth. During the nineteenth century, these pits could range from two to more than twenty feet deep. The shallow vaults required periodic cleaning, or "dipping." The most ephemeral of these structures could also be moved or replaced, resulting in several abandoned privy vault features on a site occupied for several decades. Particularly in urban contexts where deep, brick-lined privy shafts were more common during the early nineteenth century, these facilities also became convenient places to discard household trash. On the frontier farm site, however, the shallow pits were not usually used for household trash.

Cellars, wells, cisterns, and privies each have distinctive characteristics that, while they varied greatly, still allow for interpretation. Part of the predictability of the design of such facilities is reflective of their long-term functions. There were, however, a variety of short-term activities that resulted in other kinds of pits in the ground. These can be more difficult to define, as they were less carefully constructed and more idiosyncratic in their design. Archaeologists have identified several types of shallow, basin shaped pits used for the butchering of hogs, for instance. Broad, shallow pits were used to salt pork after butchering. In fact, the natural clay bases of such pits were sometimes considered integral to the curing process, as it was believed to "draw the wild taste" from the meat. Butchering and salting of pork was done in the late fall to avoid spoilage, and pits associated with these activities are often found in clusters within an activity area in the vicinity of the house, a well, or a barn.

Finally, there are many pits or other subsurface features whose original function can simply not be determined. Part of this is due to a lack of evidence, and part of this is due to the disconnection between our lives and those of the 1820s or 1830s. Certain activities, however prosaic they may have been, simply do not occur to us anymore.

CHAPTER SEVEN

Goods in the Forests

The arrival of the first American families to Illinois coincided with significant changes in Western material culture. The beginning of mass production, mass marketing, and the industrial revolution was creating a new consumer class; casual purchases of nonutilitarian goods were no longer restricted to the affluent. The industrial revolution that began in England during the eighteenth century made it possible for the middle class to indulge in a variety of fashionable luxuries and novelties. The mass production that came with the industrial revolution also began to impose a certain sameness on a range of domestic environments, and by 1800, the interiors of homes of the middle class in America were becoming quite similar to those hundreds or thousands of miles away.

Although farming communities in frontier Illinois were still without adequate export markets for surplus produce, the fact that country stores would exchange durable goods for local farm produce gave remote farm families a comfortable purchasing power. This, combined with the low prices for wholesale goods that followed the close of the War of 1812, resulted in a surprisingly well-equipped frontier.

Within the American frontier period in Illinois, there is a line that divides a time when there was probably only limited, sporadic availability of imported goods (such as cast iron cookware, manufactured cloth, Staffordshire tablewares, or sugar from the West Indies), and a time when essential and nonessential goods were plentiful. That line lay between 1815 (the close of the War of 1812) and 1820 (two years following statehood). Newspaper advertisements at St. Louis vividly dramatize this change. Prior to the war, dry goods wholesalers advertised very short lists of merchandise, made up of a hodgepodge of imported goods such as blankets, linseed oil and "a few German and English bibles."[1] By the late 1810s, however, there was such a flood of goods into the city that single ads now listed dozens of provisions and luxuries, from parasols to brass ink pots, and many merchants began to specialize in particular types of products.

To date, we have examined fewer than a dozen American sites abandoned before 1815.[2] These sites have produced very few features in the subsoil and very few domestic artifacts. Although this is due in part to short-term occupations, pre-1815 artifact assemblages from rural Illinois come closest to fitting our old stereotypical notion of the austerity of frontier life—at least in regards to quantity (figure 7.1). A closer look at the artifacts themselves reveals that many were certainly not essential to survival in the forest of the Illinois Country. Objects discarded during the very first years of the territory include not only gunflints, knife blades, and butchered deer remains, but also English teacups, brass vest buttons, and French wine bottles.

The drop in prices of English imports that followed the war, combined with the surge in immigration to Illinois after statehood in 1818, not only helped merchants fill the old warehouses along the river at St. Louis, but also led them to construct many more. The arrival of the first steamboat at St. Louis in 1817 also signaled the beginning of much more effective shipping—a trip upriver from New Orleans now took twelve days instead of three months. By 1820, merchants were stocked with a wide range of manufactured and imported goods that were affordable to anybody who could afford to buy or barter for anything. This was at a time, however, when the majority of the inhabitants of Illinois were Native Americans, when a good number of those of European descent were speaking French, and when most of the state had yet to be properly mapped.

During the frontier period in Illinois, most durable goods were imported from overseas or from manufacturing centers in the East: refined ceramics, cutlery, and gilt buttons from England; cloth from New England; iron goods, window and bottle glass from Pittsburgh; and medicines, books and shoes from Philadelphia and New York. More locally, midwestern cities such as St. Louis, Louisville, and Ohio produced paint, beer, spices, apothecary products, lead shot, and simple clothing. In the frontier settlements themselves were blacksmiths, coopers, tanners, and a few potters.

1 INCH

FIG. 7.1 All of the artifacts recovered from a short-term American farmstead in St. Clair County, abandoned before 1815. Frontier-era sites occupied after 1815 usually produce hundreds or thousands of artifacts.

Large-scale wholesale mercantile houses in Philadelphia, New Orleans, and St. Louis often assembled prepackaged crates of middling and popular goods specifically for the "country trade." This allowed novice retailers headed out to the frontier to rely on the market experience of the wholesale community, which had been shipping goods out to frontier communities since the days of the American Revolution. This also meant, however, that the decisions made by a handful of wholesalers in St. Louis warehouses reverberated across hundreds of settlements and thousands of households.

Very few durable goods were made at home, unless someone in the family was a craftsperson. Small-scale blacksmithing may have been practiced on family farms, primarily for repairing iron hardware or tools. A little woodworking may have been practiced at home as well, but the skills and tools for cabinetmaking and coopering were specialized ones. Woolen fabrics were commonly made at home, but factory-made cloth was common even during the earliest years of settlement, and soon dominated the frontier wardrobe. For most families, making cloth at home would have been an activity of choice, not necessity. Homemade clothing, however, was probably very common through most of the nineteenth century. Unfortunately, archaeologists are able to see only the buttons that fell from such garments, as any cloth that would have wound up in the ground decayed very quickly.

Their Garbage, Our Artifacts

Most of the artifacts we find out in the country are little fragments of things. When I speak of a French wine bottle or a printed platter, I am usually speaking of a vessel represented by one, two, or three pieces ranging from the size of a fingernail to the palm of your hand. This is due, in part, to the fact that most objects spent time on the ground surface before being buried in a pit somewhere near the house, and were badly broken and scattered long ago. Those items that lay protected somewhere on the ground surface and that managed to stay reasonably intact were doomed by the coming of the plow, which has effectively fractured and churned the majority of the archaeological artifacts lying in the topsoils of Illinois. But archaeologists also deal primarily in the fragmentary because most of these objects were once someone's garbage, usually discarded *because* they were broken.

Novice field technicians make plenty of notes while excavating features, but often fail to consider just how the artifacts they are so interested in actually wound up in the hole. There is a lingering assumption that the artifacts had something to do with the original function of the hole, which they usually do not—at least not on historic sites.[3] In reality, most artifact assemblages from rural pit features are composed of small portions of a number of ceramic and glass vessels (together with bits and pieces of nails, utensils, or lost buttons) that had been lost or discarded long before the filling of the pit. These were *secondarily deposited.* That is, the artifacts were thrown away a second time—usually as part of a debris-rich topsoil that was shoveled into the pit to fill it up.

Primary deposits, on the other hand, are much less common on rural early nineteenth century sites in Illinois. A primary deposit is the result of someone discarding garbage directly into a feature where it remains undisturbed until uncovered archaeologically. This form of deposition generally indicates a sample of material that was generated or discarded during a short period of time. So, if a pit used for scalding a hog was no longer needed, it would probably be filled back in. If there were a few empty bottles or broken plates to discard, they might be tossed into the hole on the Thursday afternoon that it was being filled. The most common form of primary artifact deposit is that found at the bottom of an urban privy. In the city, where there were far fewer places to toss an empty bottle or a broken plate, deep privy shafts were used for both household garbage as well as human waste. This is what makes them so attractive to both archaeologists and bottle collectors. In the rural frontier homestead, however, there is really no equivalent, as most of the privies in these contexts were very shallow, and were not used for household garbage.

The majority of artifacts found on an early nineteenth-century rural home site are related to food; its storage, preparation, and consumption. This is in part due to the fact that the most of the nonfood-related objects of the period, such as clothing, furniture, and even architecture itself, consisted almost entirely of organic materials, which quickly dissolved into the soil after having been discarded. Today, synthetic fibers, plastics, aluminum, and steel have created much more durable clothing, furniture, and fixtures. These will last longer in the ground, and will paint a much more complete picture of our lives. Of course, these future artifacts will be found primarily in the ground.

In the 1960s, historic archaeologists began using a standardized set of artifact groupings to describe debris found on historic sites. These groups consisted of "kitchen," "architecture," "furniture," "arms," "clothing," "personal," "tobacco pipes," and "activities."[4] These classifications allowed archaeologists working at different sites and within different settings to compare the basic nature of the artifact samples found at each site. Unfortunately, in most of the technical excavation reports that have followed, these categories have been left intact and not subdivided. This has tended to smooth over the detailed consumer- and activity-related patterns found in such artifact assemblages, particularly on sites postdating the late eighteenth century.

For instance, the kitchen category can encompass everything from locally made lard pots or meat forks to Chinese teacups and French wine bottles. Certainly all of these items had something to do with food, but they represent a wide range of activities, origins, functions, and symbols. By lumping a porcelain teapot and a crockery lard pot into the same category, one effectively erases the varied meanings of these things, as well as the behavioral nuances that lay at the heart of anthropological study. Most of the artifacts of a given frontier era site in Illinois could be placed in the "kitchen" or "architecture" categories, thus eradicating the need for categories at all.

The artifact assemblage from a typical early nineteenth-century rural domestic site can be immediately broken down into at least twenty basic categories, based on function and method of manufacture:

Food-related ceramics
Nonfood-related ceramics
Metallic cooking vessels
Food-related glass serving vessels
Glass packaged food products
Glass packaged nonfood products
Food-related tools and utensils
Tools used in household activities
Tools used in outdoor activities
General purpose tools
Grooming- or medical-related equipment
Grooming-related product containers
Clothing-related objects
Leisure-related objects
Arms-related objects
Home furnishings and lighting objects
Animal-related objects
Transportation-related objects
Architectural materials and objects
Food remains

These categories themselves can be broken down further, into subgroups that have more activity-related meanings. For instance, food-related ceramics can be divided into different forms of manufacture, as well as different forms of function or decoration. Glass-packaged products can be divided by type of product, or by various aspects of manufacture. The leisure, grooming and clothing-related categories can be divided into male or female, adult or child-related objects. The more subdivided an artifact assemblage, the more opportunity for observing variations or similarities when that assemblage is compared to others.

———————

Unless they are specialists, the first question a historic archaeologist will probably ask about a site will be "what are the ceramics like?" Fragments of ceramic vessels are the most abundant and articulate type of artifact available to the historical archaeologist. Throughout the history of the various European colonies in North America, a family who had the means to own anything at all probably owned ceramic vessels for cooking, storing, or serving food.

The many rapid changes in ceramic technology and fashion have made ceramic artifacts very datable—by the early nineteenth century, some of those changes occurred in increments of ten years or less. Fired clay pottery is also inherently fragile, so it is frequently broken. Most forms of pottery were inexpensive, and so broken vessels were replaced regularly. Once in the ground, though, ceramic fragments will survive indefinitely, creating little indications of the habits of those who lived on a site.

The combined fashion and fragility of ceramic vessels has made their buried fragments our clocks. Particularly during the early nineteenth century, food service vessels were so abundant, reasonably priced, and easy to break that there was little "heirlooming" of these objects. True heirlooms or precious vessels were cared for much differently, and were less likely to be broken and wind up in the ground. These vessels now reside in attics and antique stores instead. Most of the ceramic vessels used in a particular early nineteenth-century household, then, were not particularly old. So, if we know when they were made, we know that the earliest occupation of that site was probably not much later than the appearance of those kinds of pottery on the market.

Nearly all of these vessels were made somewhere else by someone else, and it is important to see such artifacts as they once were—consumer goods. In this way, broken pieces of pottery can say much about regional, national, and international trade. Because people shopped for goods for complex practical and personal reasons, ceramic artifacts can also reflect a myriad of individual tastes, habits, and traditions.

Historical archaeology recognizes two principal forms of ceramics: refined and unrefined. Refined ceramics consist of finely potted, often decorative wares, which were usually used at the table, rather than for the storage or preparation of food. Such vessels are what we would generically call china today, although 200 years ago that term was usually reserved for expensive Chinese porcelain. Unrefined wares consist of heavier bodied, more utilitarian pieces made most often for use in the kitchen—what we would generically call crockery today.

Ceramics for the Table

Most of the refined ceramics used in America at the turn of the eighteenth century were made in England. These consisted of finely potted, decorative earthenwares developed during the second half of the eighteenth century as inexpensive alternatives to Chinese porcelain, which had been a desirable commodity in wealthier European homes for generations. Although English potters also developed their own authentic porcelains, the earthenware imitations were much cheaper to produce and therefore more affordable to the middle classes.

By the 1830s, America was the largest export market for English earthenwares,[5] and fashionable and decorative wares were appearing in modest households. Across the new frontiers, settlers of the most remote creek valleys were able to purchase cheap versions of teawares that had become fashionable in London only a year or two earlier.

The clays and glazes used in the manufacture of refined earthenwares changed over time, based primary on aesthetic changes in how English potters chose to imitate porcelains. Before the mid-1700s, most of the decorative tablewares made by European potters consisted of plates, pitchers, and mugs (as well as the occasional teacup and saucer) made from a coarse, thick-bodied clay that was whitened with a tin glaze and decorated with hand-painted motifs. Many of these were derivative of Chinese decorations. In England and Holland, tin glazed wares were known as *Delft*, in France as *Faience*, and in Spain as *Majolica*. Such wares had been made for a long time in Europe, and had become an important part of the traditional material culture for their consumers. As imitations of porcelain, however, they were pretty clunky—they chipped and broke easily and did not lend themselves to effective mass production.

In the mid-1700s, English potters began producing much finer but also more durable wares that stood in sharp, modern contrast to the old tin glazed wares. In the 1750s, Josiah Wedgwood and his contemporaries developed a thin-bodied, cream colored earthenware known as creamware. This new form of pottery could be manufactured in large quantities and produce nearly identical vessels. Further, they could be made affordable and reach a bigger market. Within a few decades, refined creamwares from Staffordshire were gracing the tables of homes across much of Europe and North America. Plates and teacups were on the cutting edge of the dawning industrial revolution.

Wedgwood also managed to design fashionable wares that made them desirable among royalty and the middle class alike. After Queen Charlotte began using Wedgewood's cream-colored wares in the 1760s, they became known as Queensware. Like our use of the term *Xerox* or *Tupperware* today, *Queensware* eventually came to refer to a range of earthenware products made by many English potters. English Queenswares, or refined earthenwares, remained the principal type of affordable, decorative, and fashionable table- and teawares for most of the western world for the next century.

Know Your Ware Types

The types of refined English earthenware that are relevant to the nineteenth century midwestern frontier include creamware, pearlware, whiteware, and ironstone (figure 7.2).[6] These are for the most part modern terms used to describe the various changes in clay and glaze technology. Most of these changes centered on the quest for the perfect, cost-effective imitation of porcelain, as well as the introduction of new decorative motifs and more durable vessels.

Creamware is a thin-bodied, lightweight earthenware developed in England during the 1750s. It consists of a slightly cream-colored clay coated in a clear lead glaze, which gives the vessels a yellow, greenish cast. A wide variety of table-, tea-, and toiletwares were made in creamware. Creamware was reasonably inexpensive, yet it was used in wealthy and middle-class households alike. Refined ceramics were very much a fashion-driven industry however, and by the 1790s the popularity of creamware had fallen amongst the wealthier consumers. Between 1790 and 1820 creamware had become the cheapest refined ceramic available, and was usually undecorated. By the very early 1820s creamware was no longer manufactured, and by the 1830s, most of it had been broken and discarded.

Pearlware is a term archaeologists and ceramic collectors use to refer to English earthenware products introduced in the 1770s. These wares were designed as a more deliberate imitation of Chinese porcelain, and employed small amounts of cobalt in the lead glaze to produce a bluish cast. These new wares were always decorated—often in oriental motifs, and usually in blue—to compliment the cast of the glaze. Pearlware was gradually phased out in during the 1820s, and by the early 1840s, it disappears from the archaeological record.

Pearlware and creamware were followed in the late 1820s and 1830s by what archaeologists refer to as whiteware. Unlike creamware and pearlware, however, whiteware was not introduced as a new product. Instead, rapid changes in glazes made during the late 1820s allowed for a wider variety of brighter colors to be used underneath. These new painted or printed colors were probably introduced in America just before 1830, and thus provide another important temporal marker for archaeologists. Whiteware products are still made today.

FIG. 7.2 Nonarchaeological examples of four principal refined ceramic ware types found on sites dating to the frontier period: creamware plate (top), pearlware teapot and plate (second row), whiteware saucer and cup (third row), and undecorated ironstone cup (fourth row).

Ironstone is a much harder and heavier ware, which was introduced to American markets around 1840. It was also the first refined ceramic type to be successfully manufactured in America. When first introduced, white ironstone was designed as an inexpensive imitation of French porcelain. Many early ironstones were also decorated in printed patterns much like their whiteware counterparts. By the mid 1850s, most ironstone was undecorated, representing a shift in fashion toward all white table settings. Durable ironstone vessels continued to be manufactured throughout the nineteenth century.

The English had also begun to manufacture their own versions of true porcelain during the eighteenth century. Chinese export porcelain tea sets or French porcelain tablewares, however, remained the most desirable during the late eighteenth and early nineteenth century.

By the late eighteenth century, there were basically three main categories of refined ceramics: tablewares, teawares, and toiletwares. Tablewares could include plates, platters, bowls, mugs, pitchers, pepper pots, tureens, saucer boats, and vegetable dishes. Teawares consisted of teacups and saucers, teapots, sugar pots, creamers, tea caddies (for storing and dispensing tea leaves), waste bowls (for disposing used tea leaves), and cup plates. Finally, toiletwares consisted primarily of wash basins, wash pitchers (ewers), and chamber pots. The chamber pot was a large pot with single handle, which was kept under the bed or inside of a little cabinet, and used prior to indoor plumbing to avoid making a trip to the outhouse.

Most of the varieties of refined earthenware were available in a wide variety of colorful surface decorations. The decoration of a teacup or supper plate was probably of more interest to the consumer of 1820 than it is today. This was, in part, due to the fact that decorated plates or tea sets provided some of the few decorative elements within most households, prior to the development of inexpensive lithography, photography, or other forms of household decoration that appeared after 1840.

Like the clays and glazes used to manufacture refined earthenware, the imagery used in its decoration also changed through time—even more so, in fact. The decoration of a vessel also dictated its price—although most forms of earthenware were inexpensive. Four basic types of decorative motifs were used on most Queenswares of the late eighteenth and early nineteenth centuries: edge decorated, hand painted, banded or "dipt," and transfer printed (figure 7.3).

Edge decorated refers to the use of molded and painted rims, primarily on plates and platters. Edge decorations were manufactured in a variety of designs, but the most common during the late eighteenth and

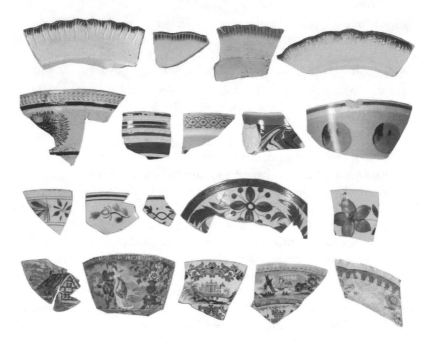

FIG. 7.3 Principal decorative motifs found on early nineteenth-century Queenswares: edge-decorated, dipt or annular, hand painted, and transfer printed. These fragments were recovered from frontier-context sites in Illinois.

early nineteenth centuries was the shell-edged pattern, which consisted of a scalloped rim painted in blue or green. Shell-edged plates appeared in the 1770s and continued to be manufactured, in slightly changing patterns, for a century.

Hand-painted designs have been applied to refined English ceramic throughout its history. Each motif was painted by hand, yet such pottery was quite inexpensive. During the early nineteenth century, hand painted designs were most common on teawares. Most of the earliest pearlware-painted designs were executed in blue and imitated designs found on Chinese porcelain tea sets. Around 1790, new multicolored painted motifs became popular.

Usually applied to bowls, mugs, or pitchers, banded or dipt (short for "dipped") decorations consist of festive, multicolored designs created by applying colored clay slips onto the pottery as it was turned on a wheel. Additional multicolored patterns were often applied in between the colored bands, creating what are referred to as "mocha" or "earth worm" decorations. Banded designs appeared in the late eighteenth century and continued to be used into the third quarter of the nineteenth century.

A slightly more expensive decorative treatment was transfer printed imagery. This involved the transfer of a copper-engraved image from an inked tissue to the body of a ceramic vessel. Transfer printing allowed for the mass production of highly detailed scenes, which could be applied to any vessel form. Printed designs were executed primarily in blue (and to a lesser extent black) until about 1830, when an explosion of red, brown, green, and purple patterns (made available by the development of whiteware), reached the American market with great success.

Though these goods were not (on a strictly utilitarian level) necessary out on the wilds of the western frontier, thousands upon thousands of fragile tea cups and dinner plates were stuffed into straw-filled barrels and shipped up and down rivers to warehouses such as those along the St. Louis riverfront. Archaeology in Illinois has yet to identify a nineteenth-century domestic site that does not contain fragile, decorative English tablewares or teawares that could have easily been replaced with durable pewter or tin vessels. This is part of what makes ceramics so interesting—they reflect not only functional needs, but also more abstract social or symbolic issues surrounding the desire to own such goods—even out in the western forests.

Crockery in the Kitchen

Before the Civil War, most Americans set their tables with refined English Queenswares. Their kitchens, however, were stocked with coarser, unrefined crockery. Local potters made a variety of traditional food preparation and storage vessels such as heavy bowls, milk pans, pots, jars, and jugs. Before 1840 in the Midwest, some potters also made vessels for the table as well, such as dishes, table bowls, and pitchers. Unlike most refined ceramics, unrefined wares were usually not meant to be decorative, although there were several notable exceptions (see chapter 11). Also unlike the refined wares, which were usually imported during the eighteenth and early nineteenth centuries, most unrefined crockery in use by 1800 was made here in America.

In most of North America, two principal types of clay were used in the production of unrefined wares, which resulted in two distinctly different products: redware and stoneware (figure 7.4). Redware appeared earliest and was the most common form of crockery in most midwestern communities. This was a low-fired earthenware, usually made of a soft, red clay and coated in a clear lead glaze. During the early nineteenth century, redware products were known simply as earthenware.[7] Redware clays are abundant and easily accessible in the Midwest (being

FIG. 7.4 Early nineteenth-century advertisement for crockery products, and archaeological examples of redware (middle) and stoneware (bottom) vessels.

basically the same clays used in soft mud brick), and can be fired at reasonably low temperatures. The craft of turning and firing lead-glazed earthenware was an ancient one—the kilns, production methods, and wares found at an early nineteenth-century redware pottery would have been familiar to a potter working in sixteenth century Europe.

During the mid-1700s, stoneware vessels began to compliment the redware crockery in many colonial households. Stoneware clays produced much more durable vessels than redware clays, but they were harder to find, and required a higher firing temperature. For this reason, redware was usually the earliest dominant form of crockery on newly settled frontiers. During the nineteenth century, American stoneware products generally did not include tablewares (such as plates, bowls, or cups) as did early redware. Stoneware was sometimes decorated, most often in cobalt blue painted or stenciled designs applied under the glazes of storage jars or churns. Over the decades, stoneware gradually replaced redware, and in Illinois, it became the dominant form of crockery by the 1850s.[8]

Glass Products

During the early nineteenth century, only a very small percentage of household products were packaged in glass. These consisted primarily of apothecary and patent medicines, and alcoholic beverages such as wine, ale, and whisky (figure 7.5). A small amount of glass tableware was also used in middle-class homes of the period. Because they were fragile and often broke, glass vessels are also usually well represented in archaeological samples.

Many of the glass bottles brought into frontier period homes in Illinois were made in America. The glass industry of the upper Ohio Valley was well developed by the 1820s, and many of the specimens found in Illinois were made in that region. Others were manufactured in the glasshouses of eastern Pennsylvania. Most of the wine bottles we encounter, however, were probably made in France. Some ales or porters may have been bottled in England, and several of the earliest medicinal bottles were also made in England.

The most common bottle type found on pre-1840 sites in Illinois is the small, unmarked vial. These were used for a variety of medicinal products, as well as for cooking extracts or household chemicals. While local storekeepers purchased the bottles filled, local druggists often bought them empty, and filled them with their own botanical compounds. Unfortunately, only small paper labels identified the contents of such bottles, and thus little can be said about their contents from archaeological excavations.

Aside from more traditional botanical remedies, new "patent" or proprietary medicines were also becoming popular in the 1820s and 1830s. Most of these products were of dubious medicinal value, and contained primarily alcohol, cocaine, and opiates as their primary active ingredients. Many were packaged in plain vials, but embossed patent medicine bottles were becoming increasingly more popular during the period, and

FIG. 7.5 Principal types of glass packaged products from pre-1840 contexts in Illinois. Top row: medicine bottles ("Essense of Peppermint," "Turlington's Balsam of Life," and "Liquid Opodeldoc"). Bottom row: liquor bottles (a figural George Washington whisky flask, a wine bottle, and an ale or porter bottle).

thus their archaeological remains are more easily identified. Some of the more common patent medicines of the period include Liquid Opodeldoc, Essence of Peppermint, and Turlington's Balsam of Life, which was packaged in a distinctive, fiddle-shaped bottle first manufactured in England during the mid-eighteenth century.

Whisky was an important food staple of the upland southern diet in the early nineteenth century, and decorative flasks (which were often filled locally at country stores) were common in Illinois by the early 1820s. Often depicting portraits of the founding fathers or American eagles, these bottles allowed mold makers at eastern glasshouses to really flex their artistic muscles. Wine was commonly consumed across the region, and most was probably French claret imported via New Orleans. The shape of the wine bottle has changed remarkably little in the last 250 years, and those used on the Illinois frontier would be very familiar to modern eyes. Only a small amount of glass for the table was in used in Illinois before 1840. This consisted primarily of flint glass tumblers, and the occasional pressed glass serving dish or salt cellar.

Various and Sundry Items

The fragility of ceramic and glass vessels, coupled with their ubiquity in the house, made it likely that at least a few pieces would end up in a pit somewhere on the farmstead. Once one departs from the ceramic and glass categories, the range of items expands rapidly, but the quantity of any given artifact falls dramatically. Items such as a knife blade or a clay marble do not break into many pieces, and are simply less likely to end up in a pit that also contains a few fragments of teacup that broke into thirty-five pieces.

Many of the nonceramic or glass artifacts commonly found on early nineteenth-century sites in Illinois are still associated with the preparation or serving of food. Metallic vessels such as kettles were found in all homes of the period. They are often poorly represented in pit feature samples, however. When they finally broke (which took a while) they did so into three or four pieces instead of two dozen. We have begun to boost our metallic vessel samples by using metal detectors on sites prior to excavations. Also related to the serving food is a wide variety of flatware found on frontier context sites in Illinois. Items in this category include Sheffield knives, pewter teaspoons, iron serving spoons, and two-tined forks.

Clothing-related artifacts consist primarily of buttons. On early nineteenth century sites, we find a variety of buttons made of animal bone, brass, pewter, or mussel shell. Despite the stereotypical notions of the austerity of frontier life, we find as many or more decorative gilt brass buttons as we do plain utilitarian bone buttons. In certain soil conditions, leather is also preserved archaeologically—and so we occasion-

FIG. 7.6 A hand forged fish spear found along Macoupin Creek in central Illinois.

ally find shoes in wells or deep privy shafts. These deep-context artifacts are more common in the cities than out in the country.

While inhabitants of the Illinois frontier used a wide range of household and farmyard tools, we see only a few of them on any one archaeological site (figure 7.6). This is in part due to their durability—as most were made of iron they broke less often and were less likely to become part of a future archaeological sample. Probate inventories of the period often list a range of common and specialized tools used primarily for woodworking. Files, gouges, augers, and small hammer heads are reasonably common archaeologically in Illinois. Some of the most common tools in archaeological contexts are (not surprisingly) axes. Those that are found on the site of a frontier farmstead were either lost in the yard or broke during use due to poor welding. We also find a number of fragmentary whetstones, used to sharpen iron tools. Whetstones have changed little since antiquity—I found a fragment of one on a Roman site in England that would have been at home on an early nineteenth century site in Illinois.

More common are small objects that were prone to loss in the house, such as brass straight pins, thimbles, or the occasional broken set of scissors or shattered writing slate. Pocket or clasp knives, with bone grips similar to those found on table knives, are also frequently encountered. The bone lice comb is the most common grooming-related artifact. Toothbrushes, also fashioned from animal bone, appear in urban contexts during the period but are far less common out in the country.

With regard to guns and ammunitions, what we find in the ground on frontier-era sites in Illinois differs sharply from the stereotypical im-

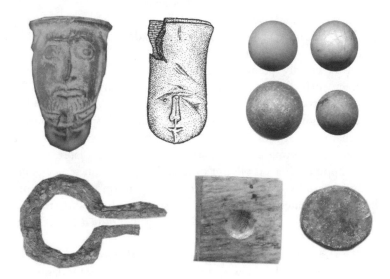

FIG. 7.7 Artifacts of leisure: figural smoking pipe bowls, stone marbles, a mouth harp, a handmade horn gaming piece, and a handmade lead checker.

age of the pioneer with rifle in hand. Arms-related artifacts from rural, early nineteenth-century sites in Illinois consist primarily of a few lead musket balls, a gunflint, and only very occasionally a piece of brass or iron gun hardware.[9] This stands in sharp contrast to households of the same period located in different cultural contexts, for instance those associated with the fur trade in Wisconsin. Early nineteenth century sites in that region produce more gunflints, lead balls, and gun parts.

There are several types of artifacts that we generally place into the "leisure activity" category (figure 7.7). These include smoking pipes, marbles, and mouth harps (or Jew's Harps). Smoking pipes dominate this category; tobacco was practically a food staple of the period, particularly in rural households of upland southern descent. With this in mind, a smoking pipe may have been no more of a leisure-related artifact than a pewter teaspoon used to stir sugar into tea. Occasionally, we also find homemade toys or gaming pieces, such as a checker fashioned from a flattened lead musket ball, or a domino cut from a piece of animal horn.[10]

The eclectic range of household wooden furnishings that would have been found in the frontier home are nearly invisible to archaeologists, save for some iron cabinet hardware, brass tacks from a studded trunk, and the occasional brass knob. At the home of a blacksmith in the 1830s village of New Salem, we recovered the small iron shaft used in a spinning wheel—an object that was otherwise made almost entirely of wood and thus nearly invisible archaeologically.[11]

There is usually plenty of nondescript iron hardware found on early nineteenth century sites in Illinois, particularly if a metal detector is used as part of the excavation. Most of the bolts, bars, and rings look surprisingly modern at first glance. Closer inspection, however, reveals that most of these items have been hand forged. Although they were used in the same manner as those made decades later, it is much easier to appreciate a simple nut or bolt when one can see evidence of its manufacture by hand. Most hardware found on early sites appears to have been related to wagons. Horseshoes or horseshoe nails seem to appear in only limited quantities on sites abandoned before 1840 in Illinois.

As for the houses themselves, architectural debris on frontier-era sites in Illinois provides a few sketches of only the most fundamental aspects of the house. As most log houses of the period were not constructed on continuous foundations, most of the soft mud brick commonly encountered on such sites was usually associated with fireplaces or chimneys. Before the Civil War, bricks were molded by hand and fired in "clamps"—sometimes by the user of the bricks himself. While most homes of the period were made of horizontal logs, there are still plenty of cut (or "square") nails found on such sites, which reflect the presence of trim, flooring, weatherboarding, or roofing. Most nails were cut and headed by machines by the 1820s, and thus hand forged nails generally appear on only those sites that predate 1820. Window glass is also far more common than the old traditions would suggest. Early nineteenth-century window glass is very thin, and has an aqua green cast. After about 1840, window glass became much thicker and clearer. The iron hardware found on these sites is simple and utilitarian. Ornamental hinges or latches are rare.

Considered together, architectural debris says only a little. Bricks, nails, and window glass speak of the chimneys, flooring, cabinetry, and windows of a log house. Indirectly, a few more details can be surmised. For instance, the presence of lath nails reflects a plastered interior. A cistern nearby reflects a system of guttering. Coal clinkers may betray the use of an early heating stove. On a site located in a plowed field, however, we usually can only approximate the size and shape of an ephemeral, frontier-era dwelling. In the end, it is what was *inside* the log houses that is best articulated archaeologically.

Consumers on the Frontier

The ultimate creation of a long list of the goods used on the frontier is only a first step. Once the hundreds of fragments of pottery and glass recovered from an archaeological site have been washed, labeled, and sorted, one is faced with the task of asking meaningful questions of the assemblage. We ask, for instance, not just *what* the residents of the frontier owned, but *how* those possessions reflected their choices and practices. Observing and understanding patterns within each household, as well as across entire communities, helps us begin to answer these questions.[12]

Did residents in different regions of Illinois, or consumers from different ethnic or economic settings, interact differently within the realm of mass-produced goods that were imported into cites such as St. Louis? In other words, what was available to whom and when? How did different households shop? The traditional assumptions were based on what seemed like common sense: that people living farther away from commercial centers like St. Louis probably had "less fashionable" goods; that farmers with very little money bought cheaper goods than those with a little more money; or that a family's ethnic background would probably be expressed in the consumer products they had in the house.

In the late 1990s, I spent a lot of time in the various curatorial facilities in Illinois, reexamining the artifact assemblages from as many frontier-context sites in Illinois that I could find. The idea was to create a database of certain frequently appearing artifact types in order to look for any patterns in consumer behavior across Illinois during the frontier period. To provide an adequate control, each site needed to reflect a short-term occupation (averaging ten to fifteen years) and to have been abandoned before the close of the frontier era in 1840. Further, only those sites that had received large-scale excavation, which encountered similar samples, could be used. Although we have been doing a lot of digging since the late 1970s, there were relatively few sites that met these criteria. While from a statistical point of view the first database sample was rather small, the synthesis provided a foundation from which to begin to look for patterns in the way residents of frontier Illinois stocked their houses.[13]

Ceramic and glass artifacts usually tell us the most about early nineteenth century consumer behavior. They are very temporally sensitive, and their ubiquity as consumer goods (as well as their inherent fragility) makes them plentiful at all sites. Thus ceramics and glass artifacts present the best opportunity to make meaningful comparisons.

That is, if they are counted correctly. Ceramic and glass artifacts began life as consumer products, in the form of complete vessels or containers. Thus, it is crucial to ascertain from any given sample of fragmentary artifacts, a minimum number of vessels that were originally present in that sample. The total number of broken fragments of an unknown number of plates or bottles says little to an anthropologist. Minimum vessel counts, with some care, can be created from any assemblage of broken artifacts—no matter how badly fragmented.[14] This is due in large part to the predictability offered by mass-produced goods.

Patterns of Consumer Behavior

Ceramic and glass assemblages from a number of rural, frontier-context sites indicate that patterns of use of certain ceramic and glass products were remarkably consistent within a range of rural households across Illinois. The proximity of a given site to wholesale markets seemed to have little effect on how well stocked a household might be. This probably reflects the success of the country retailers, who set up shop in the various frontier settlements as they were formed, and it also demonstrates the effectiveness of riverine and overland shipping long before the arrival of railroads.

Several patterns of consumer behavior appear with surprisingly predictable frequency. For instance, there are always far more refined ceramic (china) vessels recovered than unrefined vessels (crockery). In most cases this ratio is at least five to one, much higher than in other regions of the United States. We have yet to excavate a pre-1840 site in Illinois with an abnormally low number of refined vessels and an unusually high number of crocks. Such a ratio stands in sharp contrast to those from other regions in the United States. For instance, our recent excavations at a site in western Pennsylvania (which contained layered deposits dating between 1790 and 1840) produced ratios of unrefined wares two to three times higher than those commonly encountered in rural Illinois.[15]

The sheer quantity of ceramic vessels that were broken and discarded during the brief frontier period in Illinois seems surprising at first. The average number of refined ceramic vessels present in each sample, generated over a period of about ten years, is thirty-two. This means that on average, residents of rural Illinois were breaking and discarding about three cups, saucers, or plates each year. The consistent use and discard of these often fragile goods resulted in an impressive pile of broken dishes somewhere behind the house. It also inadvertently kept these households up to date with the newest fashions in inexpensive earthenwares, as those broken cups and plates were quickly replaced.[16]

Because we have examined a number of short-term sites, we can also track the appearance and disappearance of certain ceramic types in the frontier Illinois market. Creamware, introduced in the 1760s and discontinued around 1820, falls from the archaeological record very shortly afterward. This ware appears only in very small quantities on sites first occupied after 1825, and essentially disappears by the mid-1830s.[17] The rapidity of their disappearance reflects the almost disposable character of these inexpensive earthenwares.

Not surprisingly, pearlware products, which were introduced in the late 1770s and not discontinued until around 1830, most often graced dining tables and cupboards during the frontier period in Illinois. Pearlwares generally persist in the archaeological record of rural Illinois until around 1840. Again, using the average number of 3.2 vessels broken per year, we can see why discontinued ware types disappear from the archaeological record so rapidly: a set of six pearlware plates and six cup and saucer sets (or eighteen vessels in total) would last about five years, based on this breakage rate.

What modern archaeologists refer to as whiteware was accessible to remote Illinois settlements very shortly after its introduction in England in the late 1820s. For instance, one short-term site at New Salem, thought to have been occupied between 1829 and 1832, produced at least three such vessels.[18] These three vessels (not manufactured until after 1829) had been shipped from overseas, purchased as wholesale goods, sold as retail goods, and broken within three years.

The database of short-term sites within this period allowed us to see other patterns for the first time. For instance, the use of tablewares and teawares within various rural households was remarkably consistent. Vessel by vessel, teawares outnumbered tablewares at fourteen of the eighteen sites in the expanded database. That is, 78 percent of these frontier homes were using and breaking more teacups and saucers than simple dinner plates. Further, they were doing so by a margin of a little less than three to two. The lingering presence of pewter tablewares was initially considered a potential cause of lower tableware counts. The use of pewter plates, however, was in decline by the early nineteenth century, and by the 1820s it seems doubtful that they played a significant role in table service. Teacups hardly seem so important to log cabin living, but the fact is, they were.[19]

Like the vessel form assemblages, the choices regarding decorative motifs on Queenswares were similar amongst most of the frontier households. Tablewares generally consisted of edge plates and banded bowls—with more elaborate printed plates tending to be more popular in the 1830s. Variation was most apparent with respect to how teawares were decorated. Most households preferred more formal (and slightly more expensive) printed wares over painted wares. This percentage also increased during the 1830s, with the introduction of new printed colors. With regard to the ratios of edged, painted, and printed motifs, the sameness within the cupboards among each of the families represented was indeed surprising, as one would naturally expect more notable variation with regards to choices presumably based on personal aesthetics.

Although the range of crockery vessel (unrefined ceramic) types from sites predating 1840 in Illinois was found to be rather limited, the patterns of use within any given household was much more eclectic than the patterns of Queensware use. While unrefined ceramic vessels consist primarily of utilitarian pots, kitchen bowls, a few jugs, and the occasional table plate or bowl, no single pattern of use or preference emerges as the most representative of the period. This suggests that there were more variables acting on the purchase and use of crockery on the frontier, such as variations in traditional foodways. The more localized production of these goods also affected their appearance in various homes.

Very little container glass has been recovered from rural pre-1835 sites in Illinois, which, with the small sample of sites, has made it harder to establish meaningful patterns of use. Most sites produced nearly equal amounts of medicine or utility bottles and liquor bottles. The medical bottles were most often unembossed vials, while the liquor bottles consisted of a range of wine bottles, whisky flasks, and the occasional ale bottle. Glass vessels for the table, however, appear to have been largely ignored by rural settlers prior to 1840s, except for glass tumblers. Further, that preference, like many of the others visible in the database, seems to have been remarkably pervasive, and it is only in places like stores or taverns that higher quantities of liquor bottles or glass tumblers appear.

Other forms of material culture, such as flatware, clothing buttons, or household tools appear with less regularity than broken ceramic and glass, and thus are harder to place into patterns of use. Small household items are found in most frontier-context archaeological samples, but their numbers are based more on how those samples were created (i.e., how and where certain forms of garbage were disposed) than the actual number of such goods purchased by the occupants of the site.

The vast majority of the early nineteenth-century sites that we have investigated archaeologically have produced fair quantities of nonessential goods. Clearly, by the time of the American frontier in Illinois, cultural traditions had incorporated the practice of consumerism—even out in the remote forests. The artifact assemblages found on early nineteenth century home sites also suggest that frontier settlers shopped in very similar ways, often independent of variations in location, household wealth, or cultural heritage. Like the ways in which one built a house, butchered a hog, or buried potatoes, shopping at the local store appears to have been part of the well-established traditions of the western frontier.

PART FOUR

The Origins of Sangamo

CHAPTER EIGHT

The Hole in the Map

Down in the Sangamon River bottoms in August, everything is green underneath the dark shade of the massive cottonwoods. Snakes slither underfoot, and big, nearly invisible spider webs wrap around the face. Poison ivy creeps waist high, and biting flies circle incessantly. Ahead in the deer path that leads to the water lies a little pile of bloody mass, from something brought down last night. Even within the occasional patch of sunlight, there is a nagging presence that reminds us that alone, and without our machines, we are at a disadvantage. These are modern thoughts, very new to this ancient landscape.

The Sangamon River drainage is situated in the geographic center of the state of Illinois. The river is about 250 miles long, and drains over 5000 square miles of land.[1] Its headwaters lie in what was once the high prairie of Illinois, now known as Ford and Champaign Counties. The river empties into the Illinois River near the town of Beardstown. The Sangamon has always been a shallow and slow river for much of the year (figure 8.1). The channel quickly fills and floods during the rains of spring and early summer. By September, however, it is waist deep in most places. The valley itself is broad and still thick with trees. Of the 5000 square miles that it drains, about 80 percent were blanketed by prairie when the Americans first arrived. It was in the remaining 20 percent covered in hardwood forest that 12,000 years of human activity had resided. With a few exceptions, it was not until after the close of the

FIG. 8.1 The Sangamon River in late summer.

American frontier period that people began to spend their lives in the open prairies.

The name *Saquimont* appears on French maps of the Illinois Country by the mid-eighteenth century, when mapmakers began to take an interest in the tributaries of the Illinois River.[2] The place name *Sangamo Country* was probably coined by Americans during the waning years of the fur trade in the Illinois region. During the decade prior to statehood, this locale probably stretched from the Illinois River to the central part of the Sangamon Valley, including parts of ten modern day counties (figure 8.2). During these years, the seasonal hunting and trapping movements of the Kickapoo and Potawatomi (and their French and American partners) probably defined the limits of the place.

The limits of the Sangamo Country began to contract as more American farmers moved into the region. Clusters of extended family settlements began to gather into what would become loose sociopolitical boundaries. Those boundaries and population centers, then, were the basis of the new county lines that were drawn in 1821. By 1820, the Sangamo Country encompassed primarily the central portion of the valley, including all of modern Sangamon and Menard counties, as well as portions of Macoupin, Christian, Logan, Cass, and Morgan counties.

Just prior to the arrival of the first American settlers, the Sangamo re-

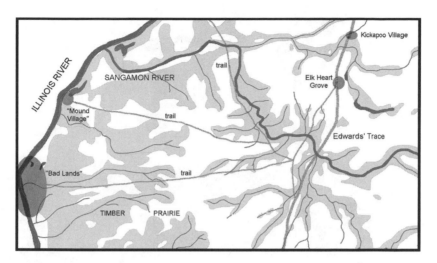

FIG. 8.2 The heart of the Sangamo Country circa 1812, encompassing parts of eight modern-day counties. The routes of the secondary, east-west trails have been deduced from county records and settlement patterns of the late 1810s and early 1820s.

gion was really only inhabited during hunting seasons, primarily by the Kickapoo. The Potawatomi, who were living at Peoria Lake, also hunted in the Sangamon valley. The closest aboriginal summer village (the most permanent form of Native American village during the period) was the Grand Village of the Kickapoo, which was located in modern day McLean County, near the headwaters of the Sangamon River. This village is thought to have been established in the 1780s, and was the principal village for the central Illinois Kickapoo for several decades.[3]

Even closer to Sangamo was a second village site, which may have begun as a seasonal encampment, but also may have been more heavily settled during the early nineteenth century. Known today as the Rhodes site, this Kickapoo village was located along the south bank of Salt Creek, less than forty miles north of the center of the Sangamo Country.[4] The site was first noticed during the 1930s, when at least one grave was disturbed by road construction.

The Illinois Kickapoo were notoriously intolerant of the continuous advances of American settlement, and their fierce independence kept most Americans out of the central and northeastern parts of Illinois until after they ceded their rights to the region in 1819. At Peoria Lake, the Potawatomi had settled along the west bank of the Illinois River during the 1750s and had maintained a strong presence in the area well into the

FIG. 8.3 Artifacts from the fur trade era of the Sangamo Country: a stone micmac pipe (modern Cass County), a fragment of a silver brooch (Morgan County), a lead bale seal stamped "St. Louis" (Scott County), a War of 1812 era brass epaulette (Elkhart Hill), and a war-era sword handle from the "Bad Lands."

nineteenth century. As the French established permanent villages along the lake in the late 1700s, the Peoria moved upriver a few miles, but continued to settle in small summer villages near the water.

Both the Kickapoo and the Potawatomi left their summer villages in the fall to spread out across the landscape for hunting and trapping during the winter. It would have been during their winter rounds that both groups spent time in what would become the Sangamo Country. Very few traces of these winter camps have been encountered archaeologically, though there is the occasional stray find: an iron trade ax, bits of trade silver, or a native-made smoking pipe (figure 8.3).

The best-understood wintering campsite in the vicinity of the Sangamo is located on a sandy terrace along the eastern shore of the Illinois River.[5] This locale served as a wintering camp for the Illinois as early as the mid-1600s, and was known as the Bad Lands during the eighteenth and early nineteenth century. Numerous aboriginal tribes (as well as the French) wintered at and near the mouth of Mauvaise Terre Creek during the 1700s, and French traders were still occupying the area as late as 1806.[6] The Tabbycat site has produced evidence of wintering activity dating from the late seventeenth century through the late eighteenth century. There is also circumstantial evidence that French and Native American fur traders may have established smaller camps further east, in the uplands closer to the heart of the original Sangamo Country.[7]

The Old Trail Again

The old overland trail between the French settlements in the American Bottom and those at Peoria crossed directly though the center of the Sangamon Valley, and it was this trail that brought the first Americans to the Sangamo Country. According to legend, some of the first Americans to travel the trace did so against their will. The story of one such event, which occurred in the summer of 1790, was retold in numerous county histories and oral traditions. As the story goes, members of the Illinois Kickapoo attacked the James Gillham farm in Kentucky, kidnapping Ann Gillham and three of her children while James was in the fields. The Kickapoo then returned to Illinois, following the old trace to their villages north of the Sangamon River. If the story is true, then Mrs. Gillham may have been one of the first Euro-American women to see the Sangamo Country. It was not until 1795 that James Gillham was able to locate his family, and with the aid of traders at the French town of Cahokia, was able to obtain the release of his wife and children. By this time, it is said, his youngest son was no longer speaking English, and did not wish to leave the Kickapoo.[8]

It was a war that first pushed the Americans up the old trace. Those living in the greater American Bottom region became aware of the region they would soon know as the Sangamo Country during the War of 1812 (figure 8.4). At the onset of the war, the northern edge of their settlements lay along an east-west line from the mouth of the Illinois River to Indiana. Although a lack of population pressure made settlement north of this line unnecessary, this line also represented the southern boundary of lands claimed by the Kickapoo. While their principal villages were located well north of the line, the region was used by the

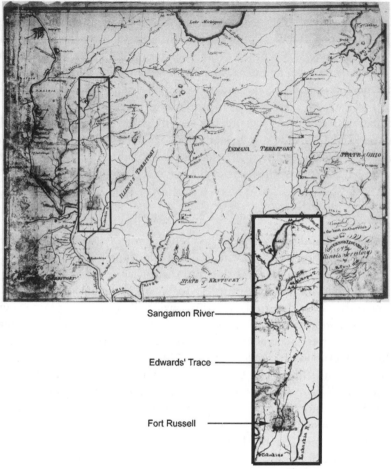

Sangamon River—

Edwards' Trace ——————

Fort Russell ——————

FIG. 8.4 René Paul's 1815 map showing the Illinois Territory, Fort Russell, Edwards' Trace, and Kickapoo villages just north of the Sangamon River.

tribe (as well as the Potawatomi and others) during their winter hunt, and also provided an important buffer zone between their villages and those of the Americans.

While technically, the war originated in disputes between the United States and England regarding shipping rights on the open seas, it also involved the lingering fur trade, westward settlement and relations with the Native Americans. In Illinois, the War of 1812 was an Indian war, which pitted Native Americans loyal to the British in Canada against Euro-American settlers who continued to occupy new land in the West. Small skirmishes, attacks, and raids were conducted by both sides. The bloodiest incident of the war occurred at Chicago, where the Potawatomi attacked soldiers and civilians who had been ordered to evacuate Fort Dearborn. On a hot August day, fifty-three Americans were brutally killed outside of the fort.[9]

During the eighteenth century, the nature and location of the French communities in the Illinois Country had never really threatened the traditional land usage of the Native Americans living in the region. Further, the French and Native Americans were codependent partners in the fur trade, and the two groups had intermarried and lived in close proximity to one another for a century prior to the arrival of Americans in Illinois. The Virginians settling the region in the late eighteenth century had no interest in communing with the natives, however. Unlike the concentrated village settlements of the French, the Virginians' desire for large tracts of land for homesteading immediately threatened the seasonal hunting traditions of the Native Americans. In Illinois, the War of 1812 was essentially an expression of two decades of tension between the various Native American tribes across the territory and the American settlers who were pushing ever northward.

With the Americans clustered in the American Bottom, the Kickapoo in central Illinois, and the Potawatomi, Sauk, and Fox north of the Illinois River, the old trail between Cahokia and Peoria became a direct connection between ancient aboriginal landscapes in the north and a young Euro-American colony in the south. The Sangamon Valley, unoccupied for most of the year, lay in between, waiting.

By the spring of 1812, the Americans headquartered at Kaskaskia began paying much closer attention to the distant French and Indian communities at Peoria Lake. Peoria had always been first and foremost an aboriginal place: the French forts, missions, and villages followed that native population. For over a century, the lake had served as meeting place for many tribes of the western Great Lakes and Illinois prairies. Now that those groups were being drawn into a war with the Americans, the military naturally regarded Peoria as a threat. By 1812, the locale (along with Prairie du Chien) was thought to be a place of "rendezvous for the discontented, the daring and the corrupt of all tribes." As there were French traders and farmers living at the lake as well, they too were automatically regarded with suspicion.[10]

In the early spring of that year, news arrived in the American settlements that the Kickapoo and Potawatomi were gathering near Peoria Lake, and it was assumed that they were planning attacks on the American settlements in the south. In response, mounted rangers were mustered from not only the Illinois Territory, but also Ohio, Indiana, and Kentucky.[11] That this militia was gathered from such a large area demonstrates that central Illinois was not simply an isolated new settlement, but in fact it represented the edge of something much larger. *The frontier*—the edge of a plow, or the edge of a blade—was in Illinois that year, and would soon be somewhere else. But that edge was always attached to something larger back east.

The rangers were assigned to guard an east-west line that was described as defining "the usual ingress to Louisiana." This was a reference to what had been traditional southward movement from Canada, headed toward the French and Indian settlements in the central and lower Mississippi valley. The line followed by the rangers began on the Mississippi River 120 miles above St. Louis, and ran easterly to the mouth of the Sangamon River on the Illinois River. From there, it followed the course of the Sangamon until the river turned to the south. The line kept running east across the prairies, until it struck the headwaters of the Kaskaskia River. This line was apparently drawn "by arrangement with the Indians," and was agreed by both parties as "the boundary for them, and us also."[12]

Such a prescribed boundary was a remarkably specific and important one, as it defined the edge of the aboriginal wilderness and the American frontier. It also defined, after the fact, a gateway between old French Canada (now under British influence) and old French Louisiana, which was under American control. That gateway had probably been conceptualized by the late 1600s, and was still relevant 150 years later. Further, that line formed the northern edge of what was about to be known as the Sangamo Country.

Two mounted troops would begin at either end of the east-west boundary line, and would ride until they met one another. This meant that one troop began its march at the mouth of the Sangamon, near modern Beardstown. The other troop began in the high prairies near the site of modern Champaign-Urbana. The two troops probably crossed paths in the vicinity of a large timbered hill, which stood 200 feet above the surrounding prairie. Within a few years, the hill (known as Elk Heart Grove) would become an important landmark, situated along the north-south Cahokia–Peoria trail, and soon to define the northern edge of a new American frontier. It was from the edge of this hill that the first groups of Euro-Americans got a good look at the Sangamo County region.

In March of 1812 Territorial Governor Ninian Edwards began plans to build a fort on Sangamon River. The site of the fort was to be where "the trail from Cahokia to Peoria" crossed the river.[13] A fort at this location would put his troops and supplies 100 miles (or one and a half days' march) closer to Peoria. From the Sangamon, he could then push to build a fort at Peoria, and thus take control of that important locale in the heart of Indian country. Had Edwards built his fort on the Sangamon, that structure would have been the first permanent Euro-American edifice in the region.[14] The fort wasn't built, however, as he was forced to use his rangers elsewhere that spring.

In August of 1812, Edwards did construct a fort on the old trail to Peoria, but it was located much further south, at the northern edge of the greater American Bottom region, or at the northern periphery of the American settlements. Strategically, this location was in a better position to actually protect the most exposed settlements, and was still located along the route to Peoria. Edwards named the fort Camp Russell after Colonel William Russell, the commander of the rangers in Illinois. Two companies of militia were stationed at the fort, armed with rifles and tomahawks. An old cannon was dragged up from the ruins of Fort de Chartres as well, and the little fortification on the trace "blazed out with considerable pioneer splendor." Local merchant William Morrison supplied ninety-three barrels of salt pork, eighty-five barrels of flour, three barrels of candles, four barrels of soap, one barrel of vinegar, and one barrel of whisky. After the war, the town of Edwardsville would be constructed just south of the remains of the fort.[15]

By the early fall of 1812, traffic had picked up along the old trail to Peoria. A company of "spies" (young and middle aged farmers living across the river from St. Louis) began patrolling the route between Cahokia and Peoria, in advance of an attack against the Indians in the north. One early morning in September, Governor Ninian Edwards led the first march against the Kickapoo and Potawatomi north of the Sangamon River. With 360 privates, Edwards struck out from Camp Russell following the old trail.

By noon, the troops had reached a point of timber known as the Lake Fork of Macoupin Creek. Apparently in no hurry, some "wild boys" in the ranks dug into an Indian grave and pulled from it a gun and silver ornaments. They soon crossed the Sangamon River and reached the hill at Elk Heart Grove, described by one member of the party as presenting a "beautiful and charming prospect."[16] Continuing northward, they reached an empty Kickapoo village before dark. The houses, covered in bark or hides, were remembered as having been decorated with paintings, which included images of "Indians scalping whites." The village was burned to the ground. The militia continued northward on the trail and did not camp until midnight, and the remains of the village began the decay that would create an archaeological site.[17]

The next morning, Edwards's troops continued north, skirting the eastern shore of Peoria Lake, and heading toward a Potawatomi village at the head of the lake (about twenty miles north of the French village). They camped within four or five miles of the village. As night fell, they waited for a possible attack on their position, but the only shot fired was the accidental discharge of one of the troop's own rifles. In the morning, some of Edwards's men encountered two Potawatomi alone in the woods. The Native Americans immediately attempted to surrender, but a captain proclaimed that he had not left home to take prisoners, and one young man was shot as he sat on his horse. In the commotion that followed, they discovered that the second individual was a female, and after some gunfire, she was taken prisoner.

The troops then proceeded to the village, which was an apparently situated below the high bluffs. At the edge of the bluff, an American soldier lost all restraint and plunged down the hill directly into the village, followed by the rest of the militia. Most of the Potawatomi retreated into the swamps along the shore of the Illinois River. The Americans' horses were immediately bogged down in the mud. Some of the soldiers chased the Indians through the cattails on foot. When the attack was over, between twenty and eighty residents of the village had been killed. None of the Americans lost their lives. Edwards's troops looted and burned the emptied village.[18]

The militia returned southward in a heavy rainstorm with eighty horses stolen from the Potawatomi, following the old trail through the Sangamon Valley and back home. This concluded the only battle of the War of 1812 in the vicinity of the Sangamo Country. Following Edwards's campaign, the old trail (which had been followed by the French for a century and by the Native Americans for much longer) would be known as Edwards' Trace.

The End of French Peoria

The French villagers at the southern end of Peoria Lake were probably trying their best to lie low during the fall of 1812. While they had partnered with the various Native American groups in the region for a century, there is no real evidence that they were convinced to plot against the Americans during this new war with the British. In fact, the French villagers at Peoria were experiencing war-related tensions with the neighboring Potawatomi themselves, and complained of stolen horses and crops. The war was disrupting all aspects of settlement and relations in the Illinois Country.

A few weeks after Edwards's march up the old trail, the Americans returned to Peoria, this time by water. In November, Captain Thomas Craig led two boats up the Illinois River in another effort to impress or subdue the Native American population at Peoria Lake. Upon his arrival at the French village, he found that many of its residents had fled, and his men helped themselves to some of the possessions they found in the vacated homes. While in their boats on the lake, Craig's men were fired upon from the shore. No one was hurt, and the origin of the fire could not be determined. Nevertheless, Craig immediately suspected collusion on the part of the remaining French villagers, and he and his men promptly "arrested" forty-two residents of La Ville de Maillet. While the prisoners were loaded onto the boats, Craig's men looted several of the dwellings, slaughtered some pigs, and burned four homes and two hay barns to the ground. The men also looted a store run by Indian Agent Thomas Forsyth, who was in fact working for the same government.

The French were taken downstream to a beach opposite St. Louis where they were left without provisions. Back at Peoria, the Potawatomi looted what was left of the village. The old town on the west bank of the river was never resettled by its builders, and what had been (partially) a French place for over 100 years was suddenly an aboriginal one again.

A year later, the Americans again returned to Peoria, to build a fortification at the site of the burnt and looted French town. The new fort, christened Fort Clark, would provide for a secure American presence in the heart of "Indian country" during the war. The soldiers building the fort complained of "many disadvantages," including having to cross the lake to cut timber for the fort. When Thomas Forsyth later visited the site of his looted store, however, he found that his and other buildings had been dismantled as convenient sources of ready-made timbers. The fort stood throughout the remainder of the war, buts its role was largely symbolic. After the war, the American government abandoned it, and its remains were salvaged and partially burned by the Potawatomi. During the next decade, however, American settlers to the south would know the west bank of the lake as Fort Clark.

The war that began in 1812 was concluded in Illinois with the ratification of the Treaty of Ghent in February of 1815. Overt hostilities between the American settlers and the Native Americans living north of the Sangamon ceased, but the Sauk, Fox, and Kickapoo of northern and

CHAPTER EIGHT

central Illinois continued to receive gifts from the British to encourage their distrust of the Americans. The Potawatomi edged further up the Illinois River, and no longer posed a threat to the Americans. The Kickapoo still claimed land on the east side of the Illinois River as hunting territory, and remained at their Grand Village (in present-day McLean County) for several more years. The Sauk and Fox kept villages at the mouth of the Rock River, which was still very remote from the American settlements to the south.

In the summer of 1815, surveyors crossed the Illinois River and began mapping lands that would become a 3.5 million acre tract of military bounty lands, known as the Military Tract. These were to be divided into eighty-acre parcels and granted to veterans of the war, most of whom still lived in the eastern states. The Sauk and Fox immediately began harassing the surveyors, stealing their equipment and removing their markers. Ultimately, few of the veterans granted property in the region actually settled (or even visited) the land, and most of it was later sold to local farmers.

Meanwhile, on the east side of the Illinois River, a new land office district was created in the spring of 1816, headquartered at the town of Edwardsville on the northern edge of the American settlements. The new district stretched northward to include the southern portion of the Sangamon River drainages, but most of this land could not yet be surveyed, as it was still claimed by the Kickapoo. The beginning of 1816 saw new maps of the wilderness north and west of the Illinois River—immigration to the territory increased and American settlement pushed against its old northern boundary. The area between, which was centered on the Sangamon River Valley, was still off limits and poorly understood.

A New Map

Although Americans had been in Illinois for over thirty-five years, and the military had been fighting an Indian war for four years, maps of the Illinois Territory were still remarkably limited. A map made in 1778 by Thomas Hutchins, which depicted a reasonably distorted picture of the geography of Illinois, was still a primary reference.[19] During the war, William Clark, Ninian Edwards, and Thomas Forsyth had made what amounted to sketch maps of the region, but these maps betray a lack of understanding of the orientation of the Illinois River and the nature of its tributaries. The uplands surrounding the Illinois Valley (in central Illinois) were basically unknown to all but the rangers and Indian traders who had spent time in the region. Ironically, Father Marquette's map of the Illinois River, drawn over 140 years earlier, was still one of the most accurate depictions of the orientation of the river itself.[20]

The first true cartographic representation of what would become central Illinois was surveyed and drawn by Major Stephen Long in the late summer of 1816 (figure 8.5).[21] As a member of the Topographic Engineers division of the Army Corps of Engineers, Long was assigned to map the Illinois River from its mouth to the head of Peoria Lake, as well as the uplands to the east. Such maps made by the corps were usually drawn for military purposes, exploring routes for the passage of troops.

The war had just ended, and Long's official assignment was to map the Illinois River as part of a reevaluation for the need to replace the existing Fort Clark, situated in what was still an important Native American locale. Not only was the resulting map the first accurate survey of that river, it was also the first to record the uplands of central Illinois, which had no obvious connection to a riverine route to Peoria.

Instead, the map, which included a survey that extended over fifty miles east of the river, was probably also designed to better document the alternate route to Peoria. This alternate was the old trail followed by Edwards's rangers during the war. Aside from those troops (and the few traders that still traveled between Cahokia and Peoria) the trail and the lands it crossed were still largely a mystery to the territorial and federal government. Officially, the land office at Edwardsville could not begin surveying the lands crossed by the old trail, as they still belonged to the Kickapoo. The region surrounding the Sangamon Valley was now a hole in the map of the future state—still claimed by Indians, still largely unknown, and still dangerous to travel.

Two independent trips to Peoria were required to create the Illinois River map of 1816. The river valley itself was actually mapped in August 1816. To survey the uplands, Long followed a meandering path northward from the recently platted town of Edwardsville to the south end of Peoria Lake. That path was Edwards' Trace, and it is the trace that essentially defines the eastern boundary of Long's map. On his return, Long made a more direct southbound journey, which terminated at the mouth of Illinois River. By anchoring this track to the mouth of the Illinois, Long tied his detailed drawings of the Illinois Valley and the adjacent uplands into the system of rectangular survey that was just beginning in Illinois

Though the final map was titled "A Map of the Illinois River," it actually gave the government its first real glimpse into uplands that lay between rapidly growing American settlements and the lands about to be gifted to war veterans. The map depicted the principal creeks that

FIG. 8.5 Detail of Stephen Long's 1816 map of the lower Illinois River and the uplands to the east.

crossed through the prairies, as well as the exact location of the trail to Peoria, as it appeared at the time. As it was quite clear that the next wave of American settlement would soon push north of Edwardsville, Long's survey produced more than a map of unsettled lands—it was also a map of the future.

CHAPTER NINE

A New Frontier

The earliest official correspondence regarding the ultimate settlement of the Sangamon River valley probably dates to December of 1816, when William Rector wrote that the lands north of the existing settlements were the subject of "much anxiety" by those who wished to relocate their families there. From "information received from several intelligent men well acquainted with the region," he felt confident that the region would sell quickly, as it was conveniently divided between prairies and woodlands, with good, well-drained soils.[1]

Two months later in February of 1817, the acting secretary of war in Washington noticed that there was a gap between the prewar settlements in the Illinois Territory, and the lands then being surveyed for military bounty lands. Nathaniel Pope echoed this concern, describing the central Illinois uplands "as fine a body of land as I have ever seen," but warning that travel between the old settlements and the new military tract would be "interrupted" by the Native Americans who claimed the region. The secretary of war immediately asked Governor Edwards to find out which Native American group claimed this land, so that a treaty negotiation might connect the two regions. The hole in the map was about to be filled.[2]

In January of 1817, Edwards answered that it was the Kickapoo who currently occupied and claimed central Illinois, and that they had moved to the "sanguemon country" around 1800. This may have been one the first official uses of the new name of the region. Edwards joined his contemporaries in extolling the virtues of central Illinois: "for fertility of soil, salubrity of climate and eligibility of situation, is not surpassed by any tract of land of equal extent, that has ever been discovered in the western country." He added, "were it now prepared for sale, there is no portion of the public lands that would sell more readily." It was probably Governor Edwards who, more than any one individual, defined the Sangamo Country during the 1810s and exposed it to American farmers.[3]

By November of 1817, preparations for treaty negotiations concerning the lands in central Illinois had begun. But a peg-legged farmer living west of Edwardsville named Robert Pulliam could not wait for the Kickapoo to leave.[4] That fall, Robert Pulliam left his wife to watch the children, and set out on the trail to the Sangamo Country with a herd of cattle that he intended to fatten in the unoccupied forests to the north. The trip was very probably also an exploratory one. Accompanied by a couple of hired hands and a cook, Pulliam built a small log dwelling in the timber on the western edge of Sugar Creek. The party spent the winter at the camp, and returned in the spring. Pulliam moved his family to the cabin on Sugar Creek in the spring 1819.[5]

Forty years later, a few historically conscious residents of Sangamon County would gather together to decide who to memorialize as the first true settler of the county. Pulliam's 1817 cabin was well remembered and became the obvious choice. Years later, however, descendants of Henry Funderburk (an early settler at nearby Brush Creek) contested Pulliam's designation. Their objection was based on the recollections of another early settler, Jacob Hinkle, who arrived at Brush Creek in the spring of 1818. He remembered seeing upon his arrival a decaying shock of fodder (or harvested corn stalks left standing in the field) on Funderburk's farm. If this was the case, then that corn would have been planted no later than the early summer of 1817, or several months before Pulliam's arrival.[6]

Gershom Flagg, writing from Edwardsville in September of 1818, related that he had heard "the hunters" say that they had found eight to ten swarms of honey bees a day on the "St. Gama," leading him to conclude that central Illinois was "truly the land of milk and honey."[7] Only a few families had yet built permanent homes in the region, however.

The territory of Illinois became the state of Illinois in 1818. Between the close of the War of 1812 (in 1815) and the summer of 1818, the population of the region had increased by 150 percent. By July of that year, the population of the new state was recorded as 35,000, but Native Americans were not counted. Responding to the northward movement of new settlements, the capital was moved from Kaskaskia to the town of Vandalia the following year.

The Kickapoo ceded their claims on lands in central Illinois by treaty in July of 1819—an act that they (and the Americans) must have seen as inevitable for several years. From Edwardsville, Gershom Flagg observed that "13 months ago there was not a family north of here and there is now perhaps 200 some 120 miles north."[8] In the late summer Ferdinand Ernst, a wealthy German agriculturist and traveler, visited the little town of Vandalia, which was about to become the new state capitol. Here he learned of the "fine lands" of the Sangamo, for which "every one is full of praise."[9] At the end of August, he and a guide set out to see the new frontier. With plenty of provisions, Ernst rode northwest across the prairies to "a fine and well-travelled road" that was in fact the old trace that had recently been mapped by Stephen Long, used by Governor Edwards and his rangers during the war, and traveled by Father Marest and his guides over a century earlier. In many ways, the trail was probably the first landmark recognized as historic by the Americans in the Sangamo Country.

On his second day, he reached the edge of the Sugar Creek timber, and spent the night near a spring. Here, he learned that there were already sixty farms along that creek alone, the majority of which were less than six months old. Genuinely impressed, or caught up in the fever of a new frontier, he gushed about the "splendid fields, covered almost without exception, with corn from ten to fifteen feet high." He predicted that "possibly no region in all this broad America will be so quickly populated" as this region "justly styled 'the beautiful land of the Sangamon.'" Ernst had the fever.

Settling at a Very Old Crossroads

Like the German traveler, most of the immigrants to the Sangamo appeared to have followed the old trace into the region. In fact, the trail (as well as two or three secondary trails that connected the overland route to the Illinois River) appears to have heavily influenced the pattern of initial settlement of the region (figure 9.1). The presence and significance of these trails has become apparent only recently, through the archival study of early preemption claims and land purchases in central Illinois. Between 1818 and 1820, a line of extended family farms sprouted along the eastern edge of the Sugar Creek timber, revealing the location of Edwards' Trace 170 years later. Similar linear patterns of settlement

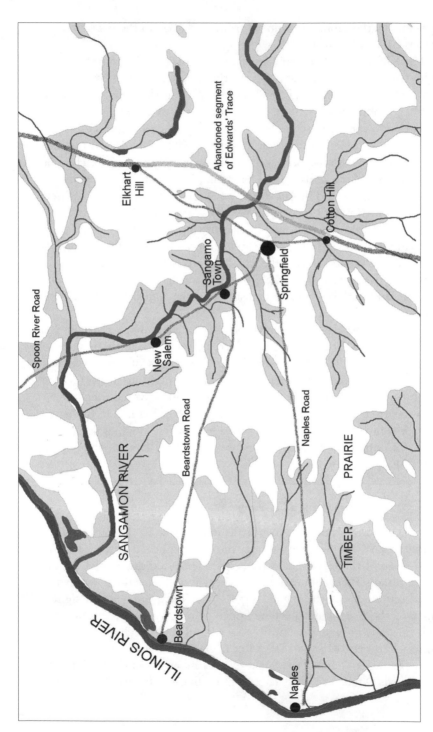

FIG. 9.1 The Sangamo Country in the 1820s showing selected towns, settlements, and presettlement trails. Note the rerouted portion of the Edwards' Trace trail, via Springfield.

were noted elsewhere in the region. In particular, a very dense line of early settlement ran westerly from Edwards' Trace, following Spring and Mauvaise Terre creeks to the Illinois River, and marking the route of an east-west trail that appears in country records of the early 1820s. At the western terminus of this route was the site of the old Bad Lands wintering grounds, thus directly connecting the heart of the Sangamo region with an important eighteenth-century fur trade locale.

The trail to the Bad Lands was an example of several secondary routes that connected the Illinois River to the overland Edwards' Trace corridor. Such a network of trails was probably formed as a result of the winter hunting traditions of the Illinois, Potawatomi, and Kickapoo, as well as their French trading partners. Further, the future political and economic center of the Sangamo Country—the new town of Springfield—would be founded at the intersection of these two old routes, along an otherwise unimpressive, damp prairie.

Two additional secondary trails appear to have predated the arrival of the first Americans, and these too seem to have served as east-west connections between the Edwards' Trace corridor and points along the Illinois River. Perhaps not coincidentally, they also met at what would become the site of the first town in the Sangamo Country. One of these trails left Springfield and headed northwest, following points of timber until it reached the Illinois River at the site of another wintering camp occupied seasonally by the Kickapoo. Known as Mound Village during the 1810s (due to the presence of a large prehistoric burial mound at the edge of the river), the locale may have been occupied by the French as well. The ruins of a building made of vertical poles (possibly a French-style vertical log dwelling) was apparently discovered by Thomas Beard, the first American settler of the area, upon his arrival in 1819. Beard's settlement ultimately became the site of Beardstown. Two years later, Springfield's first merchant Elijah Iles used this trail to haul twenty-five tons of merchandise into the heart of the Sangamo Country (see chapter 12).

About ten miles west of the site of Springfield, another secondary trail veered off the route to Mound Village, following the western edge of the Sangamon River timberline, ultimately reaching the Illinois River opposite the mouth of the Spoon River. This trail would soon become known as the Spoon River Road, and was probably an important route for veterans who had received land grants in the Military Tract. It was along this road that the second and third towns in the Sangamo Country—Sangamo Town and New Salem, would later be platted.

From what we have learned from patterns of early land occupation in the region, it is now clear that pioneers such as Pulliam, Iles, and Beard did not hack their way through virgin prairie grass and timber to reach their new homes. They followed well-worn trails that had provided a living for French hunters and trappers for a century, and Native Americans for much longer. Several of these trails intersected with Edwards' Trace, forming a hub that would become the center of the Sangamo Country frontier.

Sangamo Country Becomes Sangamon County

Somewhere in the neighborhood of 500 families settled in the Sangamo Country between 1817 and 1821.[10] These families were clustered in extended family locales, identified by specific place names and defined largely by the natural topography. The earliest of these were in the southern portion of the region, along Edwards' Trace, and included the Sugar Creek, Horse Creek, and Cotton Hill settlements. Further north on the trace, in the central portion of the region, were the communities of Fork Prairie and Springfield. To the west, along the road to the Illinois River, was Island Grove and Diamond Grove. To the northwest, along the trail headed to the Military Tract, were Richland and Clary's Grove. Finally, along the northern periphery of the Sangamo Country, were the settlements at Indian Point and Elk Heart Grove. Some of these names were later applied to towns platted nearby, or to townships that would later encompass such settlements.

The settlements in the Sangamo Country were first recognized as a distinct political entity in July of 1819, when the region was defined as its own election district in what was then Madison County. That county encompassed most of the northern tier of prewar settlements in the greater American Bottom region, and technically, it had no real northern boundary, stretching indefinitely northward into the wilderness. The new Sangamo District included all of the fledgling settlements on the Sangamon River, as well as its tributaries. By March of 1820, the Sangamo District of Madison county had grown large enough to prompt its division into three separate townships: Sangamo, Fork Prairie, and Springfield. The latter may have been the first formal reference to the place name of Springfield, which would become the political center of the state of Illinois seventeen years later.[11] In 1821, the heart of the old Sangamo Country was defined as Sangamon County, which encompassed most of the new settlements in and around the valley. Between Sangamon County and the Illinois River, what would have been considered the western portion of the Sangamo *Country* ten years earlier was defined as Greene County in 1821, and as Morgan County in 1823.

Most of the earliest services or trades within the Sangamo Country were informal ones, located within the various extended family settlements. Animal-powered mills, blacksmiths, taverns, and small dry-goods stores appeared within a year of the earliest permanent settlement, and these commercial activities were completely unregulated and untethered to formally platted communities. They were also often fleeting and transitory, as was much of the settlement of the time.

The first town to be organized in the Sangamo Country was ultimately the most successful. With the creation of the new county in January of 1821, state law required the immediate selection of a temporary seat of county government. Residents of a community along the southern timberline of Spring Creek, aided by a storekeeper recently arrived from Kentucky (see chapter 12), began planning a formal community that would ultimately serve as county seat. In the meantime, the farm of John Kelly was chosen as the site of a temporary seat of government. For the last year or so, the region surrounding Spring Creek and the Kelly farm had been informally known as Springfield.[12]

Late nineteenth-century historians believed that the location of the temporary county seat was based on population density, and that the Kelly settlement would have best provided board and lodging for visiting lawyers and judges. Closer examination of the first years of settlement in the area, however, finds no evidence that the small Springfield settlement was any larger or more improved than others along Spring and Sugar creeks. Instead, it was very probably the initiative shown by Kelly and his neighbors to accommodate the creation of the new seat of government (and the town that would follow) that made Springfield the focus of the early governmental activity. In other words, it was probably politics that brought the county seat to the damp prairie at the edge of Spring Creek in 1821.

The first election of county officers was held in the early spring of 1821, and one of the polling places was the home of John Kelly. This farm was situated along the trail to Mound Village on the Illinois River, where Thomas Beard had recently settled. The day after the election, the new county court also met at Kelly's cabin—probably sitting around his kitchen table. A week later, the county commissioners gathered again, this time to stake out a site for a temporary county courthouse. They chose a spot just east of the Kelly home, near the top of a slight hillock at the edge of the timber. At the same meeting in April, the commissioners hired Kelly to build a temporary log courthouse in what had essentially been his backyard.

The Edwards' Trace was the one of the first items of business for the new county commissioners in the spring of 1821. In their first session in the new courthouse, the commissioners heard a petition for the creation of a public road "from the south line of the county to Fort Clark." This road was to:

> commence on the south line of the county at a particular point so that a direct north line will strike the best crossing on Sugar Creek [south of Springfield] near Mr. Eades. Thence to or near the head of the timber at Long Point. Thence in a straight line as may be to the river at a place commonly called Chapman's Ford. Thence on the best route in a northern direction through the settlements three and four miles from the [Sangamon] river. Thence in a straight line to the west side of Elkhart Grove. Thence to the old Kickapoo town crossing Salt Creek at or near the old ford. Thence crossing Kickapoo Creek Sugar Creek and Mackinaw [River] to the Illinois River opposite Fort Clark. Robert Pulliam viewed the said road and made a report.[13]

Of course, the road already existed, and it was the route most new immigrants to the region had followed. The petition simply requested that the new country government adopt the route, and commit to its maintenance and improvement. Other business included electing and appointing various officials, setting election districts, issuing tavern and ferry licenses, as well as issuing permits for mill dams. Road petitions were often submitted to the court as documents composed of smaller strips or scraps of rag paper, fastened together with sealing wax to form a single large sheet. The paperwork generated in the tiny wooden building near Spring Creek represented the beginning of the taming of a massive wilderness.

On June 5, 1821, the county commissioners ordered a county tax to be made for the "purpose of defraying the necessary expenses of the county." They ordered the county assessor to assess all taxable property, which included horses, cattle, carriages, stock in trade, and distilleries. As a result, the assessor compiled a list of names of inhabitants of the county who owned such property. That list, containing over 380 names, was only recently rediscovered in the local archives.

The 1821 tax list is an important document; it is the earliest known list of American settlers living in central Illinois. Such documents are surprisingly rare among the early county records of Illinois (figure 9.2).

FIG. 9.2 Detail of the 1821 list of taxable inhabitants of Sangamon County.

While some of the names included in the list are well documented in later histories, many of these individuals spent little time in the fledgling community and their enumeration on this document is the only record of their presence. It should also be remembered that the list was designed to record those with taxable property, and the population of the community probably also consisted of a number of more transient individuals or families. Such individuals were probably not included in the list, and their presence in the county may never have been recorded in any form.

The majority of the Americans that settled in Illinois during the frontier period were upland southerners. In fact, historian Solon Buck estimated that two thirds of the people in Illinois in 1818 were from southern states.[14] This generalization appears to hold true in central Illinois in 1821, based on the nativity of the men listed in the county tax list. From that list, the birthplaces of 172 of the 384 men (44 percent) were determined. Upland southerners made up 70 percent of the identified sample, and individuals from Mid-Atlantic and New England states 15 percent and 10 percent, respectively. Only 3 percent of the identified sample were born in the Midwest (Ohio or Illinois), and only 2 percent were foreign born (in England or Ireland).[15]

The African-American population the Sangamo Country region was small during the frontier period. An 1825 census of Springfield found seven blacks living in town—most of whom were probably indentured servants.[16] Free blacks did begin to buy land in Springfield and the surrounding area by the mid-1820s, however.[17]

From the Springfield community, the temporary county seat town of Calhoun was platted in the late fall of 1823, much to the chagrin of local residents, who still called the place Springfield. The name Calhoun did not take, and the town was soon known as Springfield. During the same period, a second town was platted within the limits of the county, also in hopes of acquiring the permanent seat of government. The town of Sangamo (later changed to Sangamo Town) was platted by Moses Broadwell, about ten miles northwest of Springfield and along a branch of the trail that ran to the Military Tract. While the temporary courthouse anchored Springfield, Sangamo Town was designed as a milling center. Both towns provided services such as stores, taverns, and a few craftsmen.

The first ten years of community growth in the Sangamo consisted of an influx of new settlers who clustered themselves in more extended-family farming communities, the shape and location of which was dictated by the natural topography and preexisting trails. During the mid-1820s, those communities were serviced by a slowly growing commercial economy, anchored by two formally-platted towns. By the early 1830s, however, town platting and real estate speculation exploded across central Illinois. Between 1830 and 1839, approximately two dozen new towns were platted in Sangamon County. By 1835, there were thirty-four saw and gristmills, five of which were powered by steam. Scattered across the region were forty additional animal powered gristmills.[18] At the Springfield land office, the number of acres sold tripled between 1827 and 1830. That year, nearly 102,000 acres were purchased, and in 1835 the number climbed to almost a half a million.[19]

The Frontier Pushes Northward

The Kickapoo and Potawatomi (as well as other groups) had continued to winter in parts of the Sangamo Country well into the mid-1820s. The preacher Peter Cartwright remembered them as "degraded and demoralized" by the mid-1820s, which he attributed to alcohol. George

Brunk remembered participating in "social hunts" with Bassena and Joe Muney—members of the prairie Kickapoo. William Rutledge, whose family settled along the Sangamon River in the mid-1820s, remembered Native American women cooking with Euro-American women and wearing Euro-American-style dresses.[20]

The slow close of the frontier period in Illinois began in the summer of 1832, with a series of skirmishes between the American militia and a band of the Potawatomi that became known as the Black Hawk War. In northwestern Illinois, the mouth of the Rock River had been home to the Sauk and Fox since the mid-eighteenth century. By the late 1820s, most of the Fox and some of the Sauk had been convinced by the Americans to move across the Mississippi. One band of the Sauk (led by Black Hawk) intended to remain in the region in the face of American settlement that was pushing into this part of the state.

In the fall of 1830, Black Hawk and his followers crossed the Mississippi, probably as part of their winter hunt. The Americans interpreted this as a surrender of the Rock River lands, however, and soon began establishing new farms where the Sauk and Fox had traditionally constructed their summer villages. When Black Hawk returned to Illinois the following spring and began planting corn, he found more American farms. He and some of his followers destroyed fences and other improvements and flatly stated that they wished to remain in Illinois. In response, as many as 2000 American soldiers and volunteers marched to the Rock River in a show of force that sent Black Hawk back across the Mississippi.

In the following spring, Black Hawk once again returned to Illinois, still intent on not only remaining at his summer village, but also hoping to enlist other bands to push the settlers from the region. He found no allies, however, and the resistance was his alone. Governor John Reynolds, who had marched to Peoria on Edwards' Trace in 1812, called on the militia to remove Black Hawk from Illinois. Among the volunteers that marched to northern Illinois in the early summer of 1832 was Abraham Lincoln, who had just settled in Sangamon County.

The militia that entered the Rock River valley suffered from poor leadership and a lynch mob mentality. In May, Major Isaiah Stillman and 275 men encountered Black Hawk and his band near the Rock River. Once again, Black Hawk prepared to surrender and retreat, but several of his warriors were killed when attempting to negotiate that surrender. The Americans then blindly attacked the rest of the warriors. Black Hawk fought back, killing several Americans and sending the rest into a scattered retreat. News of the incident rippled across both Euro-

American and Native American communities in the region, resulting in six weeks of panic and skirmishes.

In August, while attempting to return across the Mississippi (at Bad Axe in southwest Wisconsin) Black Hawk and his followers were brutally attacked by both Americans and the Sioux (who had been fighting with the Sauk for years). Most of Black Hawk's band was killed, and Black Hawk himself was taken prisoner. The war was over, and the summer of 1832 essentially marked the end of 12,000 years of Native American cultural presence in Illinois.

The mid-1830s saw the arrival of many facets of a new modern age in what had been the Sangamo Country, and the region's time as a frontier soon began to close. Firstly, land speculation and absentee owners consumed most of the timbered property in the region by the 1840s. What was left was land in the open prairies that had been regarded as inhospitable and less fertile, but in fact comprised some of the richest soil in the entire country. Residents who had pioneered the landscape with temporary log dwellings began to replace these with frame houses, and more carpenters and masons found work in the region. Log dwellings soon became symbols of another time.

In the spring of 1832, the *Talisman* became the first steamboat to ascend the Sangamon River, with much fanfare from the business community at Springfield. Through the shallow and log-filled river the boat made it to Springfield, but low water prevented it from actually turning around. The steamboat returned down river backwards, and did not make the journey again. Springfield would never become a port city.

Stagecoach travel arrived in central Illinois during the 1830s, and the old trails that wove across the landscape were gradually straightened to provide more direct routes between new towns and sociopolitical centers. One of the earliest railroads in the Midwest—the Northern Cross—was begun in 1837 and designed to connect the towns of Jacksonville and Springfield to the Illinois River. An engine and building materials were shipped from Pittsburgh, and within a year the first locomotive was running on eight miles of track (figure 9.3). Engine and track problems soon caused the locomotive to be replaced by horses, and the incomplete route was in disrepair within five years. Reliable rail shipping would not cross through the Sangamo region until the early 1850s.

In 1837, the state capital of Illinois was moved from Vandalia to Springfield, in part to place the government closer to the center of the growing state and its population. On the public square in Springfield

FIG. 9.3 Early nineteenth-century image of a steam powered engine and passenger car used in advertisements for the Northern Cross Railroad in central Illinois.

was constructed an impressive Greek revival statehouse, made of limestone quarried from the Sugar Creek valley. The same year, the Panic of 1837 signaled the beginning of a nationwide depression that persisted into the mid-1840s. During this period, cash was scarce and many farmers were unable to make payments to the government on their property. Further, many laborers left the cities for the countryside, looking for work in a rural economy that was still functioning on barter and notes.

In 1839, the size of Sangamon County was reduced, and divided into modern-day Sangamon, Menard, Christian, and Logan counties. This process created more governments and more county seats, as well as more election precincts, country officials, and country roads. Many of the area's first settlers had moved further west, and many others were starting to get old. What had been the Sangamo Country frontier twenty years earlier was now just four more counties in the twenty-first of twenty-six American states.

PART FIVE

The Archaeology of Sangamo

CHAPTER TEN

Overlooking Wilderness
Excavations at Elkhart Hill

In the spring of 1817, James Latham lay dying in New Orleans. There is no record of why exactly he had traveled to the port city from his farm in Kentucky, but the trip was probably made to sell farm produce. Thousands of farmers shipped hundreds of tons of pork, grain, and other products to the city each year. By the second week of April, Latham was so ill with fever and dysentery that he was convinced he would not see his family again. After three weeks in bed, somewhere in the old French city, he was surprised to find himself recovering. It was only then that he wrote to his wife, telling her of his brush with death, and warning her that she might not recognize him when he returned. He made arrangements to travel by steamboat up the Mississippi, and hoped to arrive home by the end of May. He told her that when he arrived at the landing nearest their farm, he would have a cannon fired. When they heard the "big gun," they would know he was home.[1]

Latham made it back to Kentucky, but within eighteen months, he was 300 miles to the north, in the heart of the Sangamo Country. In the fall of 1818, he came to the region to visit the new home of his son-in-law (James Chapman), who had just established a ferry across the Sangamon River on Edwards' Trace. Chapman's farm was very near the site on which Governor Edwards had planned to build a fort seven years earlier. Latham wintered along the river with his daughter and son-in-law, and it was probably during winter hunts that he was introduced to a nearby timbered hill surrounded by an ocean of prairie grass. Located about ten miles north of the Sangamon River and known as Elk Heart Grove, the hill was situated along the old trail from Cahokia to Peoria that had been recently followed by Governor Edwards.

Settling Elkhart Hill

Elkhart, as it is known today, was probably an important stop on the east-west boundary line that was patrolled by rangers during the War of 1812. Given its location and its visibility from the surrounding prairie, the hill may have served as the rendezvous point for the two troops traveling east and west. By 1819, Elkhart lay on the northern boundary of the region known as the Sangamo Country. Just ten miles to the north were the burnt remains of the Kickapoo village that Ninian Edwards had destroyed on his march seven years earlier, and the Kickapoo still maintained a permanent presence in the region.

In the early months of 1819, James Latham and his son Richard began plans to settle at Elkhart. In the spring, they began clearing a site on the west face of the hill, near a spring and along the trace (figure 10.1). With the help of Ebenezer Briggs (James's brother-in-law) they planted a corn crop and built a new cabin just above the field. That spring, most of the corn growing north of the Sangamon was to be found in fields cultivated by the Kickapoo, and the Lathams' new farm at Elkhart formed the edge of a new American frontier.

Once the crops were in the field and the cabin completed, James Latham returned to Kentucky to collect his wife and family and bring them to their new home. By the fall of 1819, the new house on the face of the hill was full to capacity, with James's sons, daughters, and in-laws. The fields were harvested, more timber was cleared, and Elkhart was now an American place.

The German traveler Ferdinand Ernst visited Elkhart in the late summer of 1819. He was following the old trace when he crossed the Sangamon, and to the north, spotted the "not insignificant" hill, covered in timber. He was impressed by the size and antiquity of the sugar maples there, which he found to be three to four feet in diameter. He also encountered the Latham farm, which already included thirty acres of young corn "enclosed by the wood of the blue ash." Ernst was also impressed by the apparent fertility of the place and took with him a sample of the soil from the base of the hill.[2] One wonders if there is still a little vial of Illinois soil in a collection somewhere in Germany.

As the Lathams developed their settlement at Elkhart, Americans began visiting the old site of Peoria and Fort Clark. In the spring of 1819,

FIG. 10.1 View of Elkhart Hill as it appeared in the 1870s, and the site of James Latham's 1819 dwelling as it appeared in 1950. Today, the site is a residential lawn.

a small group of men traveled up the trace to hunt and fish along the lake. They salvaged timbers from in and around the ruins of the burned Fort Clark to construct new houses, and made plans to settle at the site of the former French village. They planted fifteen acres of corn and potatoes and returned south for their wives and families.[3]

In 1821, James Latham was appointed subagent for Indian affairs at Peoria. Indian agents served as liaisons between Native American groups and the federal government, which had instituted programs designed to stabilize trade and relations with the many Native American communities. There is no evidence that Latham had previous experience with the Indian trade, and his appointment was probably a political one. He was, however, aware of the local histories of the neighboring Kickapoo and the subagencies at Peoria and Edwardsville. He also warned his superiors that the Kickapoo were showing "strong symptoms of lawless disposition," and that they had stolen horses and "killed up nearly every hog" at Elkhart during the previous winter.[4]

Latham probably divided his time between Peoria and the family settlement at Elkhart, where his wife remained. He temporarily lost his position at Peoria in 1822 or 1823, during which time he and his son Richard built a horse mill at the foot of the hill. Latham was reappointed to Peoria in 1824, and it was probably Richard who oversaw the mill and farms at Elkhart.

In the fall of 1826, while he was at Peoria, Latham became gravely ill. He was attended by a doctor several times in September, but he died in December. The possessions and cattle that he had kept at Peoria were hauled back to Elkhart, as was his body—the ferry keeper at Peoria charged the estate seventy cents for carrying a wagon, three horses, a corpse, and a driver across the Illinois River. Back at the family farm, Latham's estate was handled by his son Richard. The Lathams' household and farmyard possessions were inventoried, and an estate sale was held to raise funds to pay James's outstanding debts. The sale was attended by most of the Latham clan and their neighbors. Over $200 was raised, and Richard charged his father's estate $3 for the six gallons of whisky that he served at the event.[5]

Latham's widow Mary stayed on at the house for about ten more years, before moving away—possibly into the home of one of her children. The old cabin was abandoned and disassembled shortly afterwards. Their son Robert inherited part of the farm and constructed a new cabin very nearby around 1838. The site of the first dwelling at the edge of the Sangamo frontier soon became an archaeological one.

———

Local residents had told the story of county's first settler for a century and a half, and in the early spring of 2000, two members of the Elkhart Historic Society took me to the spot on the hill where Latham's cabin was thought to have stood. We followed a crisp blacktop driveway up the western slope of the hill and parked in front of a large home built in the 1950s. The house stood on several acres of timbered property that had seen little modification over the years. So, unless the site we were looking for was also the same site chosen to build the house in the 1950s (which is often the case), there was a good chance that it was well preserved.

We walked across the mown lawn, and I soon realized my guides were leading me down the gentle slope of a ravine. This was not good. Particularly during the early nineteenth century, settlers chose level, well-drained areas to build their homes. How the ravine had become known as the site of the Latham cabin is unclear. Quite commonly, the specific locations of such sites are identified by a phantom surface depression or even a pile of old logs. It still seemed possible, however, that the oral traditions had the general locale correct. Latham had been the original purchaser of the property on which we stood, and later generations of Lathams had built homes nearby. Also, their family cemetery was located just to the east.

I walked back up the slope, and noticed an area of bare earth beneath a stand of pine trees. Right there, on the modern ground surface and surrounded by a well-maintained front yard, were small fragments of pearlware. Within a few hours, a series of shovel tests established the presence of a well-preserved archaeological site dating to the 1820s. Closer inspection found that it was situated directly above a still-flowing spring, and alongside the faintly visible ruts associated with a segment of Edwards' Trace itself. The old stories were correct—there had been a cabin here. This site—where a modern yard now stood—had a played a role in the settlement of the Sangamo frontier.

Under James Latham's House

As the site of the cabin was not immediately threatened by development (as are many of the sites we investigate), we conducted only limited testing, choosing to leave the rest preserved. Our excavation units exposed a portion of what at first was believed to be a rectangular pit cellar, measuring about five by eight feet. Further work has suggested that, in fact, our units were laid directly over an entrance to a much larger cellar, measuring approximately ten by fourteen feet (figure 10.2). Additional excavations will be required to clarify the size and shape of the feature, but it is clearly a subfloor cellar once located beneath a dwelling. Based on the age of the Queensware found in the fill of feature 1, the cellar appears to have been abandoned and filled during the mid-1830s. Most of the material dates to the mid-1810s through the 1820s, strongly suggesting that the occupation of the site began as early as the late 1810s—consistent with the 1819 arrival of the James Latham family.

Most pit features on rural, frontier-era sites were filled rapidly with debris-rich topsoils after their abandonment, making the stratigraphy of the pits rather simple and not particularly informative. The layering of

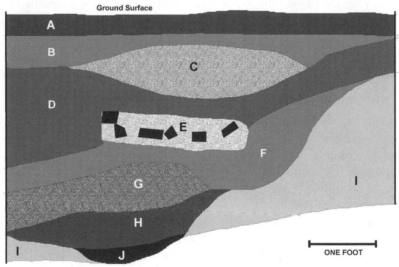

FIG. 10.2 Excavation view of the entrance to the cellar of James Latham's dwelling (top). Remnants of stairs notched into the subsoil can be seen on the left. Below is a crossectional drawing of the various layers of fill within the cellar itself.

fill within the cellar was more complex and suggested a temporal separation between zones. At the base of the feature was a layer of debris and organic soils (labeled zones J and H) from the time that the house was occupied. It is only in such layers that we are able to find artifacts affiliated with the use life of the feature itself. There was also an indication that the walls of the cellar entrance had partially slumped or caved in during the development of this layer.

Remnants of a possible decayed wooden step were also found at what would have been the base of the entranceway. Of course, after 170 years of burial in most dry soils, all traces of wood have usually decayed. What we found here was no longer wood, but instead a rectangle of a very compact, completely homogeneous, dark brown soil with square edges. It also appeared that the plank had been laid down on top of a thin layer of clay slump—indicating that the stairway was repaired or modified after it had been damaged by erosion. A similar soil anomaly was found higher up in the fill of the cellar as well, and appeared to represent a six-by-eight inch piece of timber discarded into the abandoned cellar along with soil, other organic materials, and household debris.

Above, zones F and G may represent the beginning of the intentional or unintentional in filling of the cellar (or perhaps just this entranceway) with debris-rich topsoils. Based on the complete lack of whiteware in these layers, this filling probably occurred no later than the very early 1830s, and possibly several years earlier. The prevalence of pre-1825 pearlwares suggests that this filling probably occurred between 1825 and 1830, or perhaps shortly following James Latham's death in 1826.

A particularly unusual deposit of fill soil was labeled zone E. This zone was isolated within a neatly rectangular area in cross section. It was composed entirely of mortar and brick fragments. That this activity was construction-based (as opposed to demolition-related) was reflected by evidence of wet mortar having been dumped onto piles of broken bricks, and adhering to their broken surfaces. From the well-defined edges of this zone, it suggested the contents of the base of a wooden barrel (or other wooden container) that had long since decayed. The soils and debris identified as zone E may actually represent a barrel containing the dried remnants of mortar and brick that Robert Latham discarded into the abandoned cellar in 1838 as he built a new cabin nearby.

The upper most zone of fill in the cellar represents the final filling and capping of the open pit with debris-rich topsoils that contained artifacts spanning the occupation of the James Latham site, circa 1819 to 1838. The fill soils below began to slump over time, and water-borne silt deposits were formed on the upper surfaces of the feature fill. Finally, zone A represents a layer of natural humus that developed across the site after its abandonment, and ultimately became the surface of a modern front yard.

A Glimpse into a Frontier Home

When Mary Latham moved out of the cabin built by her late husband about fifteen years earlier, she left behind thousands of little pieces of household debris scattered on the ground and shoveled into pits in the yard. The fill of the cellar feature produced a large sample of the quantity and range of goods associated with a family from the Upland South who settled in the Sangamo Country frontier during its earliest years.

Once these artifacts were washed and labeled, they were sorted into basic material and functional categories, so that the debris could be translated into specific consumer goods and the past activities associated with those goods. Presented below is a discussion of the entire range of the artifacts found in the Latham cellar, from the unusual to the common, according to the classifications we use during laboratory analysis.

Architectural Debris

As is typically the case, the architectural debris from the Latham cellar says only a little about the dwelling that once stood on the site. Fewer than forty fragments of cut nails were recovered from the feature and were well outnumbered by the fragments of Queensware found in the cellar. Most nail fragments were found in the upper levels of the fill, probably reflecting the demolition or removal of the building during the 1830s. Most are six to eight penny, and could have been used for a variety of purposes, from flooring to trim to cabinetry. One true flooring nail is also present, as are a few two to four penny nails that may have been used in cabinetry or crude furniture. The small number of nails is actually unusual for a post-1820 occupation in Illinois. Either the building was carefully disassembled and moved off-site, or the house built by James Latham in 1819 fit comfortably with our stereotypical notions of frontier architecture, and was not well finished.

Very little window glass was recovered as well—less than eight square inches in total. This may again suggest the home built in 1819 was a reasonably crude one, fitted with few windows. One fragment looks like it was casually marked with an etching stylus—perhaps as an inventory mark at the glass factory. The small quantity of soft mud brick suggests that it may have been used in the construction of a hearth or firebox, but little else. The presence of moderate quantities of baked clay daubing suggests that the chimney itself was made of logs and fire-proofed with clay.

A minimum of fifty-eight refined ceramic vessels are present in the sample—most represented by only a few small fragments. No restor-able vessels were recovered, indicating that the objects were broken elsewhere, and the fragmentary remains had been scattered prior to the filling of the cellar. It is important to sometimes pause and imagine the vessels that are now represented by a pile of small fragments. Fifty-eight plates, cups, and saucers is a lot of dishes, and all of these vessels were brought to Elkhart Hill when it was still a frontier community. From this large sample is a range of ware, vessel, and decorative types, all of which reflect both aspects of frontier trade and the consumer choices made by the Lathams. It is the variation or stability within such assem-blages (when compared to others) that allows us to look at the residents of the site as consumers.

Refined Ceramics

The refined ceramic assemblage is dominated by pearlware, although a small quantity of whiteware reflects an occupation that extended into the mid-1830s (figure 10.3). Four porcelain, one creamware, and one

FIG. 10.3 Selected refined ceramics from the Latham cellar, circa 1815–35.

yellow-glazed vessel round out the sample. The Lathams moved to the hill while a few creamware products were still found in the stores, but only one creamware vessel was found in the cellar fill. Although the manufacture of creamware persisted into the early 1820s, consumers on the rural frontier appear to have stopped buying the old-fashioned wares while they were still available. The only vessel from the Latham site is an undecorated platter; along with undecorated plates these are the most commonly encountered creamware vessels on post-1815 sites in Illinois.

At the opposite end of the ceramic spectrum of undecorated creamware are four porcelain vessels. These consist of three saucers and a cup, two of which may have been undecorated. The remaining two were painted in overglaze motifs that have largely been erased by the action of the soil. Three of the porcelain vessels are of Chinese origin, and would have been more than ten times more expensive than their earthenware imitations. The presence of porcelain on such sites is not particularly rare, however. Porcelain vessels simply make up a very small percentage of the teawares found on a given site, reflecting the better care they were given in the house. The fourth vessel—a saucer with a pink luster band painted on its rim—is probably of English origin.

The identification and division of creamware, pearlware, and whiteware vessels within the artifact sample allows us to put the site into a chronological context. The ceramics from the fill of the cellar can be divided into additional categories, however, in order to better understand the habits of the Latham family during the 1820s: by vessel form (tableware, teaware, or toiletware) and by decoration.

While the range of Queensware tablewares of the period could include plates, platters, pitchers, pepperpots, bowls, and salt cellars, the tableware category from the Latham site is almost exclusively composed of plates. A few small fragments of a pepperpot represent the only non-plate or platter from this category. Not surprisingly, most of the pearlware plates are shell edged, as were the majority of plates at the time. During the early nineteenth century, English potters manufactured four principal sizes of plates: table, supper, twiffler, and muffin. These ranged from four to ten inches in diameter. Fragments of each of these types of plates are present in the cellar sample. All have blue edges (as opposed to green, which was less common). Two are molded in an uneven scalloping known as a rococo style and predate-1815. The twelve edged plates from the site are quintessential examples of frontier-context artifacts in Illinois. We have yet to excavate a site from this era that did not produce them.

Half as many pearlware plates are transfer printed. During the 1820s,

FIG. 10.4 Fragments of two pearlware plates from the Latham cellar, shown with intact, nonarchaeological examples of the same patterns.

the overwhelming majority of transfer printed imagery was in blue, primarily due to the need to accommodate the bluish cast of the glazes used at the time. One of the plates in the sample predates 1815 and is decorated in a Chinese landscape motif popular during the late eighteenth and very early nineteenth century (figure 10.4). This vessel may be one that the Lathams brought with them from Kentucky. Another Chinese inspired plate is decorated in the Blue Willow pattern, which was first manufactured in the 1790s and is still made today.

The remaining pearlware plates, printed in an inkier, deeper blue, depict pastoral European landscapes. Three are represented by fragments large enough to identify a few of the pattern names. One of these is the "Wild Rose" pattern, which like the Blue Willow pattern, was manufactured by a number of English potters. The scene depicts a rural scene near Oxford, England. If there is a generic image in 1820s pearlware, it is the Wild Rose pattern—the same pattern has been found at sites across Illinois and up and down the Mississippi valley.

Another pattern—Moulin sur la Marne à Charenton—depicts a water mill in the French countryside. In a way, this plate illustrates the divide between the manufacture and consumption of this imagery. Very few residents of 1825 Illinois would have known where the Marne River was, or would have cared. The pattern was simply an attractive one, and the rural mill scenery would have certainly been familiar to them. One plate fragment bears the partial back-marked pattern name, *House*. During the 1820s, several potters produced patterns with *House* in the title, and this plate may have depicted Amport House, Hampshire; Esholt House, Yorkshire; or Kenmount House. All of these were historic sites in England that, again, would have been completely unknown to American consumers. Plates depicting such places would have been purchased simply as pretty pictures. Ironically, America was the largest market for such wares.

Several plates found in the cellar fill are whiteware, and therefore must have been purchased by the family after the late-1820s, or several years following Latham's death. At least six whiteware plates are present, and all are transfer printed. *Whiteware* is a modern term used primarily by archaeologists to denote a shift in the chemical composition of glazes in the late-1820s. The introduction of clearer glazes during this period allowed for the use of colors other than blue or black beneath the glaze. Previously, red, purple, or green inks would have been muddied by the blue cast of pearlware, and would not have withstood the higher firing temperatures needed for the earlier lead glazes.

One observer in England remarked on the immediate popularity of these new colors. In 1829, Simeon Shaw observed that "several of the most eminent manufacturers have introduced a method of ornamenting table and dessert services . . . using red, brown and green colors." He also observed that the old blue pearlwares had become "so common" that the new colors had gained a "decided preference in the most genteel circles."[6]

In the less-than-genteel circles of frontier Illinois, the new colors had also gained a decided preference, very shortly after their introduction. Based on the archaeology of sites occupied during the 1830s, it appears that it was the new printed patterns that were the most popular form of

Queensware between 1830 and 1840. The imagery used on Queensware of this period changed as well. Old English or patriotic American landscapes were soon replaced with exotic imagery of Africa or the Far East, as well as classical themes such as Greek ruins. Very often, the little fragments of whiteware that we unearth at frontier homesteads bear images of ancient columned temples, ruins, and classical urns.

Teawares outnumber tablewares from the cellar feature by a margin of three to two—which is the norm for the period. Like the tableware category, however, tea-related vessels are very restricted, consisting only of saucers, cups, and a single tea or sugar pot. Most of the cups and saucers are of pearlware, and these include several vessels that were made before 1820. These are among some of the earliest English wares brought to the Sangamo Country.

A teacup and four saucers are decorated in fine, hand-painted motifs and executed in the earth-tone or mineral pigments that were popular between 1790 and 1820. Unearthing wares of this type immediately signifies that we have entered the early frontier period of central Illinois. Also made before circa 1820 is a pearlware saucer decorated in a red floral motif, which has been painted on top of the glaze. As the pearlware glazes were heavily infused with blue tinting (and required high firing temperatures), it was necessary to apply colors such as red over the fired glaze. This added an extra step in the manufacturing process, and thus such products were slightly more expensive, and less common in country stores of the period. Before the late 1820s, blue was common and red was special at the table.

Among the numbers of teawares found at most sites, cups and saucer sets rarely match, and in many cases few cups are found to actually match the saucers. As these vessel pairs were traditionally sold in sets of six, the variety recovered would suggest that either an enormous quantity of cups and saucers were purchased, or that some mixing of sets occurred at country stores. Mismatched sets may have also been created by odd purchases made at estate sales.

The remaining pearlware tea sets from the cellar were probably made between 1820 and 1830, and were broken and buried by the late 1830s. These include four cups painted in much broader floral patterns than those popular a decade earlier. One broad painted saucer was backmarked by its maker—Enoch Wood and Sons. While it was somewhat common for potters to mark their printed plates and teawares, the most inexpensive painted teawares were rarely marked, and the specimen from the Latham cellar came as a surprise. Also from this period are several blue printed teacups and saucers. These are decorated in a darker, inkier hue that became very poplar in the mid-to-late 1820s. So much blue ink was used in decorating these cups and saucers that it often bled and smudged across the undecorated portions of the vessel. The 1820s were swimming in blue.

Several tea-related vessels are of whiteware and postdate the late 1820s. Notably, all are transfer printed (in red, black, and green patterns) and there was no painted whiteware found in this sample. The abundance of printed wares found elsewhere in Illinois during the period may reflect a shift in consumer tastes inspired by the new colors available during the 1830s. Those new colors were apparently more obvious and attractive when used in fashionable printed patterns than they were when applied to the old painted floral motifs. Thus, even in the wilds of the Sangamon Valley, hand-painted Queenswares may have fallen from popularity for a time.

Several of the cups purchased by the Lathams in the late 1820s and early 1830s had handles. This was somewhat unusual, as most teacups of the period (at least those shipped out to the county) were made without handles—handleless cups were far easier to ship without breaking, and they were also slightly cheaper. Clearly, however, someone was selling handled cups.

The Latham site produced no toiletwares such as chamber pots, wash basins or pitchers. Given the age and setting of the site, this was not surprising, as very few toiletwares have been found on the Illinois frontier. While wash basins and ewers may have seemed like a luxury, the rarity of the inexpensive and very practical chamber pots is somewhat surprising, and indicates that the residents of these rural communities primarily used outdoor privies.

Unrefined Ceramics

As is usual for site of this period in rural Illinois, the remains of comparatively few crockery vessels were recovered from the Latham cellar. While there is a minimum of fifty-eight Queensware and porcelain vessels, there are as few as five unrefined vessels in the cellar sample. This is due in part to the fact that small fragments of unrefined pots are much more difficult to identify and enumerate than those of decorated saucers or plates. Clearly, however, few crockery vessels were broken on the site during the 1820s and early 1830s.

The small assemblage consists of four redware vessels and one of stoneware. At least two small capacity storage pots would have been used to store lard, fruits, or leftovers. These were not designed to hold lids, and instead would have been covered by a cloth and string before they were placed in a cabinet or down in the cellar. We also recovered a small multipurpose kitchen bowl made of redware. Some of these vessels may have been made nearby, as a redware pottery shop was in operation about thirty miles to the south by 1826 (see chapter 11). It is difficult, however, to establish the source of most Midwestern redwares, as they are stylistically very similar. Also from the cellar is a stoneware jug, which is represented by only a few small fragments. As little stoneware was being made in Illinois before the mid-1830s, this jug was probably made outside of Illinois—perhaps in the Ohio Valley.

Metallic Cooking Vessels

Although the hearths of frontier homes were cluttered with cast iron cooking vessels such as pots, kettles, pans, and Dutch ovens, they are often only faintly visible in most archeological samples. Given the less fragile nature of most metallic objects, their appearance is less likely in the fill of pit features composed primarily of redeposited midden. For example, a fragment of a pearlware teacup that was broken into twenty-five pieces is more likely to end up in the fill of an abandoned pit than is an iron pot broken into only three fragments.

Only a single fragment of a cast iron pot lid was found in our excavation units. A metal detector survey of the area surrounding the cellar, however, boosted the metallic vessel sample: Recovered from these tests are a large fragment of a Dutch oven lid and two more pot lid fragments. Dutch ovens are broad, shallow vessels used for baking at the hearth. Filled with food, the vessel is covered with a lid that is fitted with a deep rim on its upper surface. This allows the user to cover the top of the lid with a layer of hot coals. Pushed into the edge of fire, the vessel then heats the food from all sides. Today, such vessels have been relegated to camping equipment, but they were the principal way to bake a variety of breads and meats on the midwestern frontier.

The metal detector survey also encountered an iron lug that was once attached to a large brass kettle. Brass kettles were shipped into the Midwest and upper Great Lakes region by the thousands during the fur trade era, and were one of the most important components of the Native American trade. Their arrival in the seventeenth century immediately disrupted a millennia-old tradition of aboriginal pottery making, and imported kettles replaced most forms of native pottery in the Midwest within two or three generations of their introduction. Such kettles, however, were widely used by American settlers as well, particularly in outdoor contexts such as boiling water or maple sap. Brass kettles similar to those traded to Native Americans in 1700 were still being sold in the Sears catalog of 1902.

Glass Product Containers

The Latham cellar produced only a small number of glass bottles, as is common in frontier Illinois. Glass-packaged medicines and foodstuffs were sold in only small amounts by country retailers before 1840. In frontier contexts, the most common forms of bottles are medicinal or liquor-related. Our sample from the Latham cellar yielded two possible medicinal bottles, and one liquor bottle.

One of the medicine bottles is a narrow, unembossed vial. These bottles were very common during the first half of the nineteenth century, and were filled with a variety of medicinal compounds, patent medicines, and household chemicals. Blown to be literally paper-thin, they are particularly fragile. In fact, given their cross-country shipping and (occasional) burial in the ground, their survival always comes as a surprise. Thousands upon thousands of these vials were blown in midwestern and eastern glasshouses, and most were probably purchased empty by druggists who then filled them at the shop. Druggists would identify the contents of the vials with small paper labels, which when discarded would quickly dissolve in the soil. So today, these ubiquitous little bottles are basically mute.

One figural whisky flask is represented only by a single, one-inch fragment. Such flasks are so distinctive, however, that one fragment easily identifies this type of bottle. While whisky flasks of the period were often heavily decorated, the piece is too small to identify a pattern on this vessel. This particular bottle was also blown in an amber colored glass, as opposed to the common aqua green. The reasons for the use of colored glass in flasks and other bottles is unclear. In most cases, such colors are rare enough to suggest that their use was probably not systematic.

Glass Tablewares

Very few glass tablewares appear to have been shipped out into the country before 1840. Their relative low value, coupled with their fragility (as well as an apparent disinterest on the part of rural consumers), seems to have kept glass stemware, dishes, and decanters out of most country stores. From the Latham cellar are two glass serving vessels—both of which are simple round tumblers. As mentioned previously, plain drinking glasses are the exception to the rule, and tumblers appear in predictable quantities on frontier-era sites. Most of those found in Illinois (on sites predating the 1840s) were probably made in the upper Ohio Valley, perhaps at Pittsburgh or Wheeling, West Virginia. There was a wide variety of domestic and imported glassware available to merchants of the period—and the pervasive absence of these goods in rural Illinois points to another broad pattern of choice on the part of these consumers. While painted teacups from England were part of life in the log cabins, stemmed wine glasses apparently were not—even though the wine itself was present in the house.

Table Utensils

A large number of table utensils were found in our excavation units—so many that they may say something about the nature of the debris sample as a whole. While a fragment or two of a plate once broken into thirty pieces is likely to end up just about anywhere on a small home site, a concentration of intact or large fragments of flatware might suggest that the artifact grouping in which they are found was more directly associated with the kitchen.

Four table (or "butter") knives were recovered from our sample of the cellar fill. Three have handles fitted with factory-made grips fashioned from polished animal bone. A fourth knife was fitted with a wooden grip, which has decayed in the ground. Prior to the early nineteenth century, table knives were used not only for cutting, but also for carrying food to the mouth. Forks were used primarily for holding foods down to the plate while cutting. Most forks of the eighteenth and early nineteenth century were fitted with only two sharp prongs. The Latham cellar produced one such fork. This, and at least one table knife, were discarded while intact and still serviceable.

A second fork, however, was made with three prongs rather than two (figure 10.5). In the Midwest, three-tined forks appear in small numbers during the late eighteenth century,[7] only to apparently fall from use until the 1840s, when they become common. This particular fork was fitted with a handle made of a section of deer antler, which may be a home-made replacement. While many of the items we uncover on frontier-era sites seem surprisingly modern, bone handled knives and two-tined forks have an archaic feel to them, quite compatible to our expectations of pioneer equipment. They are also resonant objects—so close to so many meals, and once held in the hands of the people that we study from such a distance.

FIG. 10.5 Flatware, a smoking pipe, a glass vial, and a Spanish colonial coin from the Latham cellar.

Household Tools

A few sewing-related items make up most of the household tools category from the cellar feature. Firstly, the broken blade from a pair of small sewing scissors was found in the feature fill. Scissors have changed very little since the mid-eighteenth century, and those found at the Latham site would be difficult to distinguish from a more modern pair. This is why the context of artifacts is so important—while the scissors themselves are hard to date, the age of much of the material found in association with them is easier to identify. Twelve brass straight pins were also found in the cellar, and were used in sewing, or as fasteners in dresses.

Clothing-related Artifacts

The clothing worn by the residents of early Illinois would have said much about their needs and self-images. Aspects of tradition, craft, ethnicity, economy, and trade were woven into the everyday and special clothing of the period. Yet, for archaeologists, there is little left to talk about. Everyday clothing would have been worn until worn out, and then it was probably converted to rags. Special clothing was more likely to be saved and handed down. Either way, little went into the ground, and those fabrics that did soon dissolved into the soil. Archaeology is left only with the durable accessories, such as buttons, buckles, and hasps.

The sample of artifacts from the Latham cellar includes several varieties of buttons, made of different materials and associated with different pieces of clothing. A range of everyday shirts, trousers, and dresses are represented by simple, flat buttons made of animal bone. Such buttons were cut from cattle bone and turned on lathes in American and European factories. Five such buttons were found in our excavation units. The largest single type of button from the Latham site, however, is the brass vest button. Such buttons often dominate 1820s samples, even over the cheaper multipurpose bone buttons. The reason for this is not clear.

Prior to the 1830s, most brass buttons used in the Midwest were manufactured by a number of companies in Birmingham and imported from England. Such buttons were often back marked by their manufacturers, but prior to the late 1830s, most of these markings were generic product names such as Best Colour or Treble Gilt. Such names referred to the gold color applied to the surface of the button. One button found in the Latham cellar, however, is an early American brass button. It is marked L. H. & S. W. CON., identifying it as a product of the Leavenworth, Hayden, and Scovill Company of Waterbury, Connecticut. While the American market was dominated by English imports until the late 1830s, Waterbury would become the center of domestic brass button manufacture during the mid-nineteenth century. The button found at the Latham site was made between 1811 and 1827, and represents one of the earliest American-made buttons found in the Sangamo region.

Leisure-related Artifacts

One or two long-stem clay smoking pipes are represented by several small fragments from the cellar. Native Americans introduced tobacco to Europe in the fifteenth century, and by the nineteenth century, tobacco smoking had become a centuries-old tradition in American households. The white clay pipes found at the Latham site were probably made in England, although Holland also exported a number of white clay pipes during the period. The bowl of one of these pipes is marked *TD*, which is thought to have originally referred to the initials of a mid-eighteenth century pipe maker. By the nineteenth century, however, the TD pipe had become a generic product name referring to the wares of a number of English manufacturers.

The TD pipe is also marked on its heel (at base of the bowl) with the letters *WC* or *CW,* depending on which way one orders the letters found on opposite sides of the stem. These letters may actually be the initials of a pipe maker.[8] Pipes with these markings are rare in the region, and interestingly, the only additional sites (of which I am aware) that have produced pipes marked in this way are the George Davenport Trading Post (at Rock Island, Illinois) and the Vertefeuille site in Prairie du Chien, Wisconsin.[9] Both sites were not typical American farmsteads, but were instead directly linked to the lingering fur trade of the western Great Lakes. Given James Latham's position as Indian subagent (and his tenure at Peoria), the Latham site is also indirectly linked to that trade. It is possible that, unlike the vast majority of domestic goods imported by American wholesalers in St. Louis, these pipes were brought into the region via different supply lines, as part of goods destined for the fur trade.

Coins

Quite frequently, we find silver or copper coins on early nineteenth century home sites. They are generally few in number and are of low denomination (pennies, half dimes, dimes) so they did not represent a significant loss on the part of their owners. To my knowledge, only one gold coin has been recovered during controlled archaeological excavations in Illinois, and that was found in the Mormon community of Nauvoo in a privy belonging to church founder Joseph Smith. At the Latham site, we recovered a Spanish colonial silver one-real coin, minted in Mexico City in 1795.

The use of Spanish colonial coins from Mexico and South America was widespread in America during the eighteenth and early nineteenth century, supplementing what were still small quantities of American coins.[10] One early settler of Sangamon County recalled that Spanish silver was quite common in the region, and that most such coins were treated as the equivalent of American dimes and half dimes—or "long bits and short bits."[11] Coins were not intentionally discarded, of course, and given the nature of the other artifacts found in the feature, the coin may have been lost in the house and inadvertently swept up with dirt and debris.

Outdoor Tools

Tools affiliated with outdoor activities are poorly represented in the cellar sample, again suggesting that most of the material found in this sample originated in a household rubbish pile near or under the cabin. Two gunflints were found in the cellar, however. These small, square pieces of knapped stone were used in flintlock guns. When the trigger of the gun was pulled, the flint (which was attached to a small hammer) would strike across a small piece of thumb-shaped iron known as a *frizzen*, creating sparks that would ignite the powder that propelled the ammunition out of the gun barrel.

One of the gunflints is of French origin, as were most of the flints in use in the 1820s in Illinois. A second flint is made of regional chert, and has been made in a slightly different manner than the imported varieties. It is generally assumed that these bifacially knapped gunflints were made by Native Americans, using local materials and the ancient craft of flint knapping. While there is evidence in Illinois that stone arrow points were made as late as the 1790s by the Kickapoo, flint knapping was certainly becoming a lost art by the first years of the nineteenth century. The manufacture of these little stone squares represented the very end of over 12,000 years of stone tool making in the region. By the time Mary Latham moved away from her farm on Elkhart Hill, that tradition was extinct in Illinois. Much had changed by 1840.

Down the Hill: The Kentucky House Tavern

In 1821, Benjamin Briggs (James Latham's brother-in-law) and his wife arrived at Elkhart and settled just south of Latham's farm, along the old trace and at the very foot of the hill. Living with the family was Mrs. Briggs's sister, Emily Hubbard. We know little about the Briggs family's brief stay at Elkhart, and Benjamin soon moved further north, opening a store along Edwards' Trace around 1823. His sister-in-law, however, stayed behind, marrying Richard Latham in 1824. Recent research has suggested that Richard and Emily may have set up housekeeping at the farm established by Briggses three years earlier.

Emily died in childbirth a year after their marriage, and by the end of 1825, Richard Latham had remarried. His new wife, Margaret Broadwell, had lived at Sangamo Town (twenty miles west of Elkhart) until her husband William was killed while building a barn. With Richard Latham, she would have a total of thirteen children, seven of whom died young.

At some point, Richard and Margaret Latham began accommodating travelers who passed by the front door as they followed the Edwards' Trace northward. By the late nineteenth century, their home at the base

FIG. 10.6 A rendering of the Kentucky House Tavern at Elkhart, date unknown.

of the hill was remembered as the Kentucky House Tavern (figure 10.6). Little is known about this enterprise, however, and the tavern is virtually absent in the primary documents of the period.[12] An undated drawing of a two-story structure is the only nineteenth-century image of the Kentucky House, which was said to have burned down in the 1870s. In fact, the place would have probably escaped the attention of early historians if it were not for one of its visitors, Abraham Lincoln, who is said to have stayed at the Kentucky House during his travels as a lawyer in the 1840s.

The residents of Elkhart have never forgotten where the tavern once stood, just inside the woods at the base of the hill. In the 1950s, a pageant was held near the site of the tavern, and it was a stop on hay wagon tours of the hill conducted by the local historical society. I first visited the site in 2000, which was marked only by the brick curbing of a filled, early nineteenth century well that was still visible on the forest floor.

To date, our work at the site has been limited to small-scale excavations, and there is still much we do not understand about the Kentucky House and its history. But as with many excavations, the archaeological record has managed to suggest a much more complicated history of the site than what is remembered in print. Thus far, excavations at the site have encountered a number of features dating as early as the early 1820s, through the early twentieth century.

One feature, however, has provided a glimpse of the earliest years of the site. A large unlined cistern measuring ten feet in diameter and ten feet deep was probably first constructed by Benjamin Briggs in 1821. The cistern was designed to catch rainwater from the roof of a nearby building—probably Briggs's original log house. During the mid-1820s, the cistern was abandoned and began to be filled with household rubbish. The reason for this abandonment is unknown, although water stored in cisterns was thought by some to be "dead water," unfit for drinking and easily prone to contamination. The abandonment of the cistern may also have been associated with a remodeling or expansion of buildings on the property by Richard and Margaret Latham sometime during the mid- to late 1820s.

Six episodes of fill are visible in the layered fill of the feature. The lowest represents the use-era of the cistern and is composed of thin layers of silty clay stained by minerals from standing water. These layers reflect the deposits created by the gradual slumping and peeling of the walls of the cistern while it was filled with water. Of course, this layer did not contain artifacts, as the residents of the site would not have discarded their garbage into the cistern while it was used for water.

The layers above are the soils and debris used to intentionally fill the cistern after it was abandoned, sometime during the 1820s. The earliest of these, labeled zone E, was a thick layer of pure clay subsoil that had been dumped into the base of the cistern. This soil was produced during the excavation of another deep pit somewhere nearby—perhaps a replacement cistern. Above this was zone D, which was composed primarily of several layers of fine ash (probably from the fireplace inside the house) that was mixed with organic materials and household rubbish. The ceramic vessels in this zone are partially restorable, indicating that they had not been lying on the ground a long time or subjected to widespread scattering. Zone D produced a sample of artifacts dating from only a very short period of time, circa 1820–25. Such short-term samples are rare and are quite valuable to archaeological study, as they come closer to a glimpse of the site as it was during one moment in time.

The largest single zone of fill within the abandoned cistern was labeled zone C. This zone consisted of many thin layers (or "loads") of hearth ash, organic material, and redeposited soil. Zone C contained a massive amount of ash (approximately 500 cubic feet) reminding us that fireplaces of the period were kept continually burning. The zone was also rich in domestic debris (most of which was burnt), and was probably created by successive cleanings of the fireplace, into which broken plates and bottles had been occasionally swept. Zone C was probably created over a period of several years, as the abandoned cistern was used as a convenient repository for ash and sweepings. The lack of significant layers of waterborne silt within this zone suggests that the abandoned cistern was not exposed to the weather during this period, and may have been covered over by a porch or room addition. Sometime during the mid-1830s, the mostly-filled cistern was capped with a layer of debris-rich topsoil (zone B). Finally, after the building was abandoned and demolished, a layer of organic topsoil (zone A) developed over the entire site, and the forest reclaimed the Kentucky House.

Zone D: At the Table with the Newlyweds

Most of the artifacts in zone D had probably been lying in an ash bin or trash pile under the house for only a short time—perhaps two years or so—before they were cleaned up and redeposited into the recently abandoned cistern. Many of the ceramic and glass fragments show signs of considerable burning, suggesting that they had been swept into the fireplace, where they stayed until the ash was cleaned out. The refined ceramics from this layer consist entirely of pearlwares, several of which predate the early 1820s (figure 10.7). With this in mind, the sample appears to reflect the first years of occupation of the site—by both the Briggs and the newlywed Lathams, during the 1820s.

Approximately fourteen pearlware vessels were found in this layer. The ratio of table to teawares is average for the period, with teas outnumbering plates, bowls, or pitchers. Several of the teacups are of the Chinese-style tea-bowl shape and were probably made before the early 1820s. Unusual for the period is the prevalence of printed table and teawares in this sample, making up about 70 percent of the assemblage. This would suggest that the Briggs or Lathams were setting a more formal than average table during the early to mid-1820s. Patterns include the ubiquitous Wild Rose as well as other unidentified scenic and floral patterns.

No unrefined crockery was found in this zone. The lack of pots and kitchen bowls in the archaeological sample, however, is not necessarily indicative of a lack of such vessels in the kitchen itself. Instead, the short-term nature of the deposit is probably to blame. Crockery was more durable and handled less often than Queensware plates and cups, and assemblages of household artifacts generated during a short period of time will logically contain few fragments of these wares.

FIG. 10.7 Refined ceramics (mostly burnt) from the cistern at the Kentucky House Site. A small fragment of a canary-yellow child's cup is compared with a partially intact example found in St. Louis.

Zone D contained fragments of only a few bottles, including a figural whisky flask and a "black glass" porter or ale bottle. These thick-bodied bottles, actually blown in a very deep olive-green glass, were designed to withstand the pressure of fermented beverages, and the nearly-opaque glass may have served to shield the contents from sunlight. While there were subtle variations over time, ale bottles from the 1820s and early 1830s looked very similar to those in use during the colonial period.

Very little nonkitchen-related debris was found in this zone. Only seven cut nail fragments and four square inches of window glass were recovered. No other artifact classes are present. Again, this is probably indicative of the short-term nature of the sample, and its association primarily with the debris of the dining table.

Zone C: The Tavern Years

Above the thin, single-episode of zone D soils was more than five feet of successive layers of fireplace ash, decayed organic materials, and occasional lens of redeposited topsoil. Like those in zone D, many of the artifacts from these layers are burnt, and those that aren't were found in layers of redeposited topsoil as opposed to ash. Given the volume of the feature, the ash was probably deposited over a long period. The gradual, intentional filling of the cistern appears to have ceased by the late 1830s, and it did not receive more fill until it began to slump several years later.

Zone C provides a crossection of material spanning the earliest days of the occupation of the Kentucky House site through the mid-1830s. The Queensware vessels from this longer-term sample include a larger than usual percentage of tablewares, consisting primarily of printed pearlware and whiteware plates. The tableware category also includes a number of multicolored dipt or banded bowls. These make up 14 percent of the entire assemblage—a higher than average percentage.

Anecdotally, banded wares are thought to have been popular in taverns, perhaps more so than the average home. For instance, the site of the Old Landmark Tavern in southern Illinois (first opened in 1819) produced an assemblage of pre-1830 refined ceramics that comprised 17 percent banded wares, or nearly twice the average for domestic settings of the period. If indeed taverns consumed more of these particular wares, it may have been due to the fact that they were the most inexpensive form of decorated hollowware for the table. Taverns, which served large meals to many guests, may have simply needed more pitchers and mugs.

Complicating this picture, however, is the fact that the most popular form of banded vessel was the common table bowl, and few mugs are recovered in any contexts in Illinois. The banded wares from the Old Landmark Tavern are primarily bowls; no mugs were identified. Why these small bowls would have been more useful to taverns is unknown, but this appears to have been the case.

At the Kentucky House site, the presence in zone C of more banded bowls (as well as a large number of dinner plates) may reflect the beginning of tavern-keeping at the Latham household. The morning and evening meals prepared for large numbers of people at taverns may have resulted in the use and breakage of more plates and table bowls. Teawares, on the other hand, may have been less important in such settings.

That pattern of enhanced use of tablewares was not visible in the small zone D sample, however, which dates strictly to the early and mid-1820s. This might suggest that the Lathams did not begin running a tavern at their home until the late 1820s or early 1830s, and that this change in function of the site (which may have involved remodeling) could account for the abandonment of the big cistern. In fact, the large, two-story structure depicted in the nineteenth century drawing (probably of at least partial frame construction) would have been somewhat out of place on the mid-1820s Sangamo frontier. It is possible that the Lathams first lived in a small, log structure built by Benjamin Briggs in 1821. That dwelling may then have been enlarged by frame additions, in conjunction with the formal opening of the house to travelers.

As in the earlier zone D, printed wares still dominate the Queensware assemblage from the deposits spanning the 1820s and early 1830s in zone C. This zone also reflects a shift in the 1820s fashions for printed wares. During the 1810s and early 1820s, most of the patterns sold by midwestern wholesalers consisted of pastoral and romantic European scenes like the Wild Rose pattern. Several of the teawares from zone C, however, are printed in specifically American scenes. After the close of the War of 1812, many English potters began manufacturing a number of printed patterns designed specifically for American consumers, featuring more patriotic imagery. English potters had made limited quantities of this imagery as early as the late eighteenth century, and were even producing American themes while their country was at war with America during the 1810s. During the 1820s, however, this imagery became a full-fledged fad, temporarily eclipsing the romantic European motifs.

Known to pottery collectors today as Historical Staffordshire, these wares featured images of American patriots and founding fathers, as well as American views. Popular scenes included generic American eagles, or war hero General Lafayette landing at Castle Garden, New York and visiting Washington's tomb. The relevance or marketability of some of the imagery chosen by the English potters is not always immediately obvious, and why residents outside of Kentucky would have appreciated a large platter printed with an image of the Marine Hospital in Louisville is unclear. Yet this very plate was recently excavated from a French residence in downtown New Orleans. From the cistern at the Kentucky House are teawares printed with views of the University of Maryland and Baltimore Hospital. Like the majority of the pearlwares printed in the mid-to-late 1820s, these are decorated in deep blue inks that cover most of the vessel surfaces.

Two small mugs manufactured specifically for children were also found in zone C. Small plates, mugs or miniature tea sets made for children had been around since the late eighteenth century but are rarely encountered in rural frontier contexts in Illinois. This is probably because they were not included in the generic "crates for the country trade" packaged by St. Louis wholesalers and sold to country merchants. Such items, then, were special purchases made by both the retailer and the consumer. While the rarity of specialized children's mugs on the frontier may come as no surprise, such goods were nearly as nonessential as the dozens of printed tea cups found on these sites.

One of the mugs from the cistern is glazed in a bright yellow enamel, known to collectors as canaryware. This type of English ceramic was popular for a brief time during the first two or three decades of the nineteenth century. The little yellow mug was decorated in a red transfer printed image; unfortunately, the fragment is so small that the pattern cannot be identified. Like the pearlware saucer found in the James Latham cellar, the mug was overglaze printed and would have been somewhat more expensive.

The second child's mug, also printed in red, is made of whiteware, and so must have been manufactured after the late 1820s. The shift to the clear glazes of whiteware allowed for the use of red, purple, and green inks beneath the glazes on inexpensive Queenswares. So the second red printed cup was probably cheaper than was the first, made twenty years earlier. Given the age of the children at the Latham site, the little yellow mug was probably purchased secondhand at a nearby estate sale, after the birth of Emily Latham's child (which caused her death in 1825), or perhaps following the birth of one of Margaret's children during the late 1820s.

A small amount of crockery is present in the zone C artifact assemblage. Most of the fragments are small, and it is difficult to assign specific vessel types, but there are at least four redware kitchen bowls or small capacity pots in the grouping, as well as a stoneware jug. Again, it is the jug that seems to be the earliest form of stoneware vessel brought into frontier households in the Sangamo Country. Given the small sample of redware from the much larger artifact grouping found in zone C (and the relatively small grouping found in the James Latham cellar) it seems that crockery may not have been as heavily used by the Latham clan at Elkhart, at least when compared to some of their neighbors in the Sangamo Country (see chapter 14).

Although it makes up less than 20 percent of the entire vessel assemblage, there is a slightly higher than average quantity of glassware from zone C of the cistern. This includes several bottles, two tumblers, and a jar. This layer produced another pictorial whisky flask, depicting George Washington's portrait. The remaining bottles, represented by only a few small fragments, are unidentifiable. The glass jar, which would have been fitted with a metal lid, is somewhat unusual in rural contexts and more commonly found in commercial settings in cities such as St. Louis during the period. Glass preserve jars do not become common in rural, midwestern homes until just before the Civil War.

The ashy soil used to fill the abandoned cistern at the Kentucky House contained far fewer small household items than did the soils used to fill the abandoned cellar at the home site of Richard Latham's father. The cistern produced a few fragments of table utensils, smoking pipe stems, and a fragment of a small penknife with a mother-of-pearl handle. Also present in the sample is the iron handle lug from a small brass kettle. While large brass kettles were often used for outdoor water boiling, butchering, or cleaning-related activities on many American farmsteads, this smaller kettle may have been used for indoor cooking.

Two outdoor tools were found in the cistern: a small iron musket ball mold and an iron felling ax. The mold, designed for casting balls one at a time, looks very much like a modern set of pliers (figure 10.8). Tools related to arms and munitions, as well as artifacts associated with the arms themselves, appear in only small numbers on the American farmsteads of the Illinois frontier. Given the dominance of domesticated animals over wild game in most of the food remains samples recovered, the rifles owned by early nineteenth century farmers probably spent most of the time hanging on a hook near the door. The ax was used for cutting down trees or chopping firewood. Its blade, which was made by folding over and shaping a thick piece of iron, has been broken in half, possibly due to a weak weld on the steel bit of the blade.

Missing from the large sample of artifacts found in the cistern is a range of artifacts normally associated with household sweepings, such as buttons, pins, and other small items commonly lost or discarded in the house. The material discarded into the abandoned cistern seems to be affiliated almost entirely with kitchen activities—the debris from which was swept into the fireplace before being discarded from the house. The

FIG. 10.8 Musket ball mold from the Kentucky House Tavern cistern, shown with a nonarchaeological example.

lack of sewing-related items, buttons, coins, and marbles may reflect a spatial segregation of activities within the house. That is, marbles, pins, and pipes were lost or broken far enough away from the kitchen fireplace to have been swept outside, rather than into the fireplace itself.

The upper portion of zone C, as well as the fill above, produced a large quantity of nails—many more than recovered from the lower zones. These may reflect the construction of a frame addition to the original 1821 log house, resulting in the large two-story building pictured in the drawing of the tavern. That expansion may have been responsible for the closure of the old cistern in the first place, as suggested above. More fieldwork will be necessary to explore this idea however. Thus far, our excavations have only begun to provide information about the buildings that once stood on the site and the activities that took place around them. The artifacts from the cistern, however, give us an opportunity to peer into the doorway pictured on the old drawing of the Kentucky House. From the nature of the cistern artifact sample, it would appear that this glimpse is focused very much on the dining table set by Emily and Margaret Latham during the 1820s and early 1830s.

CHAPTER ELEVEN

Earthenware at Cotton Hill

The Ebey-Brunk Kiln Site

By the beginning of the nineteenth century in America, even the most remote homes were stocked with a wide range of imported, mass-produced goods. A large number of artifacts remain for archaeologists to unearth as a result. But, as with most of the objects that surround us today, mass-produced objects come to the purchaser with a certain distance about them, as the buyer had no direct involvement with their design or creation.

The simple utilitarian crockery used in early nineteenth century households in the Midwest was another matter. The redware lard pots or stoneware vinegar jugs made at local pottery shops, while often not much to look at, were products of custom and informal learning. A shell-edged Queensware plate was a mass-produced product of an internationally popular media, but the wheel-thrown vinegar jug made near the Illinois River was still a "folk" object. Such folk objects, made and consumed locally, can often tell us more about a community than can mass-produced objects that were made elsewhere and purchased by many diverse groups.

Well into the nineteenth century, unrefined redware or stoneware crockery was still made by a local potter, who probably learned the trade from a father, uncle, or neighbor. Responses to national or international changes in technology, fashion, or trade were slower within these community-based realms of traditional craftsmanship. Crockery traditions were particularly well rooted and stubborn to change: even the design of the spoon changed more between 1650 and 1850 than did many forms of utilitarian crockery. For historic archaeologists, then, redware pots are the closest equivalent to the folk-based, community-focused character of aboriginal pottery so familiar to prehistoric archaeologists. Each is an artifact more directly tied to the place where it was unearthed.

Early nineteenth-century pottery shops in rural America did not leave much of a paper trail, however, and are very poorly documented. Earthenware potteries were family affairs, operated by only a handful of young men working on a seasonal basis. The business was a notoriously transient one, and the young men working as turners at any given shop probably moved about within the region, working at several shops, or as field hands on other farms. Particularly with earthenware, the trade was not a lucrative one, unless the shops were large and well staffed. It is probably for these reasons that years of research has produced less than a dozen period documents pertaining to the potteries of the Sangamo Country—including newspaper advertisements. Thus only archaeology stands to provide details about the potter's craft on the frontier.

The Sangamo Country was home to at least four redware pottery shops during the early nineteenth century, which was a significant cluster for the period. The presence of a potters' community here was due in part to the accessibility of the appropriate clays, but these clays were reasonably abundant in many areas of the state. More important to the creation of a "pottery district" was the presence of interrelated, interdependent families with backgrounds in pottery making traditions.

Pottery making on the early nineteenth century frontier was still a family business, built on the skills of a group of young men who were interrelated, and who passed on their expertise to other members of the family. Potters were usually farmers as well and depended on the extended family to make a decent living, much like other farmers in the neighborhood. Their niche in an increasingly international economy was to supply the local community with inexpensive utilitarian wares that were less commonly part of the inventories kept by large wholesalers in the cities. With regard to the potteries of the Sangamo Country, ongoing research is making it clear that the proprietors of each of the four "competing" potteries were actually related and members of a tightly knit community.

The first pottery to be established in the Sangamo region was located along Sugar Creek, in a community that would become known as Cotton Hill. Now known as the Ebey-Brunk site, the Cotton Hill pottery was probably constructed in 1826 by the extended Royal-Ebey-Brunk family that moved here from Ohio. The shop closed no later than 1854. This site is the only kiln in the region that has received intensive attention from archaeologists.[1]

Another pottery shop was located less than 2.5 miles from the Cotton Hill kiln, along Horse Creek. Little is known of this site, which was only recently discovered and has yet to be excavated.[2] The site may have been reasonably short term, and may have been opened after the close of the frontier period in the region (around 1840), perhaps by members of the Brunk family, who also owned the Cotton Hill pottery.

In Springfield, John Ebey, who had begun his career at the Cotton Hill pottery, opened a new shop near the public square in 1831. The restless Ebey left the Springfield area less than two year later, however, and his downtown shop was rented by a chair maker in the spring of 1833.

Fifteen miles northwest of Springfield in the town of Athens (platted in 1831), a redware pottery was opened sometime in the mid-1830s. By the early 1840s, potter Barnett Ramsey (a brother to one of the potters at Cotton Hill) was running the shop. Census records indicate that the kiln was still running in 1860, making it the longest running of the four Sangamo area shops. Unfortunately, the Athens kiln site has been heavily damaged by development, and little is yet known about the wares and history of the site.[3]

The Cotton Hill Pottery

South of the city of Springfield is a small lake—Lake Springfield—created by the damming of the lower Sugar Creek valley in the 1930s. Today, the lake serves as a source of water for the city, as well as a place to fish, water ski, or drink beer down by the water. Under the water, under the skiers, and out of view for seven decades, lies an old creek bed filled with silt. Along this submerged shoreline are some water-logged tree stumps and the occasional brick foundation or pile of stones, from a time when this was another inhabited valley in the Sangamo Country.

Along the southern timberline of the creek ran Edwards' Trace. Today, a segment of the old trail lies preserved as a deep rut in a city park overlooking the lake. The community that formed here during the 1820s and 1830s was known as Cotton Hill—a name that does not appear to have referred to a hill or a cotton crop. Surrounded by communities settled by families from the Upland South, many of the families at Cotton Hill traced their origins to Pennsylvania, New Jersey, and Massachusetts, although several had spent a generation in Ohio before moving to Illinois.

At least two redware pottery shops were in operation in the Cotton Hill area between 1825 and 1855, employing members of several of the first families to settle the area. The most substantial and better understood kiln site, the Ebey-Brunk site, was first discovered in the early 1970s, and was located less than a mile from where I grew up. It is also the first archaeological site that I visited with trowel in hand.

Various archival records and oral traditions recall the presence of at least nine potters working at a shop situated along Edwards' Trace between 1826 and 1855. Most of these men were related by marriages and had moved to Sangamon County in the 1820s. This extended family is believed to have been led to the region by a young man named George Brunk, who scouted out the locale in 1821 and returned to Ohio to collect his family and in-laws.

In the fall of 1824, Brunk led a group of sixty-three people to Sangamo. The clan included members of the Brunk, Ebey, Newcomer, and Royal families, all of whom were related by various marriages. Several of these families traced their origins to central Pennsylvania—a region with a long-standing pottery-making tradition. Further, each of these families had at least one member who was or would become a potter.

A pottery kiln was first constructed at the Ebey-Brunk site in 1826 or 1827 by the potters William and Charles Royal. The brothers were born in the 1790s in the Monongahela and Morgantown region of West Virginia. Their father, Thomas Royal, immigrated to America from England in the 1760s. Royal was a veteran of the Revolutionary War and was living in Bedford County, Pennsylvania after the war. The Royals moved to Columbus, Ohio in the early nineteenth century. Following the death of his second wife, Thomas married a widow named Ellen Brunk. Ellen was the mother of George Brunk, who would lead the clan to Sangamo in 1821.[4]

William and Charles Royal learned and practiced the pottery trade in Ohio. William's son (Thomas Fletcher Royal) later wrote an unpublished biography of his father, focusing on the path William followed to become a Methodist preacher. In his manuscript, William is said to have first "whirled the potter's wheel and fashioned the plastic clay into thousands of vessels" in or near Columbus. The family then moved to Miami County, Ohio where William built a new shop.[5]

Charles and William brought their families to Sangamon County in 1826 and joined their father at Cotton Hill.[6] They were about thirty years old at the time. Here, the brothers set up a new earthenware pottery, although William was beginning to find farming "more healthful" than pottery making. Toward the end of the nineteenth century,

Charles's daughter recalled the shop that her father and uncle established: "My father was a potter. He and my uncle William Royal made cups, saucers and plates, and earthenware, such as jugs, jars and other glazed ware. My father got lead poisoning from working with the glazed ware, so he had to give up the business and joined the Rock River Methodist conference."[7]

One of the Royals' assistants at the pottery was their brother-in-law, John Neff Ebey. John and his younger brother George were a part of the Brunk clan migration to Sangamon County in 1824. Their ancestors (originally spelled Eby) were Swiss Mennonites who fled Switzerland for Germany in the late seventeenth or very early eighteenth century. Part of the family moved to Franklin County, Ohio soon after the turn of the century, and like the Royals, John and George may have been introduced to the pottery trade there. Both of the Ebey brothers would lead long careers in the pottery business in Illinois.

Another member of the extended Brunk family, Christopher Newcomer, may have actually owned or superintended the shop, as his name appears on the only known bill of sale for crockery from the area, dated 1828. As a young boy in Pennsylvania, Newcomer was placed under the guardianship of George Ebey senior (who was John Neff's and George junior's father). Under Ebey's guardianship, Newcomer essentially became a stepbrother to John Neff and George Ebey. Like the Royal brothers, Newcomer (who was closer in age to Charles and William Royal than to John and George Ebey) may have learned the pottery trade there. Christopher Newcomer and his family arrived in Sangamon County with the Brunk and Royal families in 1824.

In late 1829, John Neff Ebey purchased the land on which the pottery was located, and probably assumed control of the shop. His family consisted of his wife Rebecca, and a son and daughter both under the age of five. Next door was the home of William Ramsey, a potter who would buy out Ebey in 1833. The Ramsey household included William and his wife (between the ages of twenty and thirty), and a second adult male between twenty and thirty. This may have been David Brunk (John Ebey's brother-in-law), who was probably apprenticing at the pottery, and who would later buy the business from William Ramsey.

Census records suggest that several of the potters were living on the kiln property during the early years of the business. In 1990, I spoke with David's great-great granddaughter Helen Brunk, and she recalled a double, or "dog trot" style log cabin that was still standing on the property in the 1910s. Dog trot dwellings could accommodate two families in separate quarters, and the cabin at the Ebey-Brunk site may have first housed the Ebey and Ramsey families, and then the Brunk and Boll families.

John Ebey probably worked at the Cotton Hill pottery until the summer of 1831. In November, he placed an advertisement in the Springfield newspaper *Sangamo Journal* announcing the establishment of a "Potter's Ware Manufactory" located in downtown Springfield. This new kiln would have been located approximately eight miles north of the Cotton Hill pottery. John Ebey sold the Cotton Hill shop to his assistant William Ramsey that year. Meanwhile, John Ebey's younger brother George briefly returned to Ohio. William and Charles Royal also appear to have left Cotton Hill by 1832 or 1833.

John Ebey spent less than two years at his Springfield pottery. While making earthenware there in 1832, he "became very anxious" to manufacture more modern stoneware.[8] Based on the experiments he had made with the clay from west-central Illinois, he relocated to Greene County in 1833. The Springfield pottery may have been abandoned shortly after departure. John Neff Ebey (as well as his brother George) would operate a number of stoneware potteries in west central Illinois during the nineteenth century, and his years of making redware in Sangamon County were virtually forgotten.

William Ramsey remained at the Cotton Hill shop for a few more years, but left around 1834. Christopher Newcomer may have resumed supervision of the pottery, as he is remembered to have hired a German immigrant named Valentine Boll to make pottery in 1833.[9] When Newcomer left the pottery business is unclear—he bought a nearby mill in 1836, although his estate still included one set of "potter's tools" upon his death in 1852.

David Brunk formally purchased the Cotton Hill kiln from William Ramsey in the summer of 1837, when the personnel at the pottery shop appears to have stabilized. David was a stepbrother to William and Charles Royal, who founded the shop ten years earlier. Brunk was training an indentured apprentice by the late 1830s. The 1840 census places Brunk on the property, with his wife and three children. Next door (but perhaps in the same dogtrot cabin) was potter Valentine Boll, living with his wife and one infant son. It is also David Brunk who features most prominently in the oral traditions surrounding the Cotton Hill pottery, probably because his descendants still live nearby today.

An 1850 census indicates that Brunk was, at the time, firing "72 kilns" of pottery annually, with the assistance of two hired men. Based on the time required to load and fire a single load (approximately five to seven days), this very high number of loads is probably a misprint. The capital investment in the property is listed as only $500, while his clay and lead stock was worth $300. He reported that he produced $1200 worth of earthenware annually, or about $28,000 today.[10]

David Brunk, with the assistance of Valentine Boll, operated a pottery into the mid-1850s. His shop may have remained at the Ebey-Brunk site (where he was living) or it may have been moved to the kiln site on Horse Creek sometime in the 1840s. Brunk was forced to close his business in 1854, however, due to illness. David was forty-six years old when he died the following year, and his life was probably shortened by twenty-five years of exposure to the ground lead used in his glazes. Unlike his restless partners, Brunk stayed in the same neighborhood for his entire career. His probate inventory included 800 gallons of "crockery ware." His was the first burial in a small family cemetery located just north of his shop, and which is still in use today.

Making Redware

Redware clay was usually mined from the side of a stream or riverbank located near the pottery shop. Both Christopher Newcomer and David Brunk owned properties centered on nearby ravines, which may have been the locations of their clay mines. Once it was brought back to the pottery, the clay was allowed to cure or season in a pit or cellar. When ready for use, it was mixed and refined in a pug mill operated by hand or horsepower. The processed clay was then stored in balls or blocks.

When ready for use on the wheel, a ball of clay was kneaded to remove air pockets and then placed on a simple foot-powered kick wheel, where it was turned and shaped into the desired vessel form. Few tools were needed—in most cases a small block of wood (called a "rib") might be used to smooth the surface of a vessel, or to create a complex rim design. Rim styles at the site suggest that most vessels were finished by hand rather than by finishing tools; the more complex styles appear to be associated primarily with pre-1835 deposits.

When pulled from the wheel, the clay vessel was allowed to air dry outdoors or inside a pole shelter. When dry, the "green" ware was glazed by immersion into a liquid bath of powdered lead, clay slip, and silica. This produced a clear glaze that enhanced or slightly altered the color of the red fabric below. Additional color could be added through the use of powdered manganese oxide, which created a brown-to-black surface finish. Copper oxide was also used as a colorant (producing a rich green hue), but its use was much less common. The lead glaze was inherently poisonous, and period recipe books and housekeeping guides often warned readers against storing acidic foods in lead glazed earthenware.

Most glazes used at the Ebey-Brunk site were simple, "clear" lead glazes. The term *clear* is somewhat misleading, as such liquid glazes included clay slips that had the potential to introduce a translucent color change to the fabric beneath. These clear glazes produced a range of yellow-orange to deep red finishes, which reflect the nature of the clays used and the temperatures at which they were fired. Many fragments found in the waster piles have an uneven gray-black finish, which was probably created unintentionally by an oxygen-reduced atmosphere in the kiln. Almost all vessels are glazed on both their interiors and exteriors. In other parts of the country, redware pots with unglazed exteriors are more common.

Most of the vessels appear to have been submersed into a liquid glaze bath while inverted, thus keeping their bases free of glaze. The rims of the pots and bowls were then wiped with a cloth, to remove glaze from the tops of the vessels. This would have allowed for the rim-to-base stacking of bowls and pots in the kiln, preventing the vessels from sticking together.

The potters at Cotton Hill commonly used small amounts of manganese oxide in the liquid glaze, producing a warm, brown color on the surfaces of pots and bowls. When fired at higher temperatures, the manganese glazes have a thick, liquid appearance. When underfired, these glazes have a slightly metallic appearance. In some cases, powdered manganese appears to have been casually dusted or brushed across the surface of the ware prior to firing, thus producing a brown-speckled or clouded effect. The potters often applied simple incised-line decorations to the shoulders of pots and bowls as well. Our excavations during the 1990s (as well as the collections made in the 1970s) did not recover any vessel fragment with capacity or maker's marks. While somewhat common on mid-nineteenth-century midwestern stoneware, the use of maker's marks on early nineteenth-century redware seems to have been unusual.

After the glazed vessels were allowed to dry for several more days, they were carefully stacked into the kiln. Most midwestern redware kilns in use during the late eighteenth and early nineteenth centuries were probably simple updraft kilns, built of soft mud brick and resembling a bottle in shape. Most were ten to fifteen feet in diameter, and were fired with wood through two opposing fireboxes. Inside the kiln, the vessels were stacked on top of each other, or separated with stacking tiles and

FIG. 11.1 Drawing of an early nineteenth-century earthenware kiln and shop in Indiana, probably very similar in appearance to the kiln at Cotton Hill. The bottle-shaped kiln is at the far left.

wedges. Glazed vessels could easily stick together during firing, thus ruining the ware. Poorly stacked kilns could result in the breakage of dozens of vessels. A kiln such as that used at Cotton Hill could hold several hundred vessels.

Once firing commenced, hardwoods were stoked into the fireboxes in such a way as to create a slow and even heat, which was allowed to rise to a temperature of approximately 1800–2000 degrees Fahrenheit. This usually took about two days. Once that temperature was reached, the kiln was allowed to cool slowly. Loading, firing, and cooling a kiln of ware took five to seven days.

After a kiln of pottery had slowly cooled, it was carefully unloaded. Undamaged wares were usually packed onto a wagon and delivered to nearby retailers, or were sold from the shop itself (figure 11.1). Christopher Newcomer sold 325 vessels to Springfield merchants Gatton and Enos in April of 1828—very possibly from the same kiln load. Those 325 pots had a wholesale value of $49.62 or the equivalent of about $1000 in today's dollars. In today's market, Newcomer's pots would have had a wholesale value of about $3 each, and would have probably retailed for around $5.

The pots that had fallen, stuck together, or warped during firing were usually tossed into a nearby ravine, open pit, or onto the ground surface behind the kiln. When archaeologists visit the site of a pottery shop, these are the wares that they find.

The Kiln Site

The archaeological remains of the pottery shop founded by David Brunk's stepbrothers were first discovered in the early 1970s. The site lies in a horse pasture, near a two-lane blacktop that is actually a paved segment of Edwards' Trace. A history class from a local university conducted some archaeological excavations in the mid-1970s, unearthing the foundation of the kiln itself. The results of this work were never reported, however, and most of the excavation records are thought to be lost. Unfortunately, just because an archaeologist digs into a site does not necessarily mean it will be properly recorded, preserved, or interpreted. Lost excavation records are as bad as lost artifacts. An archaeologist's mishandled trowel is only a little better than a developer's bulldozer.

I first visited the site in 1977 and made several collections of pottery wasters from an eroded surface near the kiln feature. In the 1990s I returned to the site and excavated several test units within a concentration of waster debris located behind the site of the kiln and pottery shop. Essentially, we were digging into a thick surface of broken pots that had been scattered across the ground surface behind the kiln during the first fifteen years of the pottery's business (figure 11.2). The excavation unit 1 and unit 2 samples appear to date primarily to the 1830s and early 1840s and are probably attributable to William Ramsey, Valentine Boll, and David Brunk.

One of the most difficult aspects of firing the kiln was keeping control of the fire. If the fire became too hot, the oxygen in the kiln would be consumed too quickly, resulting in warped and blackened pots. Loss of control of the flame could consume an entire kiln load. Excavation unit 1 encountered an eighteen-inch-thick layer of blackened, warped, and smashed bowls and pots that appear to have been the casualties of a single overfiring event. The dense pile of fragments probably reflected a single, bad day at the pottery, sometime in the mid-1830s.

Nearby, in excavation units 3 and 4 we encountered a large, ovoid pit buried beneath a surface of pottery fragments. The original function of the pit is unclear, but it was used as a convenient place to discard kiln failures upon its abandonment. Its proximity to the kiln may argue for a

FIG. 11.2 Excavation view of waster debris at the Ebey-Brunk site.

pottery-making function. The refined English ceramics that had been incidentally included in the fill help us better date the wares in the pit, and indicate that the material predates the mid 1830s. This suggests that the redware in the pit was manufactured while the shop was run by the Royal brothers and John Neff Ebey. Further, the lack of substantial silt banding and stratigraphic changes in the fill suggests that the material in the pit accumulated rapidly. This then, means that the sample of wares from the pit reflects perhaps a single season (or less) of work at the kiln, sometime in the mid-to-late 1820s. Such a tightly bracketed sample from a pottery production site is very rare.

The material recovered from our excavations is probably a reasonably representative sample of the wares produced at the shop between the late 1820s and the early 1840s. This sample would have been created by the natural attrition within each kiln load over successive firings, attenuated by the occasional disaster—such as the overfiring event seen in unit 1. Over 100 gallons of redware sherds were recovered from within the four excavation units. The four excavation units and feature 1 produced a conservative minimum of 126 identifiable vessels (not including kiln furniture). These probably constitute less than 25 percent of the vessels actually recovered. There are a lot of broken pots buried at a kiln site.

The Wares of Cotton Hill

The various types of vessels found at the kiln site can be divided into three principal categories, based on how they were intended to be used: food preparation, food storage, and food service. The most common type of vessel found in our excavations is that associated with the preparation of food in the kitchen. Nearly half of all identifiable vessels are deep, multipurpose kitchen bowls. These are slightly ovoid in profile, with tapered bases. Kitchen bowls made later in Illinois tended to lose their ovoid shape. Most of the Ebey-Brunk vessels are finished with simple tapered rims, and many have shoulder-incised lines that add a slight touch of decoration. Shoulder incising actually appears to be more common on bowls than on pots, perhaps because bowls were kept in view more often than storage pots.

The capacity of the kitchen bowls from Cotton Hill ranges from approximately one half to one gallon, and most measure about ten inches in diameter at the rim, making them equivalent to what we would call "mixing bowls" today (figure 11.3). Many of these bowls are very similar in shape and diameter to pots made at the pottery, with the bowls simply designed to be more shallow.

Milk pans—broad, shallow bowls designed to separate cream from milk—are a common vessel in American redware. Remains of only four such pans were recovered from our excavations at the Ebey-Brunk site, however, and all of these were associated with the pre-1835 feature 1. The scarcity of these vessels probably reflects the infrequent specialized dairy production in the kitchens of most of the customers at Cotton Hill. When needed, small amounts of cream could have been skimmed from milk stored in the smaller, more multipurpose kitchen bowls.

The fragmentary remains of a pipkin were recovered from the feature 1 pit. Pipkins are distinctive, covered cooking pots that were designed for open hearth or stove top use. The vessels were fitted with a single handle extension positioned ninety degrees from a pouring spout. In Illinois, these vessels are usually associated with German communities dating from the late 1830s through the 1860s. The Mississippi River cities of Alton and Quincy had significant German populations during this period, and these more specialized vessels are reasonably common in archaeological features there.[11] The presence of this single vessel at Cotton Hill (in pre-1835 contexts) may reflect a realm of specialized products that were not yet produced on a regular basis, but instead may have been made by special request. Ironically, we have yet to recover

FIG. 11.3 Kitchen bowls and pipkin fragments from the Ebey-Brunk site.

evidence of the manufacture of these vessels after the presumed arrival of German immigrant Valentine Boll at the site in 1833.

Vessels associated with food storage represent about a third of our sample and consist of pots, jars, and jugs. Pots dominate the storage vessel assemblage (figure 11.4). The term *pot* is used here to refer to wide mouth storage vessels without lids. Those designed to accommodate lids are more accurately referred to as *jars*, although the two terms were commonly mixed during the nineteenth century. Wide-mouth pots were probably covered by their users with cloth, secured with a string beneath the rim.

Pots were used for both the short and long-term storage of soft, wet

FIG. 11.4 Pots from the Ebey-Brunk site. Note the unusual horizontal strap handles (middle-left).

foods such as lard, butter, honey, fruits, vegetables, or meats. Most of the pots recovered from Cotton Hill appear to have been reasonably small, holding one to two gallons. A few larger vessels probably did not exceed three gallons. Given the size of the pots and the dominance of pork in the local diet, lard may have been one of the more common foodstuffs stored in these vessels. At least four smaller pots, with capacities of one pint and rim diameters of five to six inches, were also recovered. These would have been more appropriate for butter or fruit preserves.

Several of the pots recovered from feature 1 were more carefully made, with thinner bodies, minor incised decorations, or more lustrous glazes. These products have a more finished appearance than the bulk of the pots recovered from the site, and probably reflect the work of the more experienced potters such as William or Charles Royal. The production of these slightly fancier wares seems to have faded quickly, however, and was replaced with more heavier-bodied, strictly utilitarian products.

Each of the excavation units at the site produced a few pots fitted with unusual side handles: ribbed strap handles attached horizontally to two sides of the pot. The use of such handles at Cotton Hill seems to have been unique and was really not a very good idea, as they would have been far more brittle than solid "lugs" used by most potters during the period. I have yet to see such a pot outside of the kiln site itself, suggesting that such designs may not have sold well.

As opposed to the wide mouth pots, jars were vessels with more pronounced shoulders and necks, and with more restricted openings that were usually designed to accommodate wooden or ceramic lids. Only three jars were found in our test unit samples. These vessels did not accommodate inset lids (like later jars often did) and would have been covered in the same manner as the pots made at the site. The small number of jars at the kiln site is paralleled at the majority of the frontier-era farmsteads we have excavated in Illinois. True preserve jars in stoneware or glass appear in much larger numbers during the 1850s.

The image of the jug has become one of the stereotypical icons of rural nineteenth-century life in America—most commonly pictured with two or three X's painted across the side, signifying hard liquor. Jugs were used to hold a variety of liquids on the frontier farm, not just whisky. Accustomed as we are to plumbing, it also easy to forget the constant need for water—and jugs would have kept water accessible, clean and reasonably cool. Surprisingly few jugs, however, were recognized in the test unit assemblage from the Ebey-Brunk site. The reason for this is unclear, but might have something to do with the increasing competition from stoneware jugs. Perhaps not coincidentally, jugs seem to be the most common type of stoneware vessel found on farmsteads predating the late 1830s.

Vessels for use at the table were also made at the Cotton Hill pottery, although they make up less than 20 percent of the combined assemblage from the site. Feature 1 produced the majority of these wares, indicating that the manufacture of vessels for food service was clearly more important during the earliest years of the pottery. Food service vessels from the site include dishes, table bowls, pitchers, and cups.

We found fragments of at least six undecorated dishes in our excavations. The vessels are flat based and slightly footed, unlike the rounded bottoms of the traditional pie plates or chargers that were common in the eastern United States during the eighteenth century. Also unlike many of the eastern varieties, these vessels are wheel thrown, rather than drape molded over a wooden form. Most of the dishes are ten inches in diameter. Three of these vessels are flat and shallow, and might be more accurately described as plates. One flat rimmed plate is decorated with three concentric lines, much like those on the shoulders of pots or bowls.

At least three dishes, all recovered from feature 1, are slip decorated (figure 11.5). This form of decoration involved the application of colored clays to the surface of air-dried vessels, using a funnel-like cup. While festive, multicolored slip-decorated redware dishes were made for over 150 years in New England and the mid-Atlantic states, the tradition did not travel well during the early nineteenth-century migrations into Illinois. Prior to the excavations of the Ebey-Brunk site, it was generally assumed that no such wares were made in Illinois, and the fragments of these three dishes from feature 1 were a welcome surprise.

Two of these dishes are decorated in their centers with a tulip motif, executed in creamy yellow and manganese brown slips. The edges of both dishes are encircled by a single wavy line bracketed by two bands. Such imagery is common in the decorative arts of Pennsylvania, where the Royals and Ebeys traced their lineage. The third dish is decorated in a more abstract and unusual design: a wavy grid-and-dot pattern in the center, encircled by a wavy line and band pattern as well as two rows of manganese brown splotches made with thumb prints. There is something remarkably unrestrained and modern about this form of decoration, and such dishes stand out in sharp contrast to the endless piles of broken, undecorated pots and bowls. Art was possible at such shops in Illinois, but it was rare.

Several finely potted table bowls were also recovered from feature 1 (see figure 11.5). Five of these vessels are similar in form and size to the Chinese-style waste bowls used in tea services. Each has a flat rim, below which are one to four incised lines. The bowls are eight inches in diameter at their rims. Two are glazed in a rich copper green. Three others are clear lead glazed, producing even, creamy yellow to brick red finishes. These delicately potted and carefully glazed vessels are more similar to English Queensware products than to any other vessel recovered from the site.

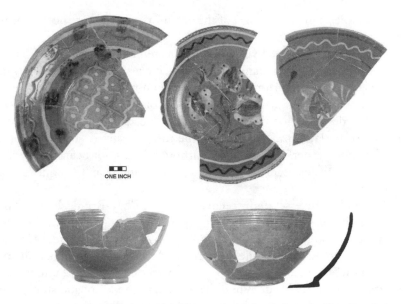

ONE INCH

FIG. 11.5 Slip decorated dishes and finely potted table bowls from the Ebey-Brunk site.

Small pitchers for the table were also produced at Cotton Hill, and our excavations produced pieces of at least three such vessels. In 1829, Springfield storekeeper Elijah Iles sold a pitcher he described as a "potter's pitcher" (for 18 cents), which may have been a reference to locally made wares. Small rim fragments of several drinking cups were recovered from our excavation units. Most appear to have been straight-walled beakers or tumblers, although one thin rolled handle was probably attached to a teacup. While Thomas Royal's daughter recalled that her father and uncle made "cups, saucers, and plates," teacups in redware were really a hopeless idea in the face of the thousands of inexpensive, highly decorative, and very fashionable teacups imported from England each spring and fall.

Very few vessels from the Ebey-Brunk site are not related to food storage, preparation, or service. "Other vessels" make up only 6 percent of the combined excavation unit assemblage and include a few flowerpots, a chamber pot, and a possible ink well. The flowerpots were reasonably large, measuring approximately one half gallon, and look very much like those in use today. The chamber pot appears to have been uncommon on the rural frontier, but was much more common in the cities. In Springfield, merchant William Carpenter referred to these vessels as "night crocks."[12] By the mid-nineteenth century, chamber pots had become an important part of the inventories of redware potters near St. Louis.

A large, kettle-shaped vessel was recovered from feature 1. Measuring seventeen inches in diameter and nine inches tall, the unusual vessel is unglazed on its exterior, and lead glazed on its interior. The vessel is finished with two lug handles and a thick rounded rim. The vessel was probably designed for use at the pottery, perhaps in the production of glazes or clay slips. Adhering to the interior surface are traces of a hard, white, plasterlike substance. Although it has not been tested, the substance may be a lead-based residue, left behind from the liquid glaze baths.

The only nonvessel items recovered at the Ebey-Brunk site (not including kiln furniture) are smoking pipes. American potters working in redware and stoneware often made smoking pipes on the side. Unlike the white clay varieties made in England, American pipes are usually of the "elbow" or "stub-stemmed" variety, with a ceramic bowl into which a reed stem was inserted. While the majority of redware and stoneware elbow pipes made before 1840 were only minimally decorated, the medium did offer an opportunity for a potter to be a bit more expressive. Anthropomorphic "face pipes" had become quite popular with American potters by the 1830s. Alas, the pipes made at Cotton Hill consist of plain, unglazed bowls. The consistent lack of decoration on these goods is surprising, and points to the rarity of those shops that did produce more decorative wares during this era.[13]

Items made exclusively for use in a pottery kiln are the most obvious indications of the discovery of a kiln site. Kiln furniture includes devices designed to aid in the staking and protecting of vessels in the kiln. Excavations at Cotton Hill have yielded several forms of kiln furniture made by the potters working at the shop.

Saggars are vessel-like objects used to stack and protect wares in the kiln during firing. Two principal forms of saggars were recovered at the site. Both forms are wheel thrown, and were designed to be used for multiple firings. The first and most common across the site were evidently used during most of the history of the pottery. They look somewhat like inverted shallow bowls, or dog dishes, with single holes in their bases. They appear to have served as pedestals or platforms, on which pots or other objects were placed.

The second type of saggar appears as a seven-inch-tall segment of round pipe (eight inches in diameter), with no rim or base. These saggars are pierced with two one-inch openings on opposing sides of the midsection of the device. As opposed to the first type (used as platforms or pedestals), these saggars would have been used to completely encircle finely potted wares such as table bowls or pitchers, allowing larger vessels to be stacked nearby and above. The side openings allowed for the even distribution of heat within the saggars. Like the table bowls themselves, these saggars are rare at the site, and appear to have been used primarily during the earliest years of the pottery.

Setting devices are small objects used to prop, separate, and stabilize vessels in the kiln during firing. At the Ebey-Brunk site, these consist of a variety of tiles and cut or pinched wedges. Rectangular setting tiles are common across the site and measure approximately three inches long by six inches wide. Most are one inch thick. The fragmentary tiles have been heavily used and exhibit glaze dripping and vessel adherence scars on both of their broad surfaces.

Both cut and pinched wedges were used to level and separate pots that were stacked on top of each other, on tiles, or on pedestal saggars. Most wedges are small, measuring one inch long or less. Small pinches of clay were also used to level or stabilize pots in the kiln. These little artifacts, many of which preserve the potter's fingerprints, are some of the most charming objects one finds at a kiln site. They capture such a momentary gesture on the part of the potter, pinching a little ball of damp clay a very long time ago.

Several sherds of heavily burnt English pearlware plates were also recovered from feature 1. It appears that the potters at Cotton Hill used broken plates from their homes as setting devices in their kiln to level or stabilize the wares. So, within ten years of their manufacture in the potteries of England, fragments of fashionably modern, richly blue-printed plates were propping up new batches of traditional, utilitarian lard pots in a kiln at the edge of a prairie thousands miles away.

Making and Buying Redware in Illinois Before 1840

During the very first years of American settlement of Illinois, redware (like most everything else) was imported by wholesalers in St. Louis. Kitchen crockery was not an important part of their stock, however, and country merchants who bought imported Queenswares and other goods at St. Louis appear to have bought little crockery there.[14] When redware kilns appear in the 1820s in Illinois, local households could buy more crockery, but most of the potters' wares were not well marketed beyond the immediate region in which they were manufactured. During the early nineteenth century, then, local merchants bought local crockery, or bought little at all. The result is an eclectic pattern of crockery consumption between households of various regions within Illinois.

In the St. Louis region, for instance, proximity to larger and more diverse markets was probably responsible for a range of imported wares not seen elsewhere in Illinois. This included slip decorated redware dishes and pie plates imported from the Upper Ohio Valley, and French kitchen bowls imported through New Orleans. In northwestern Illinois, the lack of a regional pottery industry prior to 1840 appears to have essentially resulted in farmsteads with very little crockery in the kitchen (based on archaeological information), or cooks who took much better care of this less-replaceable pottery.[15]

The Cotton Hill district provided raw material and a market for at least nine potters during the earliest days of redware manufacturing in Illinois. Here, these young men developed their craft while studying the nature of local and regional clays. Most of the potters left Sangamon County in the mid-1830s, spreading out across west central Illinois. The Ebey brothers had correctly predicted the importance of stoneware clays, and within fifteen years, stoneware vessels were the dominant form of crockery in most regions of the state.

The more we learn about the Sangamo area potteries, the more pivotal the role of the Cotton Hill shop becomes. Very recent research has shown that the pottery at Athens was in fact established by William Royal just prior to his departure from central Illinois. It was at the Athens shop that Royal "ceased to turn the potter's wheel" and decided to follow the ministry. Also working at the Athens shop for a time were members of the Goble and Sackett families, who would later establish two redware potteries in and near Galena, Illinois. The wares of the long-lived Galena shops are perhaps the most familiar to collectors of midwestern redware. The Athens pottery was later operated by Barnett Ramsey—a brother of William Ramsey who had run the Cotton Hill shop prior to 1837. Barnett took his family to the Oregon Territory in 1851, where he is credited with establishing one the first potteries in the northwest.[16] It is not an exaggeration to say that pots made fifty years and 2000 thousand miles distant were in fact the descendants of those made at Cotton Hill.

The output of the Cotton Hill pottery changed over time, and those changes are visible in our excavation units.[17] Most noticeably, food service vessels played a much more important role at the pottery before the mid-1830s. The small demand for redware dishes and table bowls in the 1820s and early 1830s diminished even further during the close of the frontier era in Illinois. A slight decline in the manufacture of pots (over bowls) may also have occurred in the 1830s, possibly due to the increasing competition of more durable and less toxic stoneware pots pioneered by potters such as George and John Ebey. Plain, multipurpose kitchen bowls were always an important product at the kiln, however, they became more important over time.

With our expectations of the potential visibility of custom, tradition, and ethnicity in these folk artifacts, what can we really say about the community that was serviced by the Cotton Hill pottery? The range of vessels recovered at the site is very limited, and there can be a frustrating muteness to dozens upon dozens of medium capacity storage pots and kitchen bowls. These vessels were so useful and multipurpose that they ultimately say very little about the habits of their users. A general lack of decoration and variety within the dominant vessel categories also makes any story about the potters' craft itself a short one.

The limited range of goods at the Cotton Hill pottery actually appears to be quite representative of the needs of much of the population during the period, however. The range of crockery vessel forms recovered from sites predating 1835 in Illinois is generally limited to small to medium capacity pots, jugs, multipurpose kitchen bowls, and the occasional refined table vessel. Vessels that bespeak of more specific foodway traditions (such as pipkins, mush mugs, porringers, pie plates, or bean pots) are rarely encountered anywhere in frontier Illinois contexts. The wares at the Ebey-Brunk site, then, appear to reflect the norm across the state during the frontier period.

The collection of generic pots and bowls from Cotton Hill may actually say something through its apparent monotony. The restricted nature of these crockery assemblages is probably reflective of the needs of the principal ethnic group to settle Illinois before 1835: upland southerners of Scotch-Irish ancestry. Broadly speaking, dietary traditions associated with the Upland South include a preference for pork, wild game, and whisky, to the lesser importance of beef and diary-related products.

The lack of milk pans, pipkins, and slip decorated pie plates (tied more directly to New England and Pennsylvania German dietary traditions) may reflect the dominance of upland southern culture prior to 1840, and its effect on regionally produced material culture such as redware. So the heaps of medium capacity pots and bowls may indirectly describe kitchens dominated by pork products and lacking in large quantities of dairy products. In this way, what is present at Cotton Hill, combined with what is not present, may reflect a reverberation of dietary preferences that stretched back to medieval Scotland, Ireland, and northern England.

While the tablewares manufactured at Cotton Hill made up only a small percentage of our sample, their presence is still surprising and the most immediately interesting aspect of the assemblage. The continued manufacture of redware food service vessels such as dishes, pitchers and bowls in the face of the popular, inexpensive, and decorative English refined wares is very noteworthy. Prior to the introduction of inexpensive English creamware and pearlware during the eighteenth century, colonial American redware potters produced large quantities of tablewares, competing with those imported from England.[18] The Ebey and Royal families would have been quite familiar with such wares while living in Pennsylvania. By the early nineteenth century in Illinois, however, the manufacture of redware dishes and table bowls for the purposes of competing with English pearlware imports seems very unlikely. The inexpensive and fashionable tablewares and teawares from England were readily available at even the most remote Illinois community during the 1820s, and archaeological sites from that period make it clear that very few families did without them.

John Ebey and the Royal brothers would not have made redware dishes to sell to those who could not obtain or afford those made in England. Instead, such vessels seem to reflect a little miracle of persistence of certain tabletop traditions. What those traditions were, however, has apparently been nearly forgotten in Illinois. The old timey, festive, slip-decorated platters may have been used primarily during the holidays by a few immigrants from Pennsylvania or Ohio. Why some of the customers at Cotton Hill preferred undecorated "dirt dishes" and locally made tea bowls over the inexpensive, more refined, decorative, and fashionable wares from England is unclear.

For the most part, potters such as those at Cotton Hill provided the kitchen crockery that was either too heavy or too inexpensive to bother importing. This allowed local residents to dictate the nature of what the potter made, and to inadvertently foster very old folk traditions. In central Illinois before 1840, the majority of the local farmers needed only a few pots and bowls. Some of the immigrants from the mid-Atlantic states, however, had been raised with a lot more crockery in the house and appear to have created a small market for a few more specialized vessels. These products might have been more sentimental than practical, reflecting traditions that were largely forgotten by the end of the nineteenth century.

Potters such as David Brunk continued to find a market for their traditional redwares until just prior to the Civil War, but after 1860, very little redware was being sold in central Illinois. By the 1880s, most of the fragile vessels had broken and were replaced with stoneware. By the turn of the century, most of the redware made at Cotton Hill remained only in the area's archaeological record. The last recorded use of a redware vessel made at Cotton Hill was in the 1970s, when a small lead glazed bowl was still being used to water chickens on a Brunk family farm in Sangamon County.

CHAPTER TWELVE

The Origins of a State Capital

The Iles Store Site

Soon after the temporary county seat was established, a twenty-five-year-old store clerk named Elijah Iles arrived at the Kelly settlement. Iles was originally from Kentucky and had previously settled in Franklin, Missouri where he also worked as a buyer for land speculators. It was there that he had heard of the "richness" of the Sangamo Country. This detail, from one of his several published recollections, is an interesting one, as settlement in the region generally followed a westward course, and the seductive tales of the Sangamo Country apparently led at least some recent settlers of Missouri to backtrack into Illinois.

Iles first visited the Springfield area in the spring of 1821. He returned to Missouri, settled his business affairs, and then moved to the Sangamo Country. He boarded with the Kelly family temporarily while he contracted for the construction of a log storehouse to be built near the planned site of the courthouse.[1] This was to be the first commercial structure in the new community of Springfield. Iles traveled to St. Louis to purchase a stock of goods and opened his store that summer. John Kelly completed the new courthouse about the same time.[2]

Elijah Iles published three accounts of his first years at Springfield, and each described his store slightly differently. Each account mentions an initial visit to the site of Springfield, followed by a return to Kentucky to settle his affairs. Upon his arrival to the site of Springfield, Iles may have made arrangements with another individual for the construction of a store building, or he may have built one himself. In an 1883 recollection, Iles stated that he "bargained for the erection of a store house . . . eighteen feet square, with sheds on the sides for shelter. The house was to be of hewn logs, covered with boards with heavy poles laid on to the keep the boards from blowing off. The plank for the shelves and counter had to be sawed with a pit saw." In another recollection (published two years earlier), Iles remembered erecting a cabin, sixteen feet square "with sheds," implying that he built the building himself. In a much earlier recollection (1859), Iles again suggested that he erected the building, which he described as a "hut with a cabin fifteen feet square."[3]

After his second visit to the Springfield area (when he supposedly contracted for the construction of the log building), Iles traveled to St. Louis to purchase wholesale goods. He remembered that most were purchased at auction. He then chartered a boat to ship the goods up the Mississippi and Illinois rivers to the mouth of the Sangamon. Here he found a vacant cabin, into which he loaded his goods. He believed that John Beard, who settled the site of Mound Village in 1819, had constructed the building.

At Mound Village Iles found a trail that led away from the riverbank, toward the southeast. He followed the trail on foot and reached the site of Springfield. He then hired wagon teams to follow the trail back, and to haul the goods stored in the riverside cabin to his new store site. Iles claimed that his stock consisted of twenty-five tons of merchandise, which took more than a month to transport.

William Davis, a hunter for a land office surveying party working in the vicinity of Springfield, visited the site of the store in the spring of 1821. His shoes had recently fallen apart, and the young man saw that Iles was "putting up a place in which to open a stock of goods." He approached Iles, who opened a box of shoes, and according to Davis, made the first sale at the new store.[4] The first retail purchase in Springfield may have been a pair of shoes sold to a barefoot surveyor.

Iles officially opened his store in June of 1821 and lived in the building as well. He later remembered that "for some time my sales were about as much to Indians as to the whites." He also recalled that it was from the Kickapoo that the community first obtained the bluegrass seed used in area pastures throughout much of the nineteenth century. Erastus Wright also remembered members of the Kickapoo and Potawatomi visiting the area, who referred to the fledgling community as "log town."[5]

In the fall of 1824, John Williams was hired as a store clerk and received a salary of ten dollars a month plus board. Just prior to his marriage to Malinda Benjamin in 1824, Iles built a shed and a brick chimney with open fireplace, which was attached to the rear of the store "for a cooking and dining place." The addition "soon gave place to a more comfortable cook and bedroom."

Town Planning on Spring Creek

In 1822, the informal Springfield community was still located on government land, which would soon be placed at auction and sold to the highest bidder. Those who had improved the properties surrounding the new courthouse would have been actively anticipating the auction and preparing to purchase lands that included not only their improvements, but also the property that would ultimately become a county seat. While speculative towns came and went on the early nineteenth century frontier, those that received a seat of government were insured traffic, longevity, and high real estate values. A town could not yet be platted at Springfield, as the land had not yet been surveyed. Once that survey had been completed, however, a platted community would be necessary for the survival of the seat of government. It was newcomer Elijah Iles who would spearhead the creation of this new government town, positioning himself at its center.

In the spring of 1822, the Springfield Land District Office was created by an act of Congress. Located in the Springfield settlement and along the same trail, the office would be in charge of auctioning lands that extended from the Sangamon valley south to Edwardsville. Iles began informally laying out streets for a new county seat town at about the same time.[6] The platting of a town was usually a reasonably straightforward affair—even if the town was planned as a county seat. In most cases in central Illinois (during the frontier period), would-be proprietors of a town would improve or occupy government land and await its availability for purchase. Then the individual (or sometimes a partnership of two or three men) would purchase an 80- or 160-acre parcel. Following this purchase, a local surveyor would be contracted to plat the lots and streets of the new town, often conforming to topographical concerns or preexisting trails and improvements. If that town was competing for a seat of county government, the plat would include a public square property, which would be gifted to the county for the construction of a permanent courthouse.

Although Elijah Iles and John Kelly were in an excellent position to purchase the lands surrounding the new courthouse (and then to plat a town across one or both of their parcels), the preparations for what would become the town of Springfield were much more complex. Over the next year, Iles added to his town-platting venture a state representative (Daniel Pope Cook), two employees of the General Land Office (Pascal Enos and Thomas Cox), and the county sheriff (John Taylor). Each was to purchase a portion of the lands surrounding the site of town, and each would gain a share of lots.

Complicating matters, on August 21, 1823, Governor Edward Coles formed a commission that was to select thirty-six sections of government land to be reserved from public auction. These lands were to be sold later, and the proceeds of the sales earmarked for education. Among these restricted properties was the quarter section immediately south of John Kelly's farm, which was to be Sheriff John Taylor's portion of the town site property. Later that month, Iles's complex plans for the county seat community were put in more jeopardy by the sudden death of his partner John Kelly.

In a recently discovered letter from Iles to Representative Cook (who was actually living in Edwardsville at the time) Iles reported Kelly's death and expressed his concern that Taylor's improvement had been selected for use by the state. With the land auction less than three weeks away, Iles asked Cook, "if you see any speculators speaking of going on to purchase, to hold out an idea the Town will be moved in consequence of the Location." This was clearly an effort on Iles's part to confuse speculators and to discourage them from bidding against him and his partners.

The need for such complexity is unclear. Although Iles was understandably worried about the possibility of his improvements being purchased from beneath him at public auction, this rarely occurred in 1820s Illinois. Squatters' rights were a long held tradition, and enforced by local mob rule if not a law from Congress.[7]

The auction of public land at the Springfield office was opened on November 6, 1823, and despite their apparent concerns, Iles and his partners purchased their land the following day. None of the men were bid against, and each parcel sold at the minimum price of $1.25 per acre. John Taylor was able to disengage his soon-to-be-valuable property from the state-selected Seminary Lands.

Ignoring the place-name Springfield, the plat of "Calhoun" was recorded a month later. The position of the plat fell across both Iles and Enos's property—reflecting their partnership—as well as across the lands held by Cox and Taylor, who had also clearly been involved in the business venture. What is surprising, however, is that combined, their properties contained only four blocks of town lots, or less than 20 percent of the plat. This would seem to have been hardly profitable for them, and yet would have added an unnecessary legal complexity to the new town.

The plat of Calhoun consisted of a rectangular grid of twenty-three blocks and a public square. Iles's store fell on lot 4 of block 8 (figure 12.1). The temporary courthouse, which had been constructed along the old trail (Jefferson Street), was now situated in the heart of a fledging commercial district pioneered by Elijah Iles. The new public square (which was to be given to the county if the town was chosen as permanent seat of government) was placed on the extreme eastern edge of the plat, however, and well away from the valuable commercial property near Iles's store.

To modern eyes, the conflicts of interest surrounding the creation of Calhoun abound, and in fact, they did not go unnoticed during the 1820s. In 1826, area resident William Hamilton (son of Alexander Hamilton and former employee of the General Land Office in St. Louis) accused Enos and Cox of improper conduct with regards to their purchase of Springfield area properties while running the land office. The charge was retracted two months later, and later historians took little notice of the affair.[8]

Peter Cartwright described the town as it appeared in 1823 as "a few smoky, hastily-built cabins, and one or two very little shanties called 'stores.'"[9] In 1825, the town of Springfield was chosen as the permanent seat of Sangamon County—the name "Calhoun" having fallen from use. An informal census conducted at Springfield in early 1825 enumerated 236 individuals: 70 males over the age of twenty-one, 159 women and children, and 7 "people of color." The census also described a business community that had grown considerably in two years, which included five lawyers, three stores, three shoemakers, three blacksmiths, three carpenters, two taverns, a distillery, an ox powered gristmill, a physician, saddler, tanner, tailor, tinner, butcher, bricklayer, cooper, and a hatter.[10] Most of these businesses would have been located in the immediate vicinity of Iles's store.

In 1826, a new courthouse was constructed on the public square at the eastern edge of the plat. The old courthouse across from Iles's store was converted into a store. Gradually, however, commercial activity began to shift toward the new courthouse square. By the early 1830s, this became the heart of the town of Springfield, and the original core of the

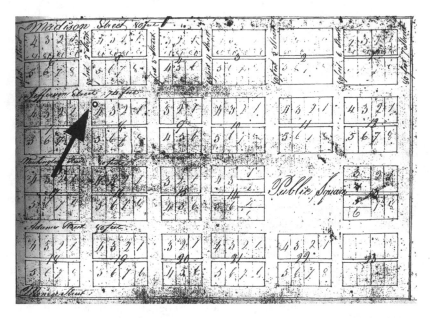

FIG. 12.1 Plat map of Calhoun (Springfield) recorded in 1823, showing location of the
Iles Store site.

community anchored by Elijah Iles's store would become increasingly
less significant in the business affairs of the town.

Iles sold his stock of goods to his clerk John Williams in 1830 or
1831, retiring from the retail business and moving to a nearby farm.
Williams moved his goods out of the building in the spring of 1833, re-
locating to the public square. Looking for a new tenant in April, Iles advertised to rent "the oldest and yet considered the best stand for a mercantile house in the town of Springfield." He stated that the property
included a "storeroom, warehouse and a good cellar." [11]

In July 1833 William Bassett announced that he was opening a new
dry goods store at "Major Iles Corner," previously occupied by John
Williams. Goods "recently purchased at Philadelphia" could be ex-
changed for country produce.[12] In March of 1836, John Hay purchased
the building and converted it into a residence for his family, thus con-
cluding the mercantile history of the old store building. The structure
was remodeled at least once during the mid-nineteenth century, and was
demolished in the 1890s.

Eliza Farnham described a scene in 1836 that may have been quite
similar to the view of the yard behind the Iles Store, when purchased by

the Hay family: "the near view is diversified by the rears of several wooden stores of different lengths, the ground about each being picturesquely ornamented with broken crockery, soiled sheets of wrapping paper, rifled boxes and crates."[13]

A Forgotten Archaeological Site

Eventually, the earliest history of Springfield (centered on the corner of Jefferson and Second streets) would be nearly forgotten. In 1837, the town became the state capital, and the brick courthouse built on the public square in 1826 was replaced by an imposing Greek revival statehouse. Shortly after the Civil War, a much larger statehouse was constructed five blocks to the southwest, and the building on the square once again became a county courthouse. A century later, the commercial district surrounding the square had become known as the "old" part of town. In the 1960s, the Old Capitol was renovated—an act inspired by the fact that Lincoln had worked in the building as a lawyer. True to fashion for the times, however, the archaeological signature of that historic building and the surrounding area was completely removed during the construction of an underground parking lot.

Four blocks to the west, however, at least one site associated with the frontier era of Springfield remained partially intact. Perhaps due in part to the fact that Lincoln had *not* slept there, the site was spared not only significant development, but also the bulldozers associated with 1960s monument building.

I had been watching the intersection of Second and Jefferson streets for years, just in case earthmoving or building demolition might momentarily expose an area of undamaged subsoil. This intersection saw much activity during the frontier period, and even small utility trenches or building projects had the potential to expose (and destroy) traces of a very different time. Our moment came in February 2003, when Curtis Mann (manager of the Sangamon Valley Collection of Lincoln Library) drove past the site and saw that a large, mid-twentieth century building had just been demolished. He called me, and we immediately visited the site.

Fortunately, the recently demolished building had not been equipped with a basement. Had it been, there would have been almost no archaeological deposits left on the property. Instead, a concrete slab floor had been peeled off of the ground by bulldozers a few days earlier. This had exposed and smeared the clay subsoil beneath and then covered it back over with several inches of disturbed soil and demolition debris. When

I arrived at the site, the surface had frozen solid, making it impossible to test with a shovel. In places, however, it looked very likely that intact subsoil was present and thus there was a strong possibility that archaeological remains had survived as well. Further, along the western edge of the lot was a small pile of sandy limestone slabs, which had been unearthed during the recent digging of a footing trench. The trench itself was already filled with concrete, so we could not see that they were removed from a feature or imported fill soils. The stones looked very suspicious, however, as they were unworked and of poor quality for modern construction. A few also exhibited traces of a very soft, sandy lime mortar. Somebody had very probably encountered an early nineteenth-century feature while digging the trench.

It can be very difficult to picture a place like Springfield in 1823 while standing in a place like Springfield in 2003. Buses and traffic, diesel fumes, pavement, concrete and steel, and constant motion quickly obscure thoughts of small log buildings, muddy paths, chickens and pigs, and a quiet that is nearly extinct. It is perhaps for this reason that few people (even in the preservation business) expect to find 175-year-old archaeological features and artifacts still lying beneath today's urban environment. Many of the remains that managed to survive the late nineteenth and twentieth century are destroyed with the assumption that they are already gone. In fact, the site that we were about to excavate (and which was about to be destroyed by construction) was located four blocks down the street from state historical preservation offices. Nonetheless, our crew was there on a volunteer basis, depending on the patience of the construction crew and landowners. No one in any agency had even bothered asking archaeologists to examine the site.

We made arrangements with the landowners and construction crew to set up a small-scale archaeological excavation at the corner of the property as soon as the soil thawed. Once that thaw came, the construction crew would soon need to resume their work, and so we would have very little time.

Because the building constructed by Elijah Iles in 1821 was still standing seventy-five years later, it was depicted on several types of late nineteenth century maps that had no equivalent during the early nineteenth century. Documentation of the physical environment, particularly in the cities, blossomed after the Civil War. At the Iles site, this would potentially make it much easier to find the subsurface footprint of the building, although because it stood for so long, that footprint had probably been modified somewhat as well. Our biggest concern was what might have happened to the early nineteenth-century archaeological deposits between the 1890s and the 1960s.

There is one form of map that can be remarkably useful to historic archaeologists working in urban environments. Beginning in the 1860s, the D. A. Sanborn Company began publishing detailed maps of cities, designed to assist fire insurance companies in their assessment of the fire hazards associated with various building types. Fire insurance maps of the late nineteenth century offer a wealth of details about the built environment of the time, including building positions, sizes, and methods of construction. The earliest fire-insurance map of Springfield (published in 1884) shows a two story wooden structure (measuring approximately twenty-five feet square) situated along the western edge of the lot, less than ten feet from the front (or northern) lot line. A large addition is shown attached to the building on its southeastern corner.

There are also at least two nineteenth century photographs of the Iles store building (figure 12.2). The first, probably dating to the 1880s or 1890s, shows a rectangular two-story clapboarded structure with a gabled end facing Jefferson Street. On the east side of the structure is a two story addition, also clapboarded. The second photo of the store was taken during the demolition of the historic building in 1896. In this image, the log core of the building has been exposed, as has the timber frame addition on the east side of the building. The original structure is fashioned of hewn logs. The front of the building is fitted with three windows (two up, one down) and a doorway on the northwest corner. Additional structures can be seen to the south and southeast of the building, but their age and method of construction is unknown.

As soon as the thaw came, we returned to the site. The surface was a greasy mess of wet clay and demolition debris, creating a rainbow of disturbed soil that obscured the subsoil. In that messy rainbow, however, alongside bits of asphalt and shattered PVC pipe, were pieces of 1820s pearlware teacups, reminding us that were on the right track. Using the Sanborn maps as a guide, I simply walked out across the site with a tape measure and a shovel. Within fifteen minutes, the shovel blade struck the southern edge of a large, deep feature. Such guided precision in archaeology is a luxury not afforded to those who work on prehistoric sites, and actually, one rarely has such a guide when looking for pre–Civil War structures either. It was its persistence for over seventy-five years that put the frontier-era store on the semimodern maps

We spent the rest of the day exposing the limits of the large feature,

FIG. 12.2 The Iles Store building as it appeared during the late nineteenth century, and during demolition in 1896.

which we soon learned was a filled cellar (figures 12.3, 12.4). In between disturbances caused by utility and construction trenches, we placed a test unit along its western edge, near the pile of limestone found by the construction crew. We found what we looking for about eighteen inches below scraped surface. Beneath the disturbance created by a utility trench was a partially intact remnant of a stone wall (figure 12.5). The wall was composed of the same sandy limestone that I had seen on the surface weeks earlier, and this was indeed the same feature hit by the construction crew. The wall was constructed of large, flat, unworked stones laid with a soft, sandy mortar. The upper courses of stone had been removed

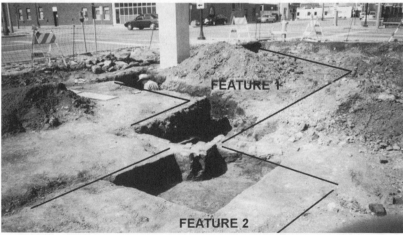

FIG. 12.3 The Iles Store site prior to and during excavations. The state capitol building can be seen in the background.

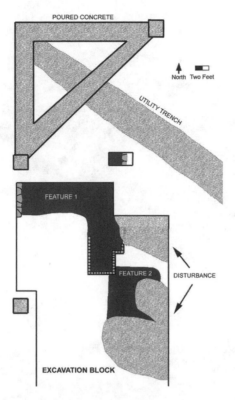

FIG. 12.4 Base map of excavations at the Iles Store site.

by utility trenches, and only the bottom four courses of stone remained. The cellar that the stones had lined was only about four and a half feet deep originally, and had a clay floor. The location of the feature and the method of its construction told us we were standing in the cellar built by Iles in the spring of 1821.

The little remnant of the stone wall eighteen inches below the surface at Second and Jefferson was not much to look at. But the unassuming feature really had an impact. The little stone wall was perhaps the first of its kind in the city, and the cellar is probably the oldest surviving archaeological feature in Springfield—barring any prehistoric features that may be preserved under a parking lot somewhere.

As the old store building stood until the 1890s, the fill of the abandoned cellar contained only very late nineteenth-century debris. As we expanded our investigations, we soon learned that what we now called feature 1 had been heavily damaged since the demolition of the log building in 1896. The cellar measured twelve feet wide on its east-west axis.

FIG. 12.5 In-situ section of stone wall associated with the 1821 store building, and mid-nineteenth-century brick coal chute modification.

As the northern wall of the feature was obscured by construction-related trenches, the north-south length of the cellar was no longer evident. Based on the information depicted on the fire insurance map, it was probably between ten and fourteen feet long.

Originally, there was a set of stairs accessing the cellar from the outside, at the rear of the building. That entranceway would have been about four feet wide and five feet long, and fitted with a set of wooden steps. Often, commercial buildings in frontier contexts in Illinois are distinguished by exterior entrances (as well as larger surface areas) for storing goods securely under the floor of the building. Heavy crates and barrels could not have been easily lowered and raise from a trap door, as were the contents of small pit cellars associated with typical dwellings of the period. Even in the bigger cellars such as feature 1, storekeepers would have loaded and unloaded their goods while bent over in the dark.

Sometime during the mid nineteenth century, however, the cellar entranceway at the rear of the old store building was rebuilt and modified. The entrance was lengthened by three feet, and the old wooden stairs were replaced by a brick-lined ramp. No brick was found elsewhere in the construction of the cellar. The modification probably converted the old exterior entrance into a coal chute, as coal heating had become the norm in cities like Springfield by the 1850s.

Behind the Store

On St. Patrick's Day the taverns at the corner of Second and Jefferson were busy by early afternoon. Celebrants in green paper top hats walked in and out of buildings that stood where the first courthouse and Carpenter's grocery had stood 180 years earlier. Several of those who crossed the street to see what we were doing (and to offer us holiday beer) were surprisingly impressed with the pile of old stones, when we told them of their long history.

After recording what was left of the main cellar, we turned our attention to the area behind the building. As we cleaned the recently bulldozed surface, we soon found that there had been extensive damage to what had been the backyard of the store building as well. More utility trenches crisscrossed the lot, and several large backhoe gouges pockmarked the clay subsoil. Directly behind the remnants of the store cellar, however, we encountered a second early nineteenth century feature, which was still partially intact.

Feature 2 was a smaller, earthen-walled cellar that was probably once located beneath a rear addition of the store building. Iles recalled that he added a kitchen after his marriage in 1824, and this feature was probably constructed as part of the addition. The pit cellar measured eight feet wide. It was probably about ten feet long originally, but its exact dimensions are unclear due to bulldozer disturbance. The feature extended to a depth of sixteen inches below scraped surface, or approximately two and a half feet deep originally. The footings of the building probably added another eighteen inches of depth to the facility. The pit was carefully constructed, with vertical walls, sharp corners, and a flat bottom. It was, however, really too broad and too shallow to actually get down into and fully utilize as storage space. Such pits probably functioned more as cool, dry, and prepared surfaces under the floor, on which containers of food were kept and accessed through one or more traps in the floorboards.

The kitchen addition built by Iles in 1824 was probably replaced or removed by the John Hay family sometime after their arrival in 1836, when they converted the entire building into a residence. The feature 2 cellar appears to have been filled as part of this remodeling episode. The northwest corner of the feature was later superimposed by the lengthening of the feature 1 entrance, indicating that feature 2 and the kitchen addition had already been removed prior to the installation of the coal chute.

Upon its abandonment, feature 2 was filled with redeposited topsoil and yellow clay backdirt from an excavation elsewhere on site. To our pleasant surprise, the artifacts contained in the fill soils dated to the 1820s and early 1830s, and were directly associated with the early years of storekeeping years at the site.

Artifacts from Iles's Store

Stores such as Elijah Iles's stocked the goods that ultimately wound up in area homes. It follows then, that the artifacts found at such store sites should be similar in character to those found at area domestic sites. The patterns of use of such goods at individual homesites, however, would have presumably been reflective of a family's particular habits, tastes, and needs. A store site, then, may or may not produce similar artifact assemblages.

On one hand, stores were stocked with a range of goods designed to satisfy the needs of a wide range of the population. So the archaeological signature of those stores would presumably contain a wider range of goods than those associated with the more specific needs of individual customers. As the archeological record shows, consumer habits of residents of pre-1835 rural Illinois were surprisingly similar. That similarity must reflect practices, habits, and preferences that were widespread across the rural population of the period. If storekeepers were in tune with such practices and needs, they would have tailored their inventory accordingly. This would suggest, then, that artifact assemblages from store sites might closely resemble those of the homes of their customers.

However, the assemblages found at store sites and home sites were created under different circumstances. One could easily assume that the debris discarded at stores would have reflected the breakage of unsold goods (in the store or during shipping) rather than the natural attrition that comes with home use. Complicating this, however, is the fact that most storekeepers of the period (including Iles) lived on the store property, and their own consumer habits were blended into the commercial archaeological signature of the site.

With these issues in mind, a frontier-context store assemblage might actually resemble more closely those of individual homesites, but with exaggerated quantities of certain fragile goods, and perhaps a wider range of goods than found on the average farmstead. The artifact assemblage from feature 2 at the Iles site fits this model.

The character of the artifact sample from feature 2 suggests that it was once part of a back door rubbish pile, composed of household sweepings and discarded domestic and storekeeping debris. Because some of the glass artifacts are still in large pieces, some of this debris may have been left in an area protected from heavy foot traffic. The assemblage is dominated by fragmentary Queenswares, the bases of broken glass tumblers, and small items such as buttons that may have been swept out of the building along with dirt and other debris. This material was then redeposited into the feature 2 cellar upon its abandonment, along with wall plaster and nails from remodeling. The undisturbed portion of the feature produced a sample of artifacts dating to the first fifteen years of the site.

The Queenswares from feature 2 consist primarily of pearlware and whiteware vessels dating to the late 1810s through the mid 1830s—or corresponding primarily with Iles's tenure of the site (figure 12.6). Little about the ceramic assemblage would be out of place on a strictly domestic site of the period. The ratios of tablewares and teawares at the store site are identical to the domestic average of the period, probably reflecting the "typical" consumer behavior of the Iles and Williams families who were living above the store. It is unlikely that breakage during shipping would produce such similar vessel type assemblages.

The Iles Store site reflects a higher than average percentage of printed

FIG. 12.6 Selected refined ceramics from the small feature 2 pit cellar at the Iles Store site.

wares, however. A similar pattern has been noted at other store sites,[14] probably reflecting an effort by these storekeeping families to present a slightly more formal atmosphere at the table. It has also been argued that a higher percentage of transfer printed wares within a particular artifact assemblage represents the elevated socioeconomic status of its users. While printed pottery was slightly more expensive than painted or edged pottery, the relatively low cost of *all* of these wares (when compared to other common household goods), as well as their abundance on a range of frontier homesites, suggests that printed earthenware probably does not really reflect the wealth or economic pretensions of its users.[15] Instead, the slightly more expensive wares were perhaps more subject to changes in the fashions and aesthetics of middle-class home furnishings than were other forms of Queenswares.

Several teacups in the Iles assemblage are decorated in painted or printed motifs that were popular before the mid-1820s (figure 12.7). These would have been the earliest types of English Queensware prod-

Cup fragment

Saucer fragment

FIG. 12.7 Fragments of pearlware teawares from feature 2 at the Iles Store site, shown with intact, nonarchaeological examples.

ucts brought to Springfield. Whether they were actually offered for sale at the shop (and were broken before they were sold) or they were owned by Elijah and Malinda Iles is unknown.

The tea-related vessels from the Iles pit cellar also include two items that were less common on the frontier—a pearlware and a whiteware cup plate. These vessels, measuring about three inches in diameter, were part of the traditional tea set, designed to play a small role in the rather complex ritual of taking tea. Tea was poured from teapot pot to cup, and then from cup to saucer, where it would cool. In the meantime, the cup (now dripping slightly with tea) would be placed back on the table, where it might stain a linen tablecloth. In came the cup plate, on which the dripping cup could be placed, thus rescuing white linen from staining. All of this was apparently played out in some of the log houses on the Illinois frontier.

Portions of only two crockery vessels were recovered from feature 2— a lead-glazed redware pot, and the rim of a salt-glazed stoneware pot. Such small samples from early contexts are typical of the period. The redware pot may have been made at Cotton Hill, or perhaps at John Ebey's downtown Springfield kiln. The stoneware pot, however, was brought to town from somewhere else.

While the general ceramic and glass assemblage at the Iles Store site is similar to the domestic norm of the period, the table glass category is made significantly larger by the presence of a number of flint glass tumblers (figure 12.8). These drinking cups were plain, round, and undecorated, very thin-walled, and extremely fragile. The presence of a number of such tumblers at the site probably reflects the dispensing of liquor by the single serving at the store, which was a common practice of the period. The larger number of tumblers was perhaps the most obvious indication of the special function of the Iles site, although they played roles in what was customary social activity, rather than store inventory.

Another glass vessel designed for use at the table was found in the pit cellar. An intricately molded cup plate represents another reasonably uncommon type of artifact for the period. Cup plates were one of the first products to be mass-produced by pressing machines in American glasshouses. They were decorated in a wide variety of geometric or floral patterns. The plate found at the Iles site was three inches in diameter, and was probably manufactured at Pittsburgh or Wheeling West Virginia. Together with the two ceramic examples, the item probably was a piece from Malinda Iles's more formal table setting.

Artifacts related to home furnishings are usually rare on rural sites dating to the frontier period. The cellar behind the store produced only a few such items, but the sample is still larger than usual. Fragments of a pewter or white metal cap and font were once attached to an early form of oil lamp. Lamps of the 1820s and 1830s would have been fueled by whale oil or camphene, but appear to have been rather rare on the midwestern frontier due to the cost of the fuel. A very small fragment of a pearlware figurine was also found in the pit cellar. Molded earthenware figurines were a sideline to the Queensware industry of Staffordshire England, but were produced in large quantities during the late eighteenth and early nineteenth century. These little figures—usually of people or small animals—do not appear to have been part of the typical country store stock in Illinois, and are very rarely found on pre-1840 homesites. They are occasionally found in urban contexts. The broken figurine discarded behind Iles's store was probably a lamb or dog. Fragments of a mirror, and a trunk or upholstery tack round out the furnishings category.

Perhaps not surprisingly given the function of the site, two coins were found in feature 2. A Mexican Republic eight-real piece, minted in Durango, is dated 1826. An eight-real was worth one dollar, and could actually be cut into "bits" to make change—hence the expression two

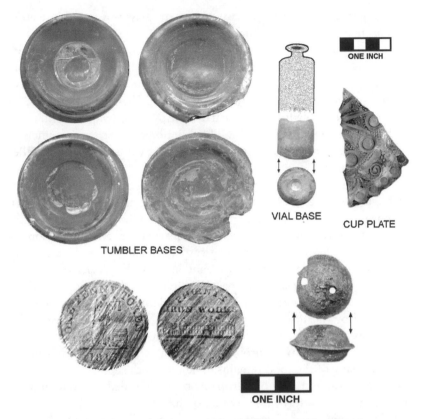

FIG. 12.8 Selected glassware, a token, and a hawk bell from the Iles Store site.

bits for a quarter. While Spanish colonial coins are common on frontier-era sites, coins of the Mexican Republic are less so. The use of foreign coinage during the early nineteenth century (across the county) reflected the shortage of coins minted in America. It should be remembered, however, that perhaps more than half of Iles's sales were conducted in credit and trade, as opposed to hard currency.

Even more unique is a Scottish, one-penny copper token. Dated 1813, the obverse of the token reads PHOENIX IRON WORKS above a view of the Phoenix Iron Works building in Glasgow. During the late eighteenth and early nineteenth century, tokens were issued by merchants as supplements to government-issued currency in times of low production, as well as to encourage purchases at a particular business. This example was probably carried by an immigrant to America in the 1810s, where it ultimately found its way to the Sangamo Country, and to Iles's store counter.

A larger than average quantity of window glass was found in feature 2. This may be the only artifact type found at the site that could more confidently be interpreted as broken store inventory. Crates of window-panes may have been damaged during their long journey down the Ohio River, or overland to central Illinois, and the broken pieces may have been discarded behind the building. Additionally, several large pieces have been intentionally cut into narrow strips, measuring one and a half inches wide and five inches long. The function of these strips is unclear, but Iles or one of his shopkeepers may have cut window glass for smaller cabinet windows.

Feature 2 produced a number of animal bones. Like much of the rest of the assemblage, these appear to be related primarily to the kitchen practices of the Iles or Williams families, as opposed to food products sold at the store. The sample includes a nearly equal amount of domes-ticated and wild animals, including cattle, swine, goat, and chicken, as well as squirrel, rabbit, turkey, dove, and buffalofish.[16] A lack of evidence of on-site butchering suggests that those living on the site consumed the food. It is also quite likely that much of the domesticated and wild foods consumed by the Iles and Williams families were obtained in trade at their store. Also mixed in with the food remains were the bones of at least four rats, who were probably responsible for the gnawing marks seen on many of the food remains. The rat bones support the idea that the debris from feature 2 had probably been discarded in a hidden-away area such as beneath the house or a porch.

Archaeological evidence of the waning years of the Indian trade in the Sangamo region is very scarce, particularly on sites associated with American settlers. Elijah Iles, however, recalled that during his first years at Springfield, his sales "were about as much to Indians as to the whites." From feature 2 (found precariously near the edge of an area re-cently disturbed by a bulldozer or backhoe) was the partially intact re mains of a small brass "hawk bell." This was the most exciting artifact from the pit cellar. Such bells were quite common in the Indian trade during the eighteenth and early nineteenth century, and were sewn to clothing or clothing accessories. The bells, however, are quite rare on domestic sites of the period. With this in mind, the little bell found be-hind Iles's store may have been lost by a visiting member of the Kicka-poo, or may have potentially been part of trade-related inventory stocked by Iles during the first years of his business at "log town." Per-haps more that any other artifact, the bell signifies the gulf between now and then at Springfield.

CHAPTER THIRTEEN

Moses's Sangamo

Relocating a Lost Town

Eight miles up river from Springfield, the site of Sangamo Town—the sister city to Springfield in 1823—is a much different place than the site of the Iles Store. The modern appearance of Springfield was assured with the arrival of the county seat early in its history. Sangamo Town, which like Springfield had provided an oasis of goods and services in the ancient forests that surrounded the river, stumbled and fell while the region was still a frontier. A town once inhabited by several businesses and a number of big plans was completely gone by 1850. Today, the old trail that crossed through Springfield is four lanes wide and dotted with government office buildings and fast food restaurants. Eight miles to the northwest, the same trail is only visible in short segments as a slight swale in the forest floor. The town of Sangamo is a field and a pasture, as it has been for 150 years (figure 13.1).

When I first began researching Sangamo Town, I was struck by just how little has been said about the place, and how really forgotten and lost the site had become. A county history published in 1881 referred to the town only briefly, as the one-time competitor for the county seat, and pointed out that less than forty years after its abandonment, there was there was "no evidence" of the town.[1] During the 1960s a nearby prehistoric site was listed in the official Illinois Archaeological Survey files as "the extinct village of the Sangamo Indians," evidently recorded on the basis of some misunderstood oral tradition. In the early 1970s, amateur historian and local physician Dr. Floyd Barringer came closer,

FIG. 13.1 What was once downtown Sangamo Town as it appears today.

and located a site that he believed to be that of the entire town. The site he found was indeed part of Sangamo Town, but a small one—a later dwelling associated with one of the mills in town.[2]

Of course, most of what was first remembered about the town was contained, again, in the wake of oral traditions surrounding the early life of Abraham Lincoln. In the spring of 1831, Lincoln and two others were hired by Denton Offutt (who would later open a store at New Salem) to constructed a flatboat and to ship a load of hogs to New Orleans. The men built their flatboat at Sangamo Town in the spring of that year, setting up a temporary camp down by the water and taking some of their meals at the town's tavern. In 1866, the tavern keeper's nephew, Caleb Carman, told Lincoln's biographer William Herndon about the six weeks Lincoln had spent camping at the edge of town. During that time, Lincoln and his crew lived in a shanty down by the river. Carman remembered that Lincoln often cooked for the crew, and that they played the card game Seven Up after dark.

In 1895, Ida Tarbell's *Early Life of Abraham Lincoln* included an interpretive map of the layout of Sangamo Town, based on interviews with an elderly former resident. The map, however, was remarkably inaccurate, and bore little resemblance to the actual plat map that had been filed in the Sangamon County Court House. Tarbell concluded that "Sangamo town, where Mr. Lincoln built the flatboat, has, since his day, completely disappeared from the earth."[3]

The first real overview of the frontier community was contained in an article published in 1926 by John Linden Roll, who was a descendant of one of the village's storekeepers. In his article, Roll included a plan of town based on both the recorded plat and Roll family recollections. He was also able to piece together a general list of businesses that were operating in the village during its heyday in the late 1820s and very early 1830s: a tavern, two stores, a gristmill, a sawmill, and a carding mill. He also contributed another story to the Lincoln lore. His great uncle (a teenager at the time) had helped Lincoln build the flatboat on the banks of the river, and was present when three young men who had upset a canoe in high water were rescued by Abe, who floated down river on a log tied to a rope.

Searching for Lost Sangamo

I decided to go out and look for Sangamo Town in 1994, when I returned to the Sangamon River valley and moved into an old house just down river from the site. From the deed records, the general location of the town (within an approximately 300-acre area) could be placed on a map. The modern topographical maps showed only an empty bluff crest overlooking the west bank of the river. This strongly suggested that archaeological deposits could still be intact, as opposed to the hundreds of features and thousands of artifacts destroyed by warehouses, office buildings, and burger places down the trail at Springfield.

It was important to locate, test, and record this particular suite of archaeological sites before suburban sprawl found its way into this part of the valley. Most forms of small-scale development do not require archaeological investigations by law, and thus the perfectly natural settlement of the landscape will always have the potential to impact the remains of former settlements. Further, just about everything regarding the place was a cipher—the location, the layout, the number of buildings that were actually built there, the duration of their occupation, and the things that went on inside them. The remaining paper records—a few licenses, some voting records, minor lawsuits, and advertisements for at least one mill and a store—really only told us that a town existed, and that there were a number of families with investments there. So many obvious questions lingered—and many more would be raised the minute a shovel struck an intact feature. An entire town, abandoned at the close of the frontier era, had basically been forgotten.

On a warm morning in June, I drove the truck down a narrow dirt lane that led to the river. While I (like many others) had examined the original plat of the town, there was no way to anchor that plat to the modern topography, as it was not recorded with respect to the original government land surveys. This meant that the town could exist anywhere on the 320-acre parcel once owned by Moses Broadwell, who platted the town in 1822. Further, only very rarely do roads or trails that are still visible today (even the obviously old ones) have a relationship to those in use during the frontier period in Illinois. Only the landscape itself remains to suggest where people may have lived.

I parked the truck along the edge of a large field situated very near the edge of the river valley itself. The field was not in cultivation and was instead covered in shoulder-high grass. Over the last fifty years, modern archaeology has been very dependent on cultivated fields to locate prehistoric and historic sites. Plowing exposes the soil to weathering, which in turn exposes debris that was once buried beneath the sod. This allows a survey crew to examine most of the surface area of given landform quickly and efficiently, often without digging a single hole. A forested or grass covered site, however, is completely invisible to the eye, and the soils below the surface must be exposed by the shovel. One by one, each fifteen-inch wide hole offers the only peek at what may or may not lie beneath.

As many archeological surveys begin, I waded out into the long grass with a shovel, some plastic bags and a notebook. The first shovel test exposed a very hard, root-bound, silty topsoil, which contained absolutely no artifacts and no subsurface disturbances—just as most shovel tests do. The next two dozen tests were exactly the same. Moving further out into the field, more shoveling, over and over. In most of the tests, I found only undisturbed clay subsoil at about ten inches below ground surface. When one finds undisturbed subsoil, one stops digging.

One of the tests, however, out in the middle of the field, did not expose yellow clay ten inches down. Instead, I could see at the base of the test, a patch of swirled grays, browns, and blacks. These colors clearly represented a backfilled excavation into the subsoil, which had not been subsequently disturbed by the plow. More specifically, those colors were created by hearth ash, decomposed organic materials, and wood charcoal. At eleven inches below ground surface, I had found culture instead of nature. A little more troweling of this soil immediately produced a fragment of a pearlware cup, and the stem of a smoking pipe, both of which dated to the time of Sangamo Town. Someone was here, *then,* smoking tobacco. That fifteen-inch opening in the topsoil was the first window into Sangamo Town.

A Glimpse Untethered

The feature discovered in the shovel tests was located very near an eroded area that had recently been modified and terraced by earthmoving equipment. If that equipment had been driven a little further to the northeast, this archaeological feature would have been almost entirely destroyed. Even in the middle of a quiet, rural field, archaeological deposits are threatened by perfectly normal, modern activity.

The chance discovery of the feature in the shovel tests was followed by two large excavation units, which exposed the entire pit in plan. The feature was a large oval-shaped pit, measuring approximately four feet wide and eight feet long. It was about three feet deep at its deepest point, but it appeared to reflect several stages of use. Feature 1 at Sangamo Town probably served as an exterior storage facility, where vegetables were stored during the late fall and early winter. From its unique shape, it is also clear that the pit was used more than once (figure 13.2). The large pit appeared to have been created in two stages. The first was a four by eight foot shallow basin, less than two feet deep. This may have been filled with squash, pumpkins, cabbages or other root crops. It was then

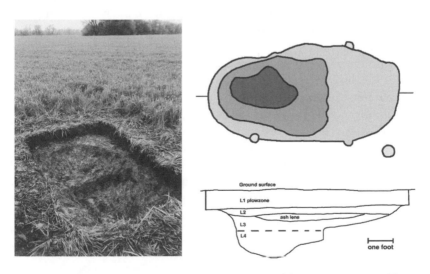

FIG. 13.2 Excavation view, plan, and profile drawings of feature 1 at Sangamo Town.

covered over for the winter. A set of five post holes found on both side of the basin probably reflect the use of poles and timbers to create a loose superstructure over the pit, which was then covered in planks and earth. Over the winter, its users would have walked out to the cellar, shoveled off some of the soil, and pulled away a few planks to retrieve some of the vegetables lying beneath. The pit was then covered over again.

At some point after its initial use, perhaps the following autumn, the eastern half of the feature was dug deeper. While most of the contours of the pit appeared to have been smoothed by long-term use, a deeper basin in the eastern end of the facility was still composed of rough, straight walls that preserved (somewhat miraculously) the marks of a shovel that cut into the clay during the early 1830s. That the shovel marks were well preserved and not eroded or slumped within the pit suggests that the pit was abandoned shortly afterwards.

The somewhat irregularly shaped pit was actually oriented in the same direction—twenty-three degrees east of north—as was the Sangamo Town plat. This indicated two things. Firstly, that the feature was built when those lot lines mattered and were visible on the landscape (in the form of buildings, streets, and fences). It also suggested that even the covering of a crop storage pit was constructed in line with the built environment of the new town.

When the pit was abandoned (perhaps to be replaced by another somewhere else on site) it was filled with organic matter, topsoil, household rubbish, and a thick layer of fine white ash. The ash layer was probably dumped in a single day when the fireplace was cleaned out and shoveled into the pit. In this ash were bits of carbonized wood, some chicken bones, the broken handle of a pair of fireplace tongs, and several brass straight pins. Such pins are often found in layers of ash, along with clusters of other small objects such as buttons, pipe stems and the occasional coin. I believe this may be due to their accidental loss near the hearth, where they were later swept up with hearth ash. It may be no coincidence that small sewing-related items are often found in hearth ash, as firelight was the brightest source of light in the dark interior of the log home. When this ash was first exposed to the damp summer air, it momentarily emitted the haunting scent of smoke from a fire that burned very near that spot 170 years earlier.

———

Based on the refined ceramics in the feature, the pit was probably abandoned by the mid-1830s. Pearlwares of the 1820s dominate the feature 1 sample, and most are very similar to those later recovered from the features at Springfield and Elkhart. In most respects, the nature of the artifact assemblage from feature 1 at Sangamo Town conforms very closely to the average for the period. English Queenswares outnumber locally made crockery by a large margin, followed by a very small number of glass bottles and glass serving vessels. Again, there are slightly more tea-wares than tablewares, and these are decorated in nearly equal quantities of painted and printed motifs. In other words, the occupants of this site were reasonably typical consumers for frontier Illinois.

While the painted tea cups and printed plates used in this particular household were really no different than countless others across the country during the mid 1820s (the feature produced yet another plate decorated in the Wild Rose pattern, for instance) that apparent sameness does not necessarily reflect a sameness for their users. Residents of downtown Philadelphia set their tableware with the same Wild Rose plates used by the Lathams, and by this family at Sangamo Town (figure 13.3). And yet, there was a difference. In the downtown Philadelphia of 1825, such a plate would have played its little part at a table that had been set within a well-established, urban, middle-class community. That plate would have found a reasonably comfortable place amongst many modern and refined things—well crafted furnishings, frame or masonry architecture, and paved streets. While eating from the plate, its owner would have enjoyed the general sense of being in the midst of then-modern civilization.

On the bluffs overlooking the Sangamon River in 1825, however, things were very different. That same deep-blue plate rested on a table within a world of contrasts. This was still primarily a wild place, and the new settlements were little spots on an eternal landscape. The progress of culture had been pushed back, and resembled what most knew as ancient. The fashionable English wares were hopelessly out of place in a forested river valley 100 miles from the nearest semblance of modernity. This would soon change, but in 1825, that blue plate stood in sharp relief against a domestic environment wrapped in hewn timbers and mud-lined fireplaces. Such contrasts—little crashes of civilization into an aboriginal forest—are detectable around each excavated fragment of a supper plate, if one listens carefully.

This particular family at Sangamo also made an effort to obtain a few types of English wares that were a little less typical to the local country stores. These included a red paste, engine-turned English teapot, a small salt cellar, and a silver luster cream pot. Elaborately turned teapots made of very fine, red clay were introduced in England in the 1760s. They

FIG. 13.3 Fragment of the Wild Rose pattern plate in-situ in feature 1, shown with intact, nonarchaeological example.

were more expensive than run-of-the-mill creamware or pearlware and were said to make better tea. The pot from feature 1 (represented by a fragment of its lid) was probably purchased in a city such as St. Louis rather than a local country store. The silver luster creamer from feature 1 probably dates to the 1810s. Earthenwares decorated in silver luster appeared in the very early nineteenth century, as inexpensive imitations of solid silver or silver plated tablewares. As imitations, they were quite effective and the glazes of metallic oxide were bright and lustrous. When unearthed, fragments of these vessels do not look as old as they really are.

Once sitting on a nearby table, along with the imported English goods, were several redware serving vessels made by the potters at Cotton Hill—at least one plate and one table bowl are similar to the early wares of the Royal brothers or John Ebey. A pot, a jug, and a kitchen bowl also appear to have been made in Sangamon County. It is very possible that the store at Sangamo Town stocked wares made at Cotton Hill: wholesale purchases made by local stores supported potters such as John Ebey during the early nineteenth century.

Reflecting its age, the glass bottles from the pit were few, but like the refined ceramic assemblage, include a few items atypical to farmsteads in central Illinois. A wide-mouth glass jar was probably used to store dry foodstuffs, and would have been capped with a loose-fitting metal lid or a large cork. A flint glass decanter, represented only by a broken stopper finial, would have added a touch of elegance beyond the typical whiskey flasks used in most households. Eliza Farnham, an educated former resident of New York, recalled that her "new bottle-case with cut glass bottles" was "much appreciated" as she set up housekeeping in Illinois.[4]

The fill of feature 1 at Sangamo Town contained a number of small items that were probably lost or broken in the house and swept into a pile or rubbish bin that was later emptied in the open pit (figure 13.4). This included fragmentary flatware, a number of brass buttons, straight pins, and pieces of broken small tools. From the flatware category are four pewter teaspoon handles, all of which appear to have been intentionally bent and broken in the same manner and to the same length — as if the handles of the damaged spoons had been salvaged for another purpose. Pewter, composed of lead and tin, was easily melted down and may have been used for repairs or even bullet making.

FIG. 13.4 Cut teaspoon handles, a fish hook, a Jew's harp, and a sequin mass from feature 1 at Sangamo Town (shown at various scales).

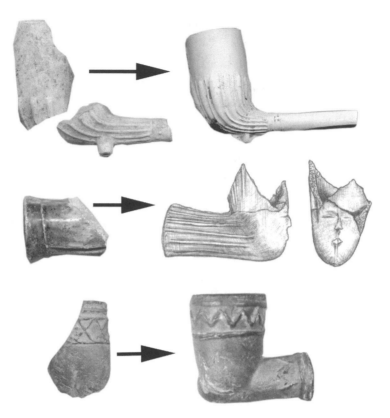

FIG. 13.5 Fragments of tobacco pipes from feature 1 (left) shown with intact examples from other contexts. Top row: English white clay pipe with example from St. Louis. Middle row: Moravian-style pipe with illustration of similar example found in St. Clair County. Bottom row: fragment shown with intact stoneware pipe bowl recovered from waster dumps at Point Pleasant, Ohio.

Fragments of several types of tobacco pipes were found in the ashy layer deposited into the pit (figure 13.5). In the early 1820s, Christiana Tillson described both men and women sitting around a fire, each with a pipe that "showed their own inventive genius," adding that "several varieties might be seen."[5] This eclecticism is visible in the feature 1 sample, which includes pipes representative of the folk traditions of two different regions of the United States, as well as those manufactured in England.

Fragments of several long stem, white clay pipes were found in the pit. These were most likely made in England. Of the wide variety of pipe styles in white clay, those that predate the 1850s are generally less elaborately molded than those of the second half of the nineteenth century. I have seen very few early-to-mid nineteenth century artifact assemblages that do not include fragments of imported long stem pipes, and these products were very common across the country.

The residents of Sangamo Town also used American-made tobacco pipes. The majority of the domestic pipes of the late eighteenth and early nineteenth century were of the "elbow" or "stub-stemmed" variety. Instead of the white ball clay used in European long stem pipes, however, American potters used traditional redware and stoneware clays for most of their products.[6]

Feature 1 contained a fragment of a distinctive earthenware elbow pipe, glazed in an apple green glaze, which was a product of what was probably the earliest successful (Euro-American) pipe-making tradition in the country. Beginning in the 1750s, Moravian potters (members of a religious sect from central Europe) began manufacturing elaborately molded stub-stemmed pipes in their community at Bethabarbara, North Carolina. Most of the pipes featured intricately molded faces peering from the front of the pipe bowls. Potters of North Carolina continued to make traditional Moravian-style "pipe heads" throughout the nineteenth century, although the molds tended to become less elaborate after the 1820s.

The specimen from Sangamo Town was probably made in the first decades of the nineteenth century at Salem, North Carolina. Very unfortunately, however, the face segment of the pipe was broken away before it was discarded into the pit. I have seen more stems missing bowls than bowls missing stems, and I can't help but wonder if some of the little faces were adopted by children in the households, to be used as improvised doll heads.

Sometime in the 1830s another significant pipe-making industry developed in the Upper Ohio Valley, and by 1840 was centered on the small town of Point Pleasant, Ohio.[7] Pipes of this tradition are also stub-stemmed, but are made of stoneware rather than earthenware. Like those of the Moravian community, many of the Point Pleasant styles are anthropomorphic (or molded with faces), though there are also geometric designs. By the 1840s, Point Pleasant pipes were in common use in the Midwest, and were manufactured by the thousands. A second broken pipe from feature 1 is decorated in a crosshatched motif, and represents one the earliest archaeological appearances for these products.

The soils in feature 1 produced two very corroded iron "Jew's harps." The name of these little musical instruments is said to have come from a corruption of an old Dutch term referring to a "child's trumpet." A Jew's (or "jaw") harp consisted of a rounded triangular frame of iron or brass, in which was a flexible steel reed. The frame was held against the lips, and the reed was plucked over the mouth, which served as resonator, like the body of a guitar. Changing the position of the tongue and lips modulated the tones, creating the familiar twangy, springy sounds that we associate with the Old West. Aside from brass harmonica reeds (which usually appear after the frontier period in Illinois), Jew's harps are the only representation of music in the archaeological record of the frontier.

I also found pieces of two pocket knives, a number of brass vest and dress buttons, and a large iron fish hook big enough for pulling the typically five or six foot long drumfish or buffalofish from the Sangamon River. A small brass coin was also found in the pit—a King George IV copper farthing dated 1824. Although Spanish silver was in common circulation in the region during the 1820s, English specie was not.

A small fragment of bright yellow sulfur was also found in the fill soils of feature 1. Compounds of sulfur were sold by apothecaries as a treatment for a variety of skin rashes and irritations. A somewhat unusual find in archaeological contexts, this fragment was probably spilled from a glass vial and swept up with household debris and deposited directly into the pit as it was being filled.

Like the Latham site at Elkhart, the pit at Sangamo Town produced both French-made and regionally-made gunflints (in this case, one of each). The frequency at which we find "aboriginal" gunflints on sites dating to the 1820s in central Illinois is somewhat surprising. Trade between Euro-Americans and Native Americans had become primarily a one-way exchange by the mid 1820s in the region, with Native Americans having little that the new farm families needed or wanted. The gunflints made of local cherts may have been made by Native Americans, but they were probably floating around the community for some time before their loss during the 1820s.

Perhaps the most unusual artifact from the wide range of items found in the shallow pit is a stitched-together cluster of metallic sequins, once sewn to a uniform or ceremonial sash. The salts that have leached from the brass or copper sequins have preserved the threads holding the cluster together. While it is difficult to tell exactly what kind of outfit these once adorned, the little rosette looks very similar to those attached to ceremonial uniforms used by fraternal organizations such as the Masons. Many of Lincoln's neighbors at New Salem later remembered the Masonic funeral held for Bowling Green, who served as a justice of the peace at New Salem during the 1830s. The unusual regalia worn by these organizations probably strengthened those memories.

The contents of the pit feature clearly dated to the time of Sangamo Town, but like most archaeological sites, there was nothing about the artifacts themselves that could identify the occupants of the site. As the town plat had not been drawn with respect to section lines, nothing could anchor it to the modern topography. The feature and the artifacts within it floated untethered, in what was again a natural landscape.

Moses's Sangamo

Moses Broadwell was born in 1764 in Elizabethtown New Jersey. He was remembered as having fought in the Revolutionary War, but little else is known about his early life. After the war, Moses married his second cousin, Jane Broadwell, and the two moved to the Cincinnati area in Ohio. The Broadwells had at least seven children in New Jersey and Ohio, including Mary, David, Sarah, John, William, Charles, and Thomas Jefferson.

In 1819, the family moved to St. Louis. Another daughter, Cynthia, was born there. St. Louis was probably planned as a temporary stop, and the Broadwells are believed to have moved to the Sangamo Country by the fall (or perhaps more likely) the following spring. The Broadwells settled northwest of where most of the extended family communities had appeared during the previous year. Their farm was situated at the edge of the Richland Creek timber, along the trail to Mound Village. A year after the Broadwells built their home, Elijah Iles hauled his twenty-five tons of merchandise down the same trail.

The family may have lived in one or two log dwellings during their first years on the property, but in 1824, Moses constructed a two-story brick residence on his Richland Creek farm. That spring, he arranged to purchase between 2000 and 5000 bricks from a local brick maker, paying five dollars per thousand.[8] His son John also built a brick house on an adjacent property, less than a mile down the trail. John and his family soon opened their new home as a tavern. The Broadwell tavern, which traded on the increasing stagecoach traffic along the old road, was later known as Clayville after the family's support of Whig candidate Henry Clay.

By the early twentieth century, John's old brick house had become a historic landmark on the road to Beardstown (figure 13.6). In the 1960s, local physician and amateur historian Emmett Pearson restored the old house and filled it with period furnishings. The Clayville Inn was opened as a house museum and folkways interpretive center, and was later operated by Sangamon State University (now University of Illinois

FIG. 13.6 Clayville Tavern and home of John Broadwell (circa 1834) as it appears today. Below is an excavation unit next to the building, showing burnt soils (light and dark bands) in crossection.

at Springfield).[9] During its years as a museum, the interpretation of its age had been somewhat of a problem. Earlier historians had assumed it was one of two brick houses built by the Broadwells in 1824. The local oral traditions, however, remembered a fire at the John Broadwell house in the early nineteenth century and suggested that this house was a replacement, built sometime before 1840.

In 2000 (several years after the investigations at Sangamo Town) I placed three test units just behind the kitchen of the old brick house, in hopes of learning more about its history and the fire remembered in the old stories. The excavations immediately encountered the most dramatic evidence of fire that I have ever seen on an archaeological site. The soils just below the surface had been intensely burned and "smoked" to a depth of eighteen inches by a very hot fire. Further, mixed into the burnt soils were shattered fragments of early nineteenth century domestic debris, including bits of Queensware, crockery, and melted glass. The ceramics in the burned soil were themselves heavily burned. They could still be identified, however, and all of them dated from the mid 1820s through early 1830s. From the burned debris, we could glimpse what was resting in the Broadwell's cupboard the day of the fire. From the age of the youngest ceramic artifacts in the assemblage, it was clear that the fire occurred in the early to mid 1830s. The standing house, then, was indeed a replacement, built on or very near the site of the original, shortly after the Black Hawk War. The old stories were correct.

Moses Broadwell came to the Sangamo Country with the intention of establishing a commercial village and milling center. His plans, well underway by 1820, outlined the most ambitious commercial enterprise in the region, at least on paper. In November of that year, he received a letter from his attorney Abram Beck in St. Louis regarding a petition for a steam mill. The petition, which Beck had forwarded to Washington, was probably a request for funding. The lawyer also mentioned at least two lawsuits, reflecting the litigious nature of the Broadwells, which would haunt them and their business associates for many years. A second, undated letter from Beck mentions a bill for incorporating the Sangamo Milling Company. That incorporation was passed as a private law in February 1821.[10]

Moses also planned to purchase several large parcels of land when they became available for sale, including a 320 acre parcel located on the west bank of the Sangamon River, about nine miles from his home. Sometime in 1822, Broadwell hired James Stephenson (the county surveyor) to survey and plat a town on this parcel, which was crossed by the trail headed for the Spoon River. The town was initially called Sangamo, but soon became known as Sangamo Town, to avoid confusion with the river and the new county.

The plat contained 101 lots, platted along the preexisting trail that was to be known as Bridge Street (figure 13.7). The presence of a formal public square signaled Moses's plans to compete for the Sangamon County seat, which had been only temporarily designated as Springfield. The final designation was to be made in 1825. As was the case with Elijah Iles's plat of Calhoun, if the town of Sangamo received the seat of government, the square would be donated to the county, and a courthouse erected there. Moses also claimed that, in the event that Sangamo was not chosen as the county seat, the square would be used for a "Seminary of Learning."

The heart of the commercial district of the new town was to be at its south end, which included a mill square or large property set aside for the construction of a saw and gristmill, and a group of twelve lots referred to as the Mechanics Block. The term *mechanic* referred to a craftsman or skilled laborer, and Moses hoped to encourage such artisans to set up shop in his new community.

In February 1823, Broadwell placed an ad in the *Edwardsville Spectator*, the nearest newspaper to the Sangamo settlements. The ad mentioned plans for three mills and two wool carding machines, which were to be in operation that spring. Although he had surveyed for a town (and advertised lots for sale) Moses would not actually be able to sell lots in the town until after November, as the land was still owned by the government and had not been yet made available for sale. Technically, Broadwell was taking a great risk in making such improvements on property that was not yet his. When the government released the land it would be sold at auction, and Moses could potentially be outbid for his own improvements. He was clearly aware of the risk, however, as he had instructed his lawyer to look into the possibly of new preemption laws as early as 1820.[11]

The land surrounding Sangamo Town was made available for public sale in November 1823. The Sangamo Town parcel was Moses's first purchase, followed by the parcels on which he and his family lived. Broadwell had evidently made previous arrangements for at least two businesses to be established in town—a tavern and a store—as there is evidence that these opened prior to his formal sale of lots. In April 1824, Jacob Carman received a tavern license for his public house at Sangamo Town. The following month a post office was established, probably in a

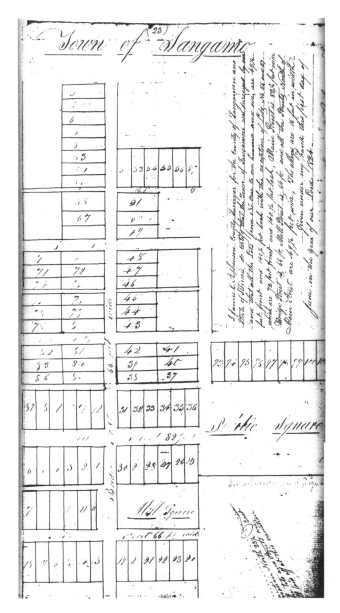

FIG. 13.7 Plat map of Sangamo Town, recorded in 1823.

store building opened by Ebenezer Brigham, who was made postmaster in June.

On the June 7, Broadwell held an auction at Sangamo Town, perhaps at Brigham's store or Carman's Tavern. A carefully printed list of terms was posted, and a copy of this document survives today. On that day, twenty-two men bid on forty-eight lots. High bids for the lots ranged from $10.50 to $61, and Moses received commitments for a total of $1415.00. Most of the bidders were area farmers, as well as a few small-scale merchants. The down payment for one lot was made in apple trees. Notably absent from the list of lots purchased were those located in what was the most prime real estate in the new town: the Mechanic's Block, and along Main Street near the public square. While most of the lots sold that day were never fully paid for or improved, several in the Mechanics Block were—and they ultimately formed the core of Sangamo Town. With this in mind, it seems Broadwell had already made several presale arrangements for these lots, which were then held back from auction.

Moses had made plans to extend Bridge Street and erect a bridge across the Sangamon River at the north end of his new town. This was to be the first of its kind, perhaps in the entire valley. The lumber for the bridge was purchased from a miller outside of town, indicating that Broadwell's sawmill had not yet been completed. Moses also felt that the timbers were completely unsuitable for his new bridge, and in November asked two area residents to formally report on the condition of the wood, prior to taking the miller to court. They testified that timber ranged from "good" and "passable" to "rough" and "rotten worthless." The bridge was never built.

The fall of 1824 was the beginning of a bad year for the Broadwell family. Just days after the bridge lumber was examined, Moses's son William was killed while raising a barn at Sangamo Town. He left behind his wife Margaret and a small house just outside of town. William's widow soon married Richard Latham of Elkhart, and moved to the base of the hill where she and her new husband established the Kentucky House tavern. Sangamon County of 1824 was a very small world.

After the snow melted the following spring, the Illinois state legislature appointed four commissioners to select a permanent site of the Sangamon county seat. The designation of the Springfield community in 1821 as the site of county government had been a temporary one, and Moses had platted his town in part to directly compete for the final choice for official seat of government. In March 1825, according to stories told in Springfield later in the nineteenth century, Andrew Elliot (the proprietor of the Buckhorn Tavern in Springfield) volunteered to guide the commissioners to each prospective site. The longtime resident of the area apparently chose the most undesirable, circuitous route to Sangamo Town, instead of following a well blazed trail that led directly to the village. The commissioners are said to have thought highly of Sangamo Town, but decided its inaccessibility made it a poor choice for the seat of government. Elliot is said to have followed an even worse route back to Springfield, thus sealing its fate as the county seat.[12]

This would have been incredibly bad news for the Broadwells, who were heavily invested in their new community. Without the seat of government, they would have to insure the success of the town through its promotion as a competitive commercial service center. Moses also scrambled to enforce previous financial commitments that various individuals had made toward the town project. His partners in the Sangamo Milling Company had apparently agreed to purchase half of the land on which the town was platted, but they immediately lost interest following the selection of Springfield as county seat. Further, most of the area farmers who had put down payments on lots did nothing more, and deeds for most of the lots were never recorded.

In the fall of 1826, when he was sixty-two years old, Moses sold a large portion of the unclaimed Sangamo Town property to his son-in-law, excepting the Mechanics Block and the Carding Mill Block. In January of the following year, he sold a large parcel of lots to his son Charles and storekeeper Ebenezer Brigham. Together, they would build a wool carding mill on that property. Three months later, Moses died in his brick home (which he described as his "mansion house") near Richland Creek. In his will, he instructed his family to continue to attempt to sell lots at Sangamo Town, which he referred to as "a plase of buisnis at some futer day not far distant."

Six months after his father's death, Charles Broadwell purchased his brother-in-law's interest in the town, and was (at the age of twenty-seven) the new proprietor of Sangamo Town. The services offered at Sangamo during the late 1820s included a gristmill (located on the mill square near the Mechanics Block), the wool carding mill (operated by Charles and Ebenezer Brigham), a general store, a blacksmith shop, a tavern, and a ferry across the river where Moses had wanted to build a bridge. The Seminary of Learning was never built on the public square, which was probably used to keep horses and cattle. The only archaeological debris found there thus far has been a horseshoe.

By the early 1830s, it was probably becoming clear to most of the residents of the community that Sangamo Town would amount to little more than a milling center. The reason for the rapid decline of the businesses is not readily apparent, but that decline was concurrent with an increase in activity in the new town of New Salem, just eight miles down river. Further, several of the individuals who had established the commercial community at Sangamo Town ten years earlier had either moved on or were getting old. Lot sales ceased, and the businesses in the Mechanics Block began to close as proprietors moved back to their nearby farms and got on with their lives.

During the early 1830s, the original gristmill was converted to steam power, but its new owner, William Porter, soon moved the equipment to another mill outside of town. Charles Broadwell constructed a new saw and gristmill along the river, well north of the Mechanics Block that had anchored the community for ten years. By the fall of 1833, most of "downtown" Sangamo Town had been abandoned. At the end of October of that year, a group of fifty-two immigrants from New York arrived with twenty-nine wagons full of possessions. The group spent the winter in several empty buildings that had once formed the core of Moses's "place of business," and then moved on the following spring. The frontier era was closing in the region, and so had downtown Sangamo Town.

For the next ten years, what had been the community of Sangamo Town became strictly a milling center, anchored by the steam saw and gristmill along the river and a wool carding mill located closer to the central part of town. The carding mill, which was powered by two yoke of oxen on a treadwheel, may have done a brisk business for a short time during the mid 1830s. Rawley Morgan, one of the later proprietors of that mill, opened a clothier's shop in a dwelling next to the carding machine, but soon moved the whole enterprise to his farm outside of town.

Overlooking the river at the extreme north end of town were two or three dwellings occupied by mill hands working at the steam mill along the river. A cabinetmaker may have lived in this vicinity for a short time as well. The steam mill received a contract to make lath for the new statehouse in Springfield in 1837. Charles Broadwell maintained varying levels of financial interest in the operation, but he was plagued by debt during the mid-1830s. In 1844, Broadwell and his family, declared insolvent by the county, packed up and left his father's town. The plat of Sangamo Town was formally vacated by the state legislature the following year. Down by the river, the Sangamo mill was sold for the last time in 1847, and was probably closed and dismantled during the early 1850s. All that is left is the archaeology.

CHAPTER FOURTEEN

Exploring Moses's Sangamo

Excavations at Sangamo Town

Over the next two years out in the big field, I found many of the places that I had read about in court documents and deed records. I began to clarify how long they stood and a little about what they might have looked like. Most of the excavations at Sangamo Town, however, revealed details not found on paper—minute and prosaic aspects of daily life in the small frontier town along the river.

The age of the artifact sample from feature 1, and its proximity to the recent mechanical terracing of the nearby slope, prompted more testing in that area in hopes of locating additional period features that might be in the path of future erosion or erosion control. On an improbable slope at the head of a deep ravine, the tests soon encountered another feature, which was much larger and which had been damaged by erosion for over a century. The feature 2 cellar was bigger than most pit cellars of the period, measuring approximately eleven by eighteen feet. When it was constructed, the cellar was probably about four feet deep, and its walls and floor were probably left as unlined clay surfaces. The orientation of the large feature was not with the cardinal directions, but with the original town survey.

It was the end of August when I began troweling into the filled cellar. The ground had not been softened by rain for weeks, and the digging was very slow. The long grass surrounding the little windows in the ground was filled with grasshoppers, buzzing and falling into the excavations. My tools and notebooks lay in the grass, and at the end of one long day of digging, I noticed that the grasshoppers had found the note-book. The margins of the pages had been completely eaten away. I was reminded of something that William Faux had written in 1823: "Grass-hoppers, so called . . . swarm in the countless millions all over this and the contiguous states. . . . They hop, jump and fly from about six to ten feet from the ground, and devour every green thing above and below. A hat left in the field was devoured overnight."[1]

The layers of fill within the large cellar described abandonment and slow decay (figure 14.1). Instead of having been rapidly and intention-ally filled with soil, the cellar was left open after the building above was dismantled and moved away. The large excavation beneath was then ex-posed to the elements. At the base of the feature was a thin layer of or-ganic soil known as a "tromp zone." This built up on the floor while the building was still standing. The few artifacts found in this zone probably fell through the cracks in the floorboards above, and include very small pieces of shattered plates and teawares.

After the building was dismantled, rains immediately began eroding the walls of the cellar and washing in topsoil from the west. The clay-rich wash and the lack of organic materials or significant quantities of debris suggests that the area surrounding the tavern was already eroded and denuded of vegetation. A few rough, sandy limestone slabs (prob-ably used as foundation piers) fell into the open pit. More rains came and deposited more soil and thin bands of silt. A tree grew out of one corner of the abandoned cellar, and root disturbance in the fill was still visible 170 years later.

During the slow excavation of the sticky clay fill within the cellar fea-ture, I began noticing that certain aspects of the artifact assemblage were somewhat unusual. The feature was producing an unusual number of redware jug fragments, and the ratio of plates to teawares also seemed high. Although there was typically little bottle glass in the feature, the

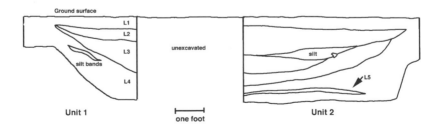

FIG. 14.1 Crossection drawing of the heavily eroded Carman Tavern cellar.

small sample included fragments of several figural whisky flasks. Together with the large size of the cellar, it seemed possible that this was a commercial site—perhaps that of a store or tavern. This was just a casual observation, but it led me to return to the paper records, and ultimately provided the key to the resurvey of the entire village.

Aside from certain aspects of the feature and its associated artifacts, I also noticed a slight swale in the field just south of the excavations. The depression had the appearance of an eroded roadbed, which appeared to wrap around the site from west to north. Returning to the deed records, I learned that Jacob Carman's tavern was situated on a corner lot, with streets on its south and east sides. Considering the large size of the cellar and the nature of the artifacts found inside, the anonymous feature was given a tentative name—Jacob Carman's Tavern on lots 11 and 12 along Mill Street.

Today, I use digital mapping software to overlay old land records onto modern maps. In 1994, I was still using pencil, ruler, and vellum. I began with a base map of the modern topography, and the two archaeological features encountered that summer. Over this was laid a second map, with the original 1822 survey drawn to the same scale. Using the tentative identification of feature 2 as the tavern, I positioned those lots over the location of that feature. In 1822, the surveyor had recorded the orientation of the plat with respect to magnetic north, so its orientation could be easily ascertained. Once the two maps were overlaid in this position, I was left with a tentative map of the entire town on the modern landscape. The only way to test the accuracy of the overlay, however, was to return to the field.

Back at the site of the possible tavern, and with maps in hand, I tried to orient myself with 1822. Specifically, I positioned three stakes in a line twenty-three degrees east of north, to the east of the big cellar feature. This line would represent the approximate location of the western edge of Bridge Street. If the map was correct, I would find archeological features on lots that had strong chains of title during the 1820s and 1830s. The closest and most obvious test of the map was to be found immediately east of the possible tavern, across Bridge Street. On the map, this was the location of the Mill Square, on the south half of which had been constructed a substantial steam mill by the mid-1830s. On the ground in 1994, however, was a deep ravine at this location. Clearly, the head of the ravine had lengthened over time, but most of the landform appeared very old, and must have looked similar during the 1820s.

So into the woods I went, sliding down the hillside into the knee-deep creek at the bottom. I followed the creek to the east, deeper into the ravine. Within twenty-five feet, I happened to look up and to my right, at the southern bank of the ravine. Sticking out of the side of the eroded surface was the corner of a brick foundation. Made of two courses of soft mud brick and covered in a thick blanket of undergrowth and trees, the feature was clearly of nineteenth century origin. It was not, however, typical of a log dwelling of the period. The building that it once supported had not been built on level ground originally, and was instead built at the edge of the small waterway in a setting that would have been very unusual for a house. It also appeared quite large, and later tests there would find no domestic debris. As I stood in the small creek, I realized that there had been no rain in weeks, and yet the stream still flowed—fed by a small spring near the head of the ravine. The size and setting of the foundation (as well as the presence of a spring-fed creek) could easily be interpreted as the site of a water powered mill. According to the plat overlay, the feature was located in the southern half of Mill Square, right where the remains of a mill should be.

The large parcel of land that contains the archeological remains of Sangamo Town is by no means covered with archaeological features and artifacts, and of the 101 lots contained in the original plat, fewer than 25 appear to have actually been improved. That the new plat overlay could lead me directly to a substantial feature in the proper setting for a mill strongly suggested that the overlay was reasonably accurate. Much more testing of the plat would follow, but feature 2 could remain tentatively identified as the tavern. Further, the site of feature 1 was also given a tentative identification—lots 28 and 29, the home of town proprietor Charles Broadwell.

Beneath Jacob Carman's Tavern

Jacob Carman's tavern at the head of the ravine at the corner of Mill and Bridge streets was one of the first businesses to open at Sangamo Town. He was born in New York state in 1785, and he and his brother Samuel moved their families west around 1820. While Samuel soon turned back and returned to New York, Jacob and his wife Mahala settled in the Sangamo Country. Jacob was issued a tavern license in April 1824, two months before Moses began to sell lots in town. In 1825, his daughter Helen married Moses Broadwell's son Charles, who would soon become the proprietor of town.

In the spring of 1831, while Lincoln and his crew were building their boat down by the water, a traveling magician visited Sangamo Town and gave a performance in Jacob's tavern. Caleb Carman (one of Jacob's nephews) remembered the visit and described the event to Lincoln's biographer William Herndon thirty-five years later. It seems that Lincoln was in the small audience that had gathered in the tavern when the magician asked for Lincoln's hat, into which he was going to break several eggs. As Caleb remembered, Lincoln declined the invitation—not out of concern for his hat, but for the magician's eggs.

Later that fall, Jacob sold the tavern at Sangamo Town to local farmer Ashel Stone. There is little evidence, however, that Stone kept the tavern open for much longer, and it was probably closed in 1832 or 1833. Meanwhile, Jacob's nephew Caleb moved down river to New Salem and managed a tavern there. For a time, the Carman tavern at Sangamo Town had probably been a busy place, serving as one of the few places of lodging and social centers along the trail that followed the west bank of the Sangamo River. Aside from a tale told of a magician and a future president, however, most of what happened in the little log building has been completely forgotten.

The artifact density in feature 2 was much lower than in feature 1, primarily because this much larger cellar (located beneath the residence on site) was not being filled with trash while the site was occupied. Instead, it was filled after its abandonment by some topsoil, a few loads of garbage, and some building materials. Most of the abandoned cellar was filled by years of rain-washed clayey soil.

As suspected in the field, the Queensware assemblage from the cellar includes a higher than average percentage of tablewares. These consist primarily of shell edged and deep blue printed plates. More plates and fewer teawares probably reflect the enhanced importance of evening meals at Carman's tavern, where travelers and locals alike would have come for supper. Like at the Kentucky House Tavern site, several of the printed vessels depict American views (such as New York Battery and the University of Maryland) as opposed to the romantic European views that were probably more common in Illinois during the 1820s. Also included in the transfer printed imagery at the Carman site are a few vessels decorated in the Chinese-inspired Blue Willow pattern, first manufactured in the 1790s and still made today (figure 14.2).

The tavern site at Sangamo Town also produced a number of undecorated creamware vessels—more than the average for the period. These include plain dinner plates, undecorated cups and saucers, and two chamber pots. While undecorated creamware would have been more prevalent in Illinois before the war of 1812, it appears to have always been outnumbered by the more decorative and only slightly more expensive pearlwares. On sites settled after 1815 (and abandoned before

FIG. 14.2 Selected printed pearlware, redware jug, and whisky flask fragments from the Carman tavern cellar. Note the cut marks on the "New York Battery" plate fragment (center).

1840), creamware usually makes up less than 5 percent of the average domestic cupboard,[2] but at the Carman tavern, it is 14 percent. This does not necessarily mean that the site was occupied earlier than 1820— it probably wasn't, given the cellar's orientation with the lot lines. Instead, more creamware in the cupboard may reflect a certain conservatism on the part of Mahala Carman, in her continued use of older everyday plates and cups. Interestingly, that conservatism was not based on the price of the goods, as the feature produced a significant number of more expensive printed vessels as well.

Included in the creamware assemblage are two plain chamber pots, which are somewhat rare on pre-1840 sites in Illinois, at least when compared to assemblages from urban contexts (figure 14.3). When they do appear, however, they are usually undecorated, and it was the chamber pot that represented the last form of creamware in use in the region. We have recovered creamware chamber pots from deposits dating to the 1840s in St. Louis, or fifteen years after most of the creamware plates and cups had been discarded. The presence of the pots at the Carman site probably reflects conveniences offered to the guests at the tavern. Many travelers from the East expected such conveniences, and were often disappointed. One wrote that "there was but one washbasin, as they called it, in the house; only one towel . . . we insisted on some sort of receptacle [for use as a chamber pot]; they brought us a kitchen kettle!"[3]

While the cellar feature produced fragments of a number of banded bowls and pitchers, the quantity is not unusually high, like that of other tavern sites in Illinois. The apparently modest number of these vessels does not, of course, compromise the interpretation of the function of the site—no single piece of evidence can do such a thing. For instance, while the Old Landmark Tavern in southern Illinois produced nearly twice the average number of banded wares, its precursor (operated on the same property by the Young family during the 1810s) did not produce a larger than average number of these vessels.[4]

FIG. 14.3 Intact examples of French salve pot and English creamware chamber pot (both excavated in St. Louis), very similar to vessels represented by very small fragments from the Carman Tavern cellar.

Instead, the lack of increased numbers of banded bowls in our archaeological sample from the Carman tavern site may serve as a reminder that, while such patterns of use did exist, they were not cast in stone. The consumer choices, practices, and traditions of a family will always be their own. The interpretation of an archaeological site is based on cumulative suggestions, rather than single pieces of definitive evidence.

The cellar feature on lot 11 produced a disproportionately high ratio of redware jugs, perhaps reflecting the need for more water, liquor, or other liquids in a kitchen that was preparing more morning and evening meals. At least one of the jugs (or rather, its very fragmentary remains) is similar to the jugs from the Ebey-Brunk Kiln site, and may have been made there. The glaze on a large stoneware pot found in the cellar, however, is indicative of much more distant manufacture. While most stoneware vessels made before 1840 in the Midwest were salt glazed (in which salt crystals were tossed into the heated atmosphere of the kiln), this pot is finished in a distinctive alkaline glaze. Such glazes, which appear more mottled and mosslike than most salt glazes, were produced by coating the air-dried vessels in a combination of wood ash and clay prior to firing. The use of alkaline glazes is traditionally associated with the Carolinas, and the pot at Sangamo Town was probably made in the southeast.[5] As few alkaline vessels are encountered archaeologically in Illinois, it is possible that the pot was brought to Illinois as part of someone's personal possessions, rather than having been purchased at a store. The Carmans may have acquired the pot at a local estate sale.

Also unusual in pre-1840 rural contexts in Illinois is a European, tin-glazed salve pot, represented by a single, small fragment. Salve or ointment pots are small, thick-bodied jarlike vessels, which were designed to be filled by apothecaries with viscous creams or medicines. The capacity of these little vessels was quite small, suggesting that the contents inside may have been expensive. The design of the distinctive vessels changed little between the seventeenth and nineteenth centuries, and they lend a European and somewhat archaic presence to ceramic assemblages dominated by fashionable Staffordshire wares and American crockery. The pot from Sangamo Town was made in France, and is coated in a green colored tin glaze. Salve pots also represent the last form of traditional French tin-glazed products to be used in Illinois and are often found in urban contexts as late as the 1840s. Few seem to have made it into the country, however.

While the bottle glass assemblage from the cellar is no larger than average, it is composed entirely of liquor-related bottles, including wine, sprits, and figural whisky flasks. Although very fragmentary, one of the flasks is molded in an American eagle motif, and another with a portrait of George Washington. Less common in domestic contexts of the period is at least one stemmed wine or cordial glass. Particularly in eastern urban contexts, inexpensive stemware had been available to middle-class families by the mid-eighteenth century, but these goods do not appear to have been common in the rural Midwest until after the frontier period.

The fill of the cellar also produced a small quantity of hog bones left over from butchering, a burnt peach pit, and a tiny fragment of glass painted in gold. That fragment may have once been part of the glass door of a mantle clock. The tavern building itself is represented by a number of machine-cut nails, some window glass, a hand-forged door pintle (or hinge), and several fragments of thick, sandy wall plaster with traces of whitewash still preserved on their exterior surfaces.

As with the Iles Store site in Springfield, the commercial function of the Carman Tavern is visible archaeologically, but is blended with the habits of the family itself. At the tavern, more evening and morning meals were served, producing more broken plates but fewer broken tea cups and saucers. Liquor may have been more important here, and both liquor and water may have been kept at the table in earthenware jugs. The Carmans offered their overnight guests chamber pots, which may have been less common at the homes of their neighbors. The building itself was equipped with a larger than average cellar, but it was still shallow, earthenwalled, and probably prone to flooding. We can also surmise that someone once ate a peach to the sound of a ticking clock behind a pane of painted glass. The remains of the peach were then tossed into the fire. Knowing this will not change our notions of Illinois history, but it does make that history a little more authentically human.

Looking for Roll's Store

The two best-documented storekeepers at Sangamo Town, Ebenezer Brigham and Jacob Roll, owned lots 1 through 3 on Main Street. From the maps drawn by John Roll, and from the deed and court records, it appears that the store building itself was probably on lot 1. With the new overlay of the town plat, and working from the position of the possible tavern cellar, I could approximate the limits of lot 1 and focus the shovel testing more specifically.

In a few hours, the possible lot lines were marked out, and I began more testing. By the end of the day, portions of three subsurface features were visible. The first feature encountered in the vicinity of lot 1 consisted of a slight depression in the subsoil surrounded by coal clinkers (mineral impurities left behind from the burning of coal) and small scraps of hand-forged iron. This was probably the site of a blacksmith shop. To the south, two deeper pit features were found at what would have been the front portion of the lot—right where one would expect a structure to be. The blacksmithing area, however, was actually located north of the lot line, in what would have been Main Street. This suggested that the plat overlay probably still needed some work.

Before beginning the excavations at lot 1, I reexamined some of the archival documents associated with Jacob Roll. I immediately found a reference to a court case between Roll and town proprietor Charles Broadwell. In 1830, Roll had sued Broadwell for breaking into his blacksmith shop. This was very good news, as Roll's ownership of such a shop provided more confirmation that the plat overlay was indeed reasonably correct. Further, it seems Broadwell felt entitled to enter the shop due to the fact that it was not actually located on Roll's property, but instead "just north of the Lot 1 lot line," technically lying in Broadwell's Main Street. Rarely do archival records provide such immediate answers to questions posed in the field. The features found on the previous day were indeed associated with lot 1 and were very likely part of the store and blacksmith shop kept by Jacob Roll.

The depression north of lot 1 may represent the earthen floor of a blacksmith shop, although as the feature was exposed within only two small excavation units, its dimensions are unknown. Most of the artifacts associated with the shop consist of pieces of iron bar stock that have been manipulated to varying degrees—from small pieces of square stock cut away from larger pieces, to those that have been hammered flat and trimmed. Some of the bulkier objects appear to have been projects that failed early in their manufacture and were quickly discarded. Other, more heavily worked pieces appear to have been trimmed from projects closer to completion.

The work conducted at the blacksmith shop was very plain and utilitarian—making simple door hinges, cabinet latches, and barn hardware, or repairing iron hand tools. Fragments of hand-made nuts and bolts may have been made on site or were left from cutting off pieces of bent or damaged hardware brought into the shop. There are also larger pieces of iron that may have been mounted on plows, which were still made primarily of wood. Most of the diagnostic items appear to have been tools used by the blacksmith himself, such as flat and triangular files and small hammers. Surprisingly, there is little evidence of horseshoe manufacture or repair at the shop.

Excavations at other blacksmith shops in the region, including that of Joshua Miller's shop at nearby New Salem, have also encountered similarly stoic artifacts, indicating that little attention was placed on the visual elements of domestic hardware on the frontier farm.[6] The 1820s and 1830s were probably a period of transition for blacksmiths on the midwestern agricultural frontier. Items such as nails and small tools had become factory products, and an increasing variety of cast iron hardware and manufactured utensils were available at little cost to the consumer. Soon after the close of the frontier period, the manufacture and repair of wagon-related hardware appears to have become the dominant activity in many of the rural blacksmith shops of Illinois.

Ebenezer Brigham first established what was the principal dry goods store in Sangamo Town during the 1820s. Originally from Massachusetts, Brigham followed Edwards' Trace up from southern Illinois in 1822 and passed through the Sangamo Country on his way to the lead mines in northwestern Illinois and southwest Wisconsin. The trip was probably an exploratory one, as American settlement of the lead mine district was only sporadic prior to 1823. At the time, the mines themselves were still worked primarily by Native Americans. Brigham soon returned southward, and this time stopped in the Sangamo Country. He was probably at the site of Broadwell's new town by the late fall of 1822, and opened his store at Sangamo Town by early 1823, when in February of that year he billed a local estate for goods. This would suggest that Brigham's store was the first business to open in town.

In 1826, Brigham and Charles Broadwell purchased a wool carding machine and set up a carding mill on the northwest end of town. Wool production in central Illinois was common, but was not conducted at a large scale during the 1820s. Like other forms of farm produce, wool simply provided a little extra income for area farmers, as well as raw product for homemade woolens. A year earlier, Brigham was joined in the retail business by Jacob Roll. Born in New Jersey, Roll had spent time in the Cincinnati area before moving to Illinois, and the Roll family had been associated with the Broadwells there. In the summer of 1825, Jacob and his wife Sarah left Cincinnati with a keelboat loaded with their family's possessions, as well as goods for the store at Sangamo Town.

They piloted the boat down the Ohio to the Mississippi, where they turned northward. Thirty miles up that river, the keelboat capsized in shallow water. Roll managed to salvage some of the cargo and continued the journey. The Rolls arrived at Sangamo Town in early October and bought acreage for a farm nearby.[7]

In 1827, Ebenezer Brigham decided to return to the lead mines in the north. He sold his interest in the store on lot 1 to his partner and loaded his possessions on a keelboat (which he christened the *Good Luck*) immediately after the Sangamon River thawed. Brigham would become the first permanent settler of Dane County Wisconsin, establishing a store and inn before becoming a member of the territorial legislature. Jacob Roll ran the store at Sangamo Town for several more years, and probably set up his blacksmith shop in late 1829 or early 1830. Why he built the shop outside of his property line is unclear, but the fact that he did indicates that Main Street was not well traveled by that time, and the property limits in the town may have been somewhat casual and unclear. In the fall of 1830, Charles Broadwell informed Roll that the shop was built on his property, and he demanded possession of the building "built of logs and covered clapboards." Roll apparently refused, and Broadwell forced his way into the shop. In November, the issue was taken to court, and Roll lost the suit. There is archaeological evidence that Broadwell may have literally dragged the building across Bridge Street to the east, as a second scatter of blacksmith debris was later found on lots under his ownership.

Roll continued running the store at Sangamo Town for another year, but appears to have left town by December of 1831. That month, Charles Broadwell ran an advertisement in the Sangamo Journal for a "store for rent." Broadwell described the store as "shelved and countered in a neat and convenient manner" and as measuring sixteen by twenty feet. There is no evidence that he found another storekeeper for the shop.[8]

Beneath the Store at Sangamo Town

About forty feet south of the concentration of blacksmithing debris, my shovel tests revealed a larger, deeper disturbance in the subsoil. Without a careful removal of the plowed topsoil, one can only approximate the size and shape of features seen in the small shovel test windows. The big disturbances seem to float underfoot, without definite size and shape. So, the shovel tests were replaced by two large excavation units, which were designed to expose the limits of the feature. Two days later, after the removal of the disturbed topsoil, the dark feature could be seen in plan against the compact yellow subsoil. Measuring eleven feet long and five feet wide, the rounded rectangle immediately spoke of frontier architecture. The feature 7 pit cellar at Sangamo Town, positioned on the front of lot 1 (and oriented with respect to the town lot lines) was probably once located beneath Brigham and Roll's store.

Even before cutting into the fill of the feature, it was clear that the soils used to fill the abandoned cellar were different than the more typical dark, organic topsoils mixed with ash. This soil was composed of a tiny patchwork of browns, reds, and grays, composed of burnt clay, tiny fragments of soft mud brick, and sandy lime plaster. After the excavation of the soils down to the base of the cellar (which was about four feet deep originally), the sequence of events that led to its infilling could be read in cross-section. The old cellar on lot 1 was essentially filled with the building that once stood above it.

Specifically, it appears that the log building that served as a store was fitted with a cat's clay chimney and brick fireplace, was finished with a plastered wall interior, and was built upon piers made of limestone slabs. When the building was dismantled (and the logs probably hauled away for reuse somewhere else), the remnants of the chimney, fireplace and the debris left behind from the demolition was pushed into the old cellar. A few of the stone slabs were tossed down into the pit as well, and the rest were probably carted away. From the refined ceramics found in the fill, this probably occurred in the mid-1830s, or shortly after Charles Broadwell tried to rent the "neat and convenient" store.

Deeper in the pit, below the demolition debris, was evidence that the cellar was at least partially exposed to weathering or erosion before the chimney was demolished. This was reflected by a thin lens of waterborne silt on the north end of the cellar, and evidence of erosion-related damage to its eastern wall. With this in mind, it appears that the building may not have been removed all at once, and may have stood empty and only partially dismantled for a year or so. Similar to what was found at the Carman Tavern site, the archaeology at lot 1 suggests that Broadwell was in no real hurry to clean up the abandoned lots and partially dismantled buildings in town. This might indicate that he had largely given up hope of attracting new business to the Mechanics Block by the mid-1830s. Again, Eliza Farnham's descriptions of the mid-1830s town of Tremont provide a good comparison to what might have been seen at Sangamo during the same period: "The adjacent lot . . . is occupied by a gaping cellar, all uncovered and affording, therefore, readier ingress than egress to sundry small pigs, chickens, etc. who perambulate the vicinity. Its walls, however, are so weatherwashed, that one of them offers a practicable way of escape."[9]

At the base of the cellar was a four-inch layer of decayed organic material that had accumulated on the mud floor while the store was still standing. Most of the larger artifacts found during excavation were found in and on this layer, and were probably lying in the dark pit while the store was still operating. A shell-edged platter, an undecorated creamware dish, and two matching redware kitchen bowls—broken and laying in a little pile—were sealed over by the slumping of the eastern clay wall of the cellar (figure 14.4).

The cellar under Roll's store produced a different type of artifact sample than did most of the pit features at Sangamo Town. The assemblage includes almost none of the smaller types of artifacts that seem to be associated with household activities and the sweeping of the debris out the back door. Instead, this sample consists of a somewhat eclectic range of broken ceramic vessels and little else. From the nature of the artifact assemblage, it appears that this particular site probably functioned solely as a store building, and that Roll (and Brigham before him) lived elsewhere—perhaps on lots 2 or 3.

The Queenswares from the feature consist entirely of creamware and pearlware—mostly edged plates and printed teas. These large fragments are partially restorable, indicating that they were probably discarded directly into the cellar when broken. Like that from the Iles Store, printed imagery dominates the assemblage, although in this case these goods may represent lost inventory rather than the possessions of the storekeeper's family.

The Brigham/Roll artifact assemblage is composed of an unusually high percentage of crockery. Consisting primarily of kitchen bowls and table service vessels, several do not resemble those made in Illinois. Instead, these are more reminiscent of the redware traditions of Ohio, where Roll had lived prior to his move to Illinois, and where he outfitted his store on at least one occasion. These include a small black glazed jug and a little table bowl decorated in large manganese splotches that make it completely unlike the redwares of Illinois.

Also from the floor of the cellar was a fragment of a large, slip-decorated pie plate. These decorative vessels were designed for open-hearth cooking as well as serving, and had become an important part of the culinary traditions in much of colonial America by the mid-eighteenth century. The use of these traditional vessels appeared to have declined during the 1830s, or did not follow immigrants from Pennsyl-

FIG. 14.4 Deposit of ceramic artifacts on the floor of the Brigham-Roll Store cellar: an edged pearlware plate, a redware slip decorated pie plate, a redware table bowl, and a redware kitchen bowl.

vania or Ohio as they moved into Illinois. While the Royal brothers or John Ebey made table plates decorated in very similar motifs, the more traditional pie plate from the store cellar was likely made east of Illinois.

Few retailers in Illinois (or wholesalers in St. Louis for that matter) sold traditional redwares made in Ohio or Pennsylvania after 1820. With this in mind, these vessels may have been amongst the shipment of goods Roll brought from Cincinnati. If this is the case, then they may have spent a few hours in the bottom of the Mississippi River in the late fall of 1825, before being salvaged by Jacob, hauled to Sangamo, and eventually buried in his abandoned store cellar.

Down the Street from Carman's Tavern

From an archaeological standpoint, most pit cellars found on frontier-era homesites are rather simple affairs: shallow, flat-bottomed rectangles excavated into the subsoil. Usually, all evidence of wooden structural details has long since decayed. One such feature, however, located just down Mill Street from the tavern at Sangamo Town, was more artic-ulate, offering a better glimpse of how it was constructed and how it functioned.

The feature was a small, rectangular pit, measuring approximately three and a half by five feet. When originally constructed, the cellar was about three feet deep. The small pit would have been located beneath the floor of a dwelling, and would have been accessed through a trap in the floor. Making this particular feature unique was evidence of an un-usual lining, still preserved as variations in soil color within the fill soils.

The pit was a carefully dug rectangle, oriented with respect to the town lot lines. Rather than leaving the walls unlined, however, its build-ers created a lining of small logs (about six inches in diameter) placed vertically around the edges of the pit, and anchored to larger corner posts. Why this labor-intensive vertical post lining was preferred over a simple plank lining is unclear, unless the pit was constructed before milled planks were readily available.

Of course, these posts had long since decayed, leaving behind only dark organic soil in their place. Their former presence was still visible, however, as subtle differences in soil color where the yellow clay walls had once slumped around the posts, leaving a scalloped yellow-and-brown pattern around the edge of the pit (figure 14.5). The users of the cellar may have also initially lined the bottom with a small amount of pea gravel, which was found scattered across its base. Near the center of the floor of the pit cellar was a shallow basin-shaped depression, mea-suring about eighteen inches in diameter. This depression was probably created unintentionally, by the repeated impact of feet landing in the small pit from the trap door in the floor above.

The little cellar was probably filled upon the abandonment of the house, although such pits may have also sometimes been closed while the houses were still in use. The pit was rapidly filled with organic ma-terial, some topsoil, and a thick layer of fine gray ash, containing chunks

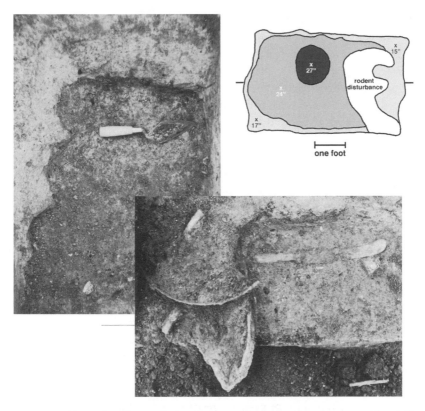

FIG. 14.5 Excavation views and plan drawing of lot 8 pit cellar, showing scalloped fill created by vertical post lining (left), and broken Dutch oven lid and table knife deposited into fill.

of wood charcoal and burnt clay. Within the layer of ash were numerous tiny fragments of eggshell and animal bone. While fragile eggshell seems inherently perishable, its calcium content allows it to survive for centuries in the ground. Also in the ash layer were two large pieces of a broken Dutch oven lid, which were nested together and dropped into the pit.

Just to the south of the pit cellar was a broad, shallow basin-shaped pit. Given its proximity to the house that once stood over the cellar, this feature may have been a "borrow pit" to obtain mud and clay for the repair of a chimney. When it was abandoned, it was partially filled with broken bricks. These showed signs of having been accidentally splashed or coated with wet mortar, which was found clinging to their broken surfaces as well as their finished surfaces. The construction debris may have been deposited into the pit after the completion of the construction or remodeling of a chimney.

The log-lined cellar feature fell on the east side of lot 8, based on the resurveyed plat. Elisha Clark purchased lots 7 and 8 in Sangamo Town from Moses Broadwell sometime before Moses's death, as Clark was forced to sue the estate in order to obtain a deed for the property. Elisha and wife Sarah arrived at Sangamo Town in 1823 or early 1824. As they had moved from Cincinnati, they may have been acquainted with the Broadwell family there. Thomas Clark (possibly Elisha's uncle) moved with him to town or followed him soon after. Very little is known about the activities of either Elisha or Thomas Clark.

By 1824, Thomas Clark had been appointed justice of the peace. The same year, Elisha was present at the estate sale held by William Broadwell's widow, and in fact, purchased a skillet and Dutch oven from the estate. Fragments of the broken lid to that very oven may have been recovered from the pit cellar on lot 8 exactly 170 years later. In the fall of 1825 Thomas Clark was appointed to superintend the opening and improvement of the navigation of the Sangamon, and in 1828, he obtained a license allowing him to sell liquor by the serving, suggesting that the family may have opened a store at Sangamo Town.[10]

In February 1830, Elisha and Sarah Clark sold lot 7 and the west half of lot 8 to James Dorrell, who was one of three young men later rescued by Lincoln after their canoe overturned in the river. The east half of the lot was not included in the sale, suggesting that an improvement was located on that half of the property. That improvement was probably the Clark family home, as both Elisha and Thomas appear to have remained in the area after February. The east half of lot 8 was also the location of the small pit cellar found in 1994.

If Thomas Clark had opened a store during the late 1820s it was probably on the property sold by the Clarks in 1830, as John Daggett soon purchased that lot. The store may have been managed by Benjamin Dunn, another area merchant. The Clarks had probably moved away from Sangamo Town by the mid-1830s, and Elisha purchased a mill at nearby Athens. The store briefly managed by Dunn appears to have been abandoned by the mid-1830s as well.

———

In general, the artifacts from the features on lot 8 seem to reflect the activities of the Clark family household, rather than the store that may have been located immediately to the west. The Queensware assemblage from the pit cellar is composed of a reasonably typical ratio of tablewares and teawares. The feature produced primarily creamware and pearl-ware, although a small number of whiteware vessels reflect the occupation of the site into the early 1830s. The tableware category, however, includes more banded or dipt vessels (bowls, a pitcher, and a mug) than any other sample in town, including the tavern. Although English potters made a variety of Queensware mugs during the early nineteenth century, this particular vessel form is surprisingly absent from the archaeological record in rural Illinois. Why the obviously useful mug seems to have been ignored by consumers on the midwestern frontier is very unclear.

While dipt bowls and pitchers may have been used more heavily in some taverns of the period, there is no other evidence that the building on lot 8 served such a function.[11] There may be a similar explanation for the enhanced use of these products by the Clark family, however. In the late 1990s, I was asked to examine an assemblage of early materials from one of the sites excavated as part of the Scott Air Force Base project in St. Clair County. The site produced a large quantity of artifacts, including Queenswares that indicated an occupation dating to the 1810s and 1820s. In that sample were an unusual number of dipt and mocha decorated bowls and pitchers—more so than any previously excavated tavern site in Illinois.

The standard archival research had yet to be conducted, but I suspected we would find that the occupants of the property had operated a tavern during the 1810s and 1820s. After an exhaustive study of the deed and census records, I found that I could not have been more wrong— the site had in fact been the home of Jesse Walker, the founder of Methodism in Illinois.

While he and his wife were not running a tavern, their use of a more than usual number of dipt bowls and pitchers may have reflected a similar social practice. As the leader of the Methodist community in the area, the Walkers' home would have been the scene of frequent meetings and gatherings. This was essentially the same scene found in many rural taverns of the period, where groups of people shared meals and visited. The use of the festive mochaware pitchers and bowls at the table may have found an important place in both settings, which differed from the average home.

The same may hold true for the Clark household at Sangamo Town. While little is known of Elisha, Thomas Clark was clearly a leader in the community. In this capacity, the Clark family may have found themselves in social settings similar to that of the Walker household—temporarily accommodating or feeding larger numbers of people on special occasions. For some reason (which is not entirely obvious anymore), certain type of ceramic vessels—decorated in a certain way—seem to have been considered particularly appropriate for such gatherings.

The small pit cellar on lot 8 also produced a good sample of the various types of painted teawares in use during the late 1810s and 1820s (figure 14.6). While the painted floral motifs on English wares were reproduced by the thousands, each was painted by hand, copied from pattern books by an artisan (usually a young woman) in the dimly lit interiors of the Staffordshire potteries. The motifs echo amalgams of very old decorative traditions, ones that originated in China and were then imitated and expanded upon, first in Holland and later in England. Like many other forms of material culture, so much history welled up behind these seemingly prosaic goods.

Four principal types of painted pearlware products are found on sites predating 1830 in Illinois: China glaze type pearlwares, mineral-pigmented motifs, and monochrome blue and polychrome broad-floral pearlwares. Painted patterns were most often applied to teawares. While English potters manufactured painted plates, pitchers and mugs, they are rare in pre-1830 Illinois.

Fine line, monochrome blue China glaze pearlware products (first introduced in the late 1770s) were designed as direct imitations of Chinese porcelain, and employed fine-line, blue-painted motifs and a heavily blue-tinted glaze, used to approximate the cast of porcelain. China-glaze products are thought to have fallen from the market by the close of the War of 1812.[12] Fragments of a China glaze cup and saucer were found in the cellar. During the 1790s, English potters introduced new, fine-line floral motifs painted in multicolored mineral pigments. These wares were also Chinese-inspired, at least at first.[13] They were manufactured until about 1820, and leave the archaeological record shortly afterward. Most of the features at Sangamo Town have produced teawares painted in mineral pigments, and pieces of six such vessels were found in the cellar on lot 9.

Replacing the more Chinese-inspired motifs of the late eighteenth and very early nineteenth century were pearlwares decorated in broader patterns and brighter colors. These were more similar to floral patterns found on Dutch delft, and often covered most of the vessel in pigment. During the mid-1820s, monochrome blue patterns were the most popular,[14] but multicolored motifs were also manufactured. Both monochrome and polychrome broad floral teawares were found in the fill of the pit. Such products, like shell edged plates, are a hallmark of the frontier in Illinois.

FIG. 14.6 Lot 8 at Sangamo Town: dipt bowl and pitcher fragments (top), and non-archaeological examples of China glaze, broad floral, and mineral pigment painted motifs shown with similar fragments from the pit cellar.

The pit cellar at lot 8 produced a slightly larger than average percentage of crockery, and like that of the Carman Tavern and Roll Store samples, this assemblage includes both locally and nonlocally made redwares. At least two large capacity pots are identical to those found in the pre-1835 pit feature at the Ebey-Brunk Kiln site. A wheel-thrown table plate (decorated in wavy, dark lines) also looks similar to the wares made by the Royal brothers or John Ebey. A large stoneware pot was probably made outside of Illinois, however, as it was discarded before the mid-

1830s and prior to the development of the stoneware industry in this state.

The feature also produced fragments of a very unusual barrel-shaped redware water cooler or "rundlet" (used for liquors). The vessel was elaborately turned and shaped in imitation of a wooden barrel. To my knowledge, additional examples of such vessels have not been found in Illinois, and the vessel from the pit cellar at Sangamo Town was probably made in the Ohio valley. A small jug with a jet-black manganese glaze (very similar to a jug found at Roll's store) was probably also brought to Sangamo Town from outside of Illinois. Rarely do features from this period in Illinois produce such a variety of redwares of non-local origins.

Like most sites abandoned before the close of the frontier period, the pit cellar at lot 8 produced very little bottle glass. The few glass artifacts recovered from the site consist of small medicine vial fragments and a part of a rectangular snuff bottle (figure 14.7). Snuff is a finely-ground, flavored tobacco which is inhaled through the nostrils. The design of snuff bottles, such as the example found on lot 8, had changed little between the late 1700s and mid-1800s.

Recovered from the nearby shallow, basin-shaped pit on lot 8 was an interesting cluster of crudely sawn disks made of deer antler. The pit also produced a utensil or tool handle (probably homemade) fashioned from antler. What the disks were made for is unclear—they may have been scraps from making handles for tools or utensils, such as the specimen recovered with them. Homemade gaming pieces made of lead and animal horn have also been found in the region, and it is possible that someone was sawing up an antler to make checkers at Sangamo Town. While we do not know exactly what was being made on lot 8, we do know that in the face of all the manufactured stuff shipped into the remote village, someone found it necessary or desirable to make something from a deer's antlers. Such contrasts, as we have seen throughout this book, are also hallmarks of the early nineteenth century American frontier.

Back to the Beginning

Over a two-year period, the new town plat overlay was fine tuned, and excavations encountered substantial archaeological features on twelve lots. From the deed records and field surveys, it appears that fewer than five additional lots were improved—so the testing has provided a pretty good look at life at Broadwell's Sangamo Town. Shortly after the exca-

FIG. 14.7 Fragmentary snuff bottle from lot 8 pit cellar, shown with nonarchaeological example.

vations at the Carman Tavern site, I determined that the first feature found at Sangamo was probably located in the yard of Charles Broadwell's home. After two seasons of work elsewhere in the village, I returned to the Broadwell site in hopes of verifying this.

Charles Broadwell married Helen Carman (whose father was running the tavern) in 1825. He probably built his home at Sangamo around this time, if not slightly earlier. The couple had seven children while living in town. In the fall of 1827, Charles bought the unsold Sangamo Town property from his brother-in-law, who had inherited the land from Moses Broadwell. Most of the individuals who would move to town (and particularly in the downtown Mechanics Block area) had already done so, and Charles focused most of his promotional activity on the mills. While he and his wife had maintained a farm outside of town, Charles advertised the property for sale in 1833, stating that he was "selling low for cash." This was probably a reference to debts he had acquired during the development of the mills. Local elections were held at his home in 1834, and he and Helen hosted a Whig Party meeting there in 1839.

Broadwell's financial troubles continued into the next decade, and he mortgaged property to secure more loans. Lot sales at Sangamo had ceased, however, and the mills were never particularly successful. By the end of 1844, county officials declared Broadwell insolvent. By 1846, Moses's dream of "a place of business at some future day" was over. Charles left his home, the town, and the county. He and his wife moved north to the new town of Pekin, opposite Peoria on the Illinois River. Broadwell managed to finance another store business in Pekin, but he died in 1854.

———·+·———

Working with a good understanding of the original town lot lines, I redirected shovel testing to the southeast of the feature 1 pit, in an area that would have been located at the front of the lot on which Broadwell built his home. These tests immediately encountered a large, deep feature in the subsoil. The discovery of the cellar now believed to have been located beneath the Broadwells' home marked the eighth and last cellar I entered at Sangamo Town. Fittingly, this cellar was the largest and most well finished cellar found within the limits of the village. Unlike any of the cellars previously examined at Sangamo Town, this one was once lined with roughly dressed limestone, although most of that lining had been removed by salvers after the house was abandoned (figure 14.8).

While much of the original appearance of the stone cellar had been destroyed, a very similar cellar (built at about the same time) has provided a more visual comparison. Less than ten miles up the Spoon River Road, Reverend John Berry arranged for the construction of one of the area's first frame dwellings in 1825. The house was constructed just to the south of the site of New Salem, which would be platted four years later. Berry's son William would eventually enter into a retail partnership with Abraham Lincoln at New Salem. That partnership, and Lin-

FIG. 14.8 In-situ stone wall section in the Broadwell cellar, shown with the nearby John Berry cellar, built during the same period.

coln's frequent visits to the Berry home, ensured the survival of the building as a historic ruin until it was dismantled by its owner in 2002.

Because the old Berry house had remained standing (used as a hay barn for over fifty years) the cellar below had been well preserved. After the house was torn down, we were allowed to briefly examine the site archeologically. This involved cleaning out the cellar itself, which had been nearly filled with decomposed straw, manure, and soil over the last seventy years. Once the fill was removed, however, we were afforded an unusually clear picture of what was one of the fanciest subterranean spaces in the region in the mid-1820s.

The Berry cellar was constructed of loosely dressed limestone slabs, laid up against the walls of a fourteen by eighteen foot excavation into the subsoil. The cellar was equipped with an exterior stairway that, surprisingly, led to the front yard of the house. While the floor of this cellar was not covered in stone, the clay surface was actually coated with a thick layer of plaster and whitewash, which must have begun to puncture and fail early in the life of the building. The walls of the cellar were also coated in several layers of whitewash. Housekeeping booklets of the early and mid-nineteenth century often encouraged the frequent cleaning and whitewashing of cellars, in order to keep unhealthy miasmas (or "bad air") at bay. The Berry site reminded us that the 1820s could indeed appear more modern than they often did in central Illinois.

The cellar under Charles Broadwell's house at Sangamo Town probably looked very similar to Reverend Berry's, yet both were unusual for the time and place. In fact, it is possible that the two men hired the same builder to construct them, given the small size of the community at the time. The Broadwell cellar measured approximately eighteen by twenty feet and was about five feet deep.[15] This cellar was also fitted with an exterior stair, located on the west side of the building. Like that of Reverend Berry's, the floor of this cellar was also left in clay, although it was not coated in plaster.

When Broadwell left for Pekin in 1844, he did not sell his house, and he probably took as much of it with him as he could—including doors, windows, fixtures, and so forth. On the floor of the cellar was debris left behind from the initial phase of abandonment of the building: pieces of hardware, a few old tools, and some recent household garbage. These items were found in very silty, waterborne deposits, suggesting that rain water began washing into the cellar soon after the family's departure, perhaps because the cellar doors or other parts of the house had been removed.

Artifacts found lying on the floor of the cellar include a D-shaped shovel handle, a Dutch oven lid, a hand-forged pan or utensil handle, and the cast-iron portion of a hand-operated coffee mill. In the rural Midwest, the consumption of coffee quickly overtook that of tea during the third and fourth decades of the nineteenth century, based on sales figures from country stores.[16] Coffee beans were stocked by most rural stores of the period and were ground at home.

After rain-washed mud had built up on the floor, someone entered the old cellar and began dismantling parts of its stone walls, probably for use in a construction project nearby. By 1845, the only remaining residents of what had been Sangamo Town were living near the steam mill on the river, and in a dwelling that had once been part of the carding mill property. The stones from the cellar may have been reused at one of those residences. Broadwell's house appears to have remained standing after the partial removal of the stone walls of the cellar, indicating that its walls were not built directly on top of the cellar itself. Because much of the building had been removed, thick layers of mud and silt washed into the entrance of the cellar, carrying small pieces of household debris that had been lying on the ground near or under the house. Finally, the house itself was demolished, and the remainder of the cellar was rapidly filled with soils containing nails, bricks, and wall plaster left behind from its dismantling.

Within the layers of soil and debris were fragments of many ceramic and glass vessels. As the debris that was deposited in the cellar of the Broadwell's abandoned home had accumulated on the ground around the house for twenty years, the cellar produced a sample of goods used by the family throughout their residence at Sangamo Town. Like the nearby feature 1 pit feature, the combined artifact assemblage from the cellar was very similar to the domestic average of the period. In fact, when compared to the various assemblages associated with the other properties in Sangamo Town, the Broadwell family's purchasing habits were the closest to the norm for the period.

Small items from these deposits include more fragmentary flat-ware and pewter teaspoons, two brass thimbles, two marbles, and several pipes—including two stoneware Point Pleasant varieties. The somewhat large and diverse pipe assemblage from the Broadwell site demonstrates that tobacco consumption was not just an important facet of upland southern households, but also of those from the east. Also recovered from the cellar fill were the heavily corroded remains of at least three tin containers. While we think of foods packaged in tin cans as a relatively recent phenomenon, canned foodstuff began to appear in mid-western cities by the 1830s, in the form of imported sardines. Small quantities of tin-packaged foods were probably sold out in the country by the early 1840s—or after the close of the frontier period.

Like other households at Sangamo Town, the Broadwell cellar assemblage contained slightly more crockery than average. In this case, that number is partly a reflection of the long-term nature of the sample, which spans about twenty years. The family used a range of crockery vessels for storage, preparation, and service. A redware cup or table bowl and a redware plate were probably made at Cotton Hill before 1835. Several redware pots in the collection appear to have been made at Cotton Hill, and also at the nearby Athens pottery.[17] Unlike several other sites in town, no obviously imported redwares are present in the Broadwell sample. Surprisingly (given the late date of the abandonment of the site), the crockery assemblage is composed of less than 20 percent stoneware. The continued importance of redware in the Broadwell kitchen probably reflects the continued health of the traditional redware shops at Athens and Cotton Hill through the 1840s. A small stoneware pot is represented only by its base, which has been neatly broken into a perfect disk by the freezing water inside the vessel.

The refined ceramic assemblage from the cellar feature is also large: a minimum of 92 vessels. As most of the 62 vessels found in the nearby feature 1 (abandoned about ten years before the house itself) are *not* represented in the debris from the cellar, there are between 120 and 140 plates, bowls, and teawares present in the combined archaeological samples from the Broadwell home. One of these vessels is a plain, white, ironstone plate. The semivitrified, thick-bodied ware identified as ironstone by archaeologists was not manufactured in any quantity until after 1840. Designed for better durability, the new (often undecorated) wares were also intended to serve as imitation of French white porcelain, which had become very fashionable in the cities. The unassuming plate found in the Broadwell cellar, abandoned by 1845, was probably one of the first to enter the archeological record in central Illinois. Throughout Illinois, the appearance of ironstone in archeological features signals the end of the frontier period, and the beginning of what was in many ways, the modern age.

———

It was cold and almost dark on the December day that I crawled out of the Broadwells' cellar. Most of the time, it is easy to forget about the rich history of the places that are now archaeological sites in the middle of open fields. This field, waiting for winter, was the location of a little cluster of real homes built of logs and clay over 170 years ago. In the woods and overlooking the shallow river were some gardens, some log piles, and several paths down the hill. Mud, dung, and always smoke. That cluster of houses had been constructed when this place had yet to become a tamed place. In less than a generation, those homes were abandoned, disassembled, and buried. As a ruin, Sangamo Town has missed the passages that would have made it an old thing modern, instead of an extinct thing buried.

Although I walked across an empty field, I also walked across Bridge Street toward Roll's Store. I carried with me a little mental map—the first of its kind since the death of the last resident nearly a century earlier. Some shoveling, some math, and then a resurrection of sorts. For the first time in 125 years, someone was walking across town, knowing how to get from here to there. With my second-hand memory, I walked down streets that only I could see. From their distant future, I haunted their now-invisible homes.

Lincoln's New Salem
History and Archaeology

The photograph was taken in the 1920s, eight miles down river from Sangamo Town. Another haunted place, and another home of Abraham. The blufftop field, also overlooking the river, had only recently been purchased by the state of Illinois for its historical significance. In the photo, my grandfather is twenty years younger than I am now. He is smiling, and standing inside a slight depression in the ground (figure 15.1). A small wooden sign is posted in front of the shallow hole, giving a name to an archaeological feature. Marked with new signs, more little cellars from another time, still sleeping. Old Salem.

The town of New Salem was platted in 1829, seven years after Moses Broadwell platted his town (figure 15.2). Reverend John Camron and his uncle James Rutledge built a mill on the Sangamon in early 1829, and had the town surveyed that fall. Both men built homes in the new town, and Rutledge's would also serve as the village tavern. This was only the third town to be platted within the heart of the Sangamo Country.[1] Like Sangamo Town, most of what has been remembered and preserved of New Salem is due to the former presence Abraham Lincoln.

New Salem was an important place in Lincoln's life. It was his first home apart from his parents, and it was here that he began piecing together a professional career. When he arrived in the early summer of 1831, Lincoln entered the storekeeping business. His first job was that

FIG. 15.1 Visiting New Salem during the 1920s. Frank Mazrim (left) stands in a depression created by an unexcavated archaeological feature.

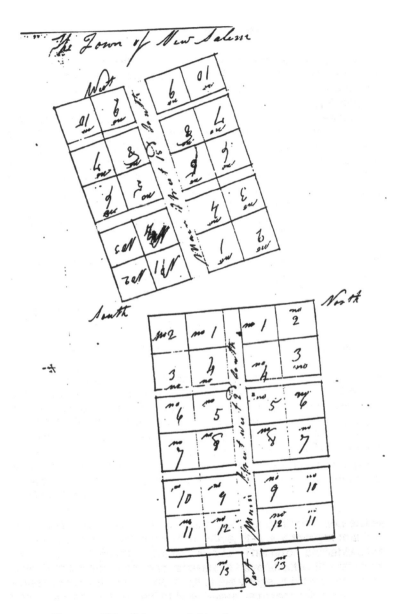

FIG. 15.2 Plat map of New Salem recorded in 1829.

of a "chief clerk" at Denton Offutt's store.[2] That store closed about a year later, and Lincoln purchased his own stock of wholesale goods in partnership with William Berry. In early 1833, the two rented a frame store building across the street from the Rutledge Tavern and ran what would ultimately be an unsuccessful business there until mid-1834. Lincoln also served as the postmaster of New Salem between 1833 and 1836. As his retail business faltered, Lincoln began working as a land surveyor. He was elected to the legislature in 1834 and spent much of his time at the state capital of Vandalia.[3] In the spring of 1837, he moved to Springfield to practice law.

Like Sangamo Town, John Camron's New Salem served as a commercial village anchored by a mill. At its peak in the mid-1830s the village included several stores, a tavern, a blacksmith, a cooper, a shoemaker, a hatter, and a carding mill. Trades such as shoemaking and hat making were more often found in the larger, better established towns. New Salem, then, was more immediately successful in attracting a range of "mechanics" and services than Sangamo Town had been, and it may be no coincidence that New Salem's peak paralleled Sangamo's decline.

In 1839 the large and well-populated Sangamon County was divided into several smaller counties to provide more effective local governmental services. The northwestern portion of the county, where New Salem was located, became Menard County. This required the establishment of a new county seat, and (unfortunately for New Salem) that seat of government was placed in the new town of Petersburg, two miles down river on more accessible ground. While the business climate at New Salem had already stalled (probably due to the Panic of 1837), the selection of Petersburg as the county seat immediately doomed the older village. Most of the residents of New Salem packed up and moved down the hill, often taking their dwellings with them.[4]

Abram Bale (whose brother Jacob was still running the saw and gristmill) arrived at New Salem in the fall of 1839 and found it nearly deserted, except for his brother's residence. Abram and his family camped in a vacant store and wintered in Petersburg that year.[5] The Bale family continued to run the mill built by Reverend Camron in 1829 and modernized it to make flour before the Civil War. By the late 1870s, however, the mill had ceased operation, and it burned down in the 1880s. Meanwhile, many of the former residents of New Salem still lived nearby, and they watched as their former neighbor became lawyer, president, and legend. Then the stories began, and visitors arrived: "Many a visitor, from far away, seeks the spot where president Lincoln spent the days of his early manhood. . . . Nothing is there to remind you that it ever existed save a part of the broken wall of the old foundation of the mill, and farther down some rotting timbers."[6]

The replica village of New Salem that stands today is an amalgam of oral traditions, primary documents, and archaeological record. The oral traditions surrounding the village were first recorded in the 1860s, or more than twenty-five years after the abandonment of the village. Many of the stories that led to the rebuilding of New Salem, as well as its furnishing with events and narratives, were told in the 1860s to Lincoln's biographer William Herndon. Those stories were related by a variety of individuals who had spent time or lived in the village during the 1830s. They were not attempts to record the history and layout of New Salem, however. Instead, they were short anecdotes, principally concerned with the activities of Lincoln between 1831 and 1837. Even with regard to Lincoln's life on the hill, the stories were incomplete and often conflicting.

Attempts to anchor the old stories about Lincoln and New Salem to the actual landscape began at least as early as 1884, when William Green (a former resident who had clerked at Offutt's Store with Lincoln) led a correspondent for the Chicago Tribune to the top of Old Salem Hill and pointed out the former locations of Lincoln-related sites.[7] During the 1890s, local enthusiast Thomas Reep began visiting the hilltop in preparation for an article he intended to write for a college literary society paper. While that article was never written, his research led to a lifelong interest in identifying the locations of specific sites in the open field that was once New Salem. Reep became a founding member of the Old Salem Lincoln League in 1917.

It was the Lincoln League that began the reconstruction of New Salem, and in doing so, conducted some of the earliest historical archaeology in the country. The league excavated the cellar on the edge of the bluff (known as the Three Graces) where Lincoln had managed the store for Denton Offutt in 1831. They also conducted excavations at another store site, remembered as the only frame building in town. It was here that Lincoln and Berry had operated their dry goods store during 1833 and 1834. At the site of this store, the Lincoln League uncovered what would be the largest cellar feature in the entire village, measuring about twenty feet square and once lined with limestone.

As legend has it, the league was not the first to unearth an artifact at this site. William Green (who owned the property for a time during the mid 1830s) is said to have returned to the site forty or fifty years later, only to find a stone inscribed "A. Lincoln and Ann Rutledge were betrothed here July 4, 1833."[8] The stone conveniently "proved" the existence of what many believe to have been a largely fictional romance between Lincoln and the tavern keeper's daughter.

Archaeology at Old Salem

As I began to assemble the archaeological data from Sangamo Town, I thought it would be a good idea to compare the material with the archaeology of New Salem. It was common knowledge that a large amount of archaeology had been conducted there, prior to the reconstruction of the village by the state of Illinois in the 1930s. I had never seen a publication or technical report, however, and I contacted Richard Taylor at the Illinois Historic Preservation Agency, to ask him for a copy. He told me there was really no such report.[9] Instead, the various records from the excavations (photos, maps, correspondence) were scattered in several archives and agencies. Dick asked me if I was interested in putting together a summary of these records, and that project was the beginning of what would become many years of new archaeological and historical research.[10]

The state of Illinois purchased Old Salem Hill in 1919. At the time, five replica cabins built by the Lincoln League were standing on the hill (figure 15.3). Other unexcavated sites were visible as the ground surface

FIG. 15.3 Replica of the Offutt Store, built by the Lincoln League in 1918. The structure was replaced by the state of Illinois in the 1930s.

depressions created by partially filled pit cellars. Small signs had been placed in front of some these archaeological features identifying the former occupants of each site. The first projects implemented by the state were designed to improve automobile access to the new park, and to install improvements such as a water tower, a museum, and custodian's residence. The old Lincoln League replicas, built of cottonwood logs (which were already beginning to dry out and warp) were left standing for another ten years before they were replaced.

In 1932, Governor Louis Emmerson released funding for a complete reconstruction of the village, including the replacement of the five Lincoln League replicas, and the construction of eight additional structures. Joseph Booton, chief draftsman for the State Architect's office, was put in charge of the reconstruction. Booton's task was to conduct the necessary research to rebuild the entire village on its original location. This would entail deed research, interviews with local residents, archaeological excavations, comparative architectural studies, and material culture research. Remarkably, Booton was given only six months to complete the bulk of his research and to render his designs, as the governor wished to cut the ribbon on the project before he left office that fall.[11] Tourist literature from that year captured some of the anticipation surrounding the reconstruction project: "The State department of Public Works and Buildings is restoring the log cabins and the early homes that stood on the original site when Lincoln lived there. Already a few, including the Onstot cabin and others, have been rebuilt. A relic house been established and is visited every year by thousands of people. . . . Restoration of the town of old Salem is proving one of the most fascinating pieces of construction work."[12]

To accomplish his task, Booton had at his disposal the original town plat, four or five hand drawn maps, several signs pounded in the ground over the years, and a large and complex archaeological site. From these he would resurvey and reconstruct the village platted a century earlier. Several maps of New Salem had been drawn during the late nineteenth century by former residents. These maps had been created in response to contextual questions about Lincoln's years in the village, but also became important supplements to the sporadic deed record of the town (figure 15.4).

Although the original plat of New Salem survived, no markers existed that could anchor it to the modern topography. Booton replaced the town plat onto the landscape using remnants of a road that was still visible across the hilltop, as well as the locations of some of the sites that had been identified by the Lincoln League. Booton's 1932 resurvey of

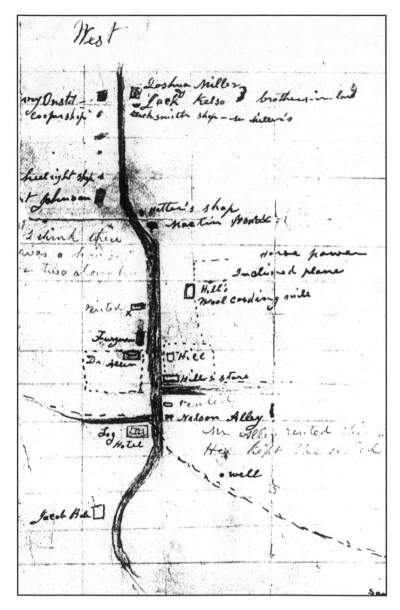

FIG. 15.4 Example of one of several maps of New Salem drawn by former residents years after the village was abandoned. This was drawn by Parthena Hill in the 1880s.

the eastern half of the village (which was the commercial heart of town) appears to have been very accurate. The western half of the village was more problematic, however, and shortly after its construction it was suggested that that route of Main Street had been misplaced. The 1994 study of the archaeological excavations on the west side of town found that this was indeed the case. The result of this surveying error (which was based on the misidentification of a late nineteenth century farm lane as the 1830s Main Street) was the unintentional shifting of the western half of the plat to the north.[13] This then resulted in the mislabeling of six archaeological sites in that half of town.

Booton's archaeological efforts resembled those of the Lincoln League, although he expanded his excavations beyond the cellar features themselves, often encountering subfloor depressions and brick chimney pads, which allowed him to approximate the shape and size of many of the structures. However, in his brief discussion of his archaeological work, he made no reference to the many hundreds of artifacts that he would have encountered, and there are no known field drawings or photographs of his work.

Two years later, under the direction of Booton the Civilian Conservation Corps began a second round of reconstruction activity. Seven more structures were to be rebuilt, and archaeology was again conducted in advance of construction. John Biggs supervised these excavations. The excavation methods had improved, and there is more paperwork associated with the fieldwork—in the form of correspondence from Biggs and a few photographs (figure 15.5).

The first individual with a background in archaeology to work at the site arrived at New Salem in 1939. Paul Maynard, a graduate student at the University of Chicago, conducted a brief field season on the hill, where he spent most of his time reexamining two sites that had been first opened by the Civilian Conservation Corps. After the close of the war, another archaeologist, Richard Hagen, spent one field season looking for sites that were pictured on the villagers' maps, but had not been previously located.[14]

After stitching together the various documents from the 1930s excavations at the site, I was able to gather a basic understanding of the archeological features found in the 1930s. Firstly, it was clear that eighteen of the twenty-two replica buildings were reconstructed on authentic archaeological remains. It was also clear that in most cases, the excavations were very surgical in nature, focusing on the footprint of the building itself and leaving the surrounding archaeological features basically undisturbed.

FIG. 15.5 View of the 1936 excavation of the First Berry-Lincoln Store Site. A stone lined cellar (partially robbed of its stone) can be seen on the right, and the remnants of a chimney footing can be seen on the left.

Seventeen cellar features were recorded by Booton, Biggs, Maynard, and Hagen. Several wells, an unlined cistern, and two exterior storage facilities were also excavated, and there are probably many more such features that are still preserved on the site. Most of the cellars associated with residences were earthen-walled, with footprints measuring between 90 and 225 square feet in plan. The largest cellars encountered during the early investigations were those associated with stores and taverns. These measured between 240 and 400 square feet. Two of the commercial cellars were stone lined, and two were equipped with exterior entrances.

There is little evidence that the archaeological projects actually retrieved and curated artifacts. At the time, the reason for the archaeological excavations at New Salem was very straightforward—to locate the sites of buildings, and to identify their shape and size. The inhabitants of those buildings were remembered in stories and were not the subject of anthropological study. For this reason, the debris associated with their lives on the hill was not of interest to the excavators, and so only a very few of the thousands of artifacts that would have been encountered were saved, such as intact tools that served as good visual relics for the early museum displays (figure 15.6).

FIG. 15.6 Examples of some of the few artifacts known to exist from the 1930s excavations at New Salem: pocket knives, an ornate hand-forged hinge, and a leather shoe possibly recovered from the well associated with the Hill residence.

Forgotten Roads and Houses

While reassembling the old excavation records, I also spent a great deal of time reexamining the reconstructed town itself. Little evidence of the archaeological features unearthed during the 1930s is visible today. Beneath most of the replica log buildings, Booton's crew completely replaced the old earthenwalled cellars with stable, limestone replicas. Under four of the buildings, however, Booton actually marked the former locations of in-situ stone footings (discovered in 1932) by placing slight pilasters in facades of his new stone cellar walls. This subtle gesture had gone largely unnoticed for sixty years. In a very few instances, the old clay walls of the pit cellars were left somewhat intact, and beneath one replica, I discovered that a portion of the original 1830s feature fill had been left unexcavated. Still preserved under the building, it is not only a little fossil of the abandonment of New Salem, but also of its resurrection a century later.

While measuring lot lines at the site of the Second Berry-Lincoln Store (so named because one of its many tenants was the retail partnership of William Berry and Abraham Lincoln) my attention was drawn to a large open area northeast of the building (figure 15.7). Platted between two deep ravines, there was never very much level real estate in New Salem. That may be one of the reasons it failed so quickly. Yet behind the store lay a large expanse of level ground, where no archaeology had been conducted, and where no buildings were reconstructed. Instead, the area has been used for an oxen pen for the park. As the area was situated in the heart of the village, the apparent absence of activity there seemed odd.

FIG. 15.7 The replica Second Berry-Lincoln Store, and the location of area CC in the background, right.

I climbed over one of the many split rail fences in the park, and within fifteen feet, encountered a small scatter of early nineteenth century artifacts, lying on top of the bare, frozen ground. This concentration consisted primarily of very tiny fragments of pearlware, cut nails, and the occasional fragment of early bottle glass. At the back of the cattle lot, two additional scatters lay at the edge of the trees. The archaeological record can be remarkably durable, and after seventy-five years of modern activity on the hill, there they were. Right there on the ground, in the mud and under the dung, lay pieces of the real thing—remains of 1830, out behind the facsimiles of 1830.

Behind the pasture, just inside the tree line of the forest that surrounds the village, was a deep, narrow swale along the edge of the ridge summit. The approximately four-foot deep rut looked distinctly different than naturally eroded gullies nearby. From inside the forest, it was also apparent that this depression extended into the open pasture itself, neatly separating two of the three artifact scatters. Not only had there been early nineteenth-century occupations on this ridge, but there had also been a trail or roadway across the ridge as well. The narrow, heavily eroded path was clearly nineteenth century in origin, and yet was not part of the plat of the village made in 1829.

Only a single known paper document places buildings in this portion of the village. On a birds-eye view drawing of New Salem made by Reverdy J. Onstot (published by the Lincoln League in 1909), two structures are depicted in roughly the same location as the artifact scatters found in 1994 (figure 15.8). Onstot had lived at New Salem as a small boy and probably created this map during the late nineteenth century with the help of other surviving former residents. Certain details pictured on the map (such as the location of wells, fireplaces, etc.) appear surprisingly accurate and are consistent with the subsequent archaeological findings.

The structures related to the new archaeological sites, however, were left suspiciously unlabeled. Further, within the rich oral tradition of the village were no references to houses or businesses in this area. Finally, the scatters of artifacts discovered in the back field fell across four town lots, only one of which appears in deed records as having been purchased during the life of the village. And that lot (5 north) was already occupied by a replica building with its own archaeological footprint—the Second Berry-Lincoln Store, first excavated by the Lincoln League in 1918.

So, the hike across the field produced three little bags of artifacts, evidence of an early road or trail, two or three potentially unknown structures dating to the New Salem era, and new archaeological information

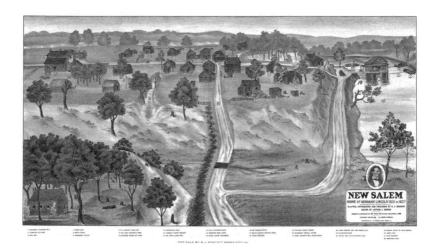

FIG. 15.8 Reverdy J. Onstot's 1909 bird's-eye view of New Salem, and detail of the two unlabeled structures associated with area CC and area AA.

concerning one of the most historic sites in the village—the store building once occupied by Lincoln. The findings immediately posed an opportunity to apply modern research methods to new questions regarding life in the 1830s village. For the next several months, the little bags of artifacts became the subject of many meetings. Eventually, I found myself carrying them up the capitol steps to the governor's office—generally not a normal part of the archaeological process.

Archaeology had not been conducted at New Salem in nearly fifty years. Further, the last time it had, the results had been difficult to digest—suggesting as they did that part of the village had been misidentified. Modern archaeology has since acquired quite a reputation for historical revisionism. Those in charge of maintaining the resurrected New Salem were quite aware that the old stories and interpretations (however accurate or inaccurate) had lived on the hill seven times longer than the original town, and had become a dependable part of the lexicon of Lincolniana. In a way, this is part of what is preserved at sites like

New Salem. Archaeology, then, would not simply represent an academic exercise, but a kind of pulling back of a very old curtain.

"There Used to Be a House Over Yonder"

The three surface scatters of early nineteenth century artifacts found in the oxen pasture were each given their own site designation. At the rear of the pasture, most distant from the reconstructed village itself, was a small scatter labeled area AA. Near the center of the pasture, but located on a slope overlooking a ravine was area BB. This scatter was later found to be heavily eroded, and was probably once part of area AA. At the front of the pasture, just behind the replica of the Second Berry-Lincoln Store, was area CC, another cluster of material similar to area AA.

Onstot's map pictures two structures on the ridge behind the building known today as the Second Berry-Lincoln Store. Both appear to be houses, one of which is larger than the other. A road is also pictured crossing the hilltop headed toward the northeast, corresponding to the rut found in the forest behind the sites. Although Onstot's map was not designed as a scale drawing of the village, it appears that the smaller of the two buildings was roughly situated at area CC, while the larger structure was in the vicinity of areas BB and AA.

The ridge behind the Berry-Lincoln Store is surprisingly absent in the rich and detailed oral traditions of the village. Thomas Reep explored Old Salem Hill at the turn of the century, accompanied by several individuals who had lived in or near New Salem during the 1830s. They were in their seventies and eighties, and had not visited the hilltop in decades. It was on the basis of these interviews, however, that many of the archaeological sites and replicas were labeled. Many years later, Joseph Booton interviewed Reep, questioning him about those early visits.[15] During their discussions, Reep spoke of a visit to the hill with "Uncle Johnny" Watkins, who had lived just south of the village during the 1830s. Several remarks made by Watkins seem to refer to the sites discovered in the oxen pasture a century later.

On the topic of roads used during the 1830s, Watkins seems to have described the road that appeared as a rut in the woods behind the pasture. Reep remembered: "You could see where an old way had gone. On the east side, it ran around the east corner of it [the Second Berry-Lincoln Store]. . . . I have a distinct recollection of him [Watkins] showing me where the slant was, anybody could see it. . . . they told me it was a wet weather road."

That road, it turns out, actually predated the town of New Salem.

More archival research (conducted after we finished our excavations) found references to the road in county records dating as early as 1824. Connecting Springfield to the mouth of the Spoon River (near present day Havana, Illinois), the road even had a name: The Spoon River Road. The route (which probably predated the arrival of Americans in the region) was used during the 1820s to reach the Military Tract, the region in northwestern Illinois that was gifted to veterans of the War of 1812. Although most of the parcels were never settled by their original recipients, many of those who chose to visit or settle the region followed Edwards' Trace to Springfield. From there they headed west on the trail that passed by Elijah Iles's store, through Sangamo Town, and across the hill that would become New Salem. The course of that trail, then, forms a virtual tour of the archaeological heritage of the Sangamo Country.

Upon the platting of New Salem in 1829, the route of the road was probably altered on the hilltop, directing traffic slightly to the east to the saw and gristmill along the river. Villagers then used the old route that passed through the northern edge of town only when the mill road (which followed a very steep course down to the river) became too muddy or washed out—hence the "wet weather road." Soon, much of the path of the old Spoon River Road was redirected, and its importance in the shaping of the cultural landscape along the Sangamon was quickly forgotten.

——————

During his visit to the site with Reep in 1890, Uncle Johnny Watkins also alluded to residences in a "cleared strip" northeast of the Berry-Lincoln Store. Reep mentioned the area toward the end of his interview with Booton, in the process of questioning him about the Dr. John Allen site (located across the street southwest from the Second Berry-Lincoln Store). He seems to have missed the significance of Reep's off-hand remark, which is the only recorded oral tradition regarding one of the two households thought to have occupied the ridge top northeast of the store building:

> Reep: "We went back to Allen's place. And there was one other house, site of a house, he pointed out to me. . . . He said, 'There used to be a house over yonder, right in there,' but I don't believe he knew who lived in it."
> Booton: "Did he point to the site now known as Allen's house?"
> Reep: "No, he pointed northeast of the Berry-Lincoln Store."

In the spring we began our excavations at area CC, behind the Second Berry-Lincoln Store. Two weeks of rain had delayed the project, but had made the ground soft and easy to cut with the trowel. During those rainy weeks, as we prepared for four months of fieldwork, I thought about the sites, and about what we expected to find. After so many meetings, I was becoming increasingly concerned about the condition of the subsurface archaeological remains in what was clearly a heavily eroded field. Those concerns evaporated three hours into our first day in the field. The first test unit of the season immediately encountered a well-preserved pit feature, clearly sealed during the early nineteenth century. By the end of the week, we had exposed two more. Old Salem Hill had more to say.

Behind the Store: Excavations at Area CC

As we began our excavations, with a small crew working inconspicuously in an empty oxen pasture, we did not expect many visitors. There were no signs announcing our presence, and there were also no partitions between the site and the visiting public. We expected to garner as much attention as someone mowing the grass. We soon learned how naive we had been. New Salem receives upwards of 100 tour busses a day during the month of May, and we found that a remarkable percentage of their riders were interested in archaeology. On the second day of our work, we found ourselves inundated. Dozens of hands reached toward the exposed soil, and shovels narrowly missed fingers and toes. By the next morning, we had surrounded ourselves with roping and caution flags, but we had also begun to integrate the research excavations into the interpretive program of the park. Digging became a way of talking about history, as well as studying history.

Our excavations at area CC immediately encountered intact archaeological features, surprisingly well preserved given the fact that most of the topsoil had been eroded or removed by sixty years of park-related activity. The first test unit revealed the edge of a large pit feature. Two additional pits were soon found in the immediate vicinity, as well as two lines of postholes and subsurface traces of the Spoon River Road itself.

Feature 1 at area CC was an oval basin, measuring about 9.5 by 6.5 feet (figure 15.9). In 1995, the pit was about 1.5 feet deep, but considering the deflation of the topsoil caused by plowing and erosion, the pit was probably almost three feet deep originally.[16] The large pit probably functioned as an exterior crop storage facility, much like the pit found near Charles Broadwell's home at Sangamo Town. Lining the pit with straw, its users would have "holed up" vegetables and fruits inside, covering the pit with a mound of wood and soil.

FIG. 15.9 The feature 1 crop storage pit at area CC, exposed in plan prior to excavation.

When it was abandoned, the pit was filled with debris-rich topsoil, as well as a few items that were probably tossed directly into the hole. One of these items was an object that would have been completely prosaic in 1830, but is quite rare to archaeology today. Surprisingly well preserved beneath less than six inches of soil (trodden by oxen for sixty years) was a simple tin cup (figure 15.10). Tinware was the most inexpensive form of cookware and tableware available to the early nineteenth century consumer. The ubiquitous character of these goods, however, is not at all apparent in the archaeological record, as tin decays rapidly in the soil. The cup found in feature 1 was originally composed of two pieces. The wall of the cup was found separated from its base, which had been connected to the vessel body by a small rim that fitted around the wall of the cup. A small loop handle had been soldered to the exterior of the vessel as well. The 170-year-old artifact looked exactly like the reproductions used throughout the village, with the exception of the corrosion.

From within a concentration of small debris that was probably swept up from inside a nearby building were several pieces of an unusual crystalline substance. The substance, which has the consistency of hardened salt, has not been identified, but appears to have been originally suspended in a solution kept inside of a round container. The inside impression of this container was preserved as the liquid evaporated, leaving a round crystalline form. It is quite possible that the material was a

FIG. 15.10 Artifacts from feature 1: a tin cup and a child's thimble.

medicinal compound, which dried out inside of a glass bottle that was broken before the substance was deposited into the pit.

We continued to conduct our work in full view of the many tourists who watched as we unearthed a number of objects from feature 1. The artifact that seemed to create the biggest stir among visitors (as well as the interpretive staff at the park) was a surprisingly common one—a small, brass, child's sized thimble. The discovery of a single thimble is not a pivotal one, yet visitors and staff were genuinely thrilled to see the little brass artifact. "Is this were they found *the thimble?*" "Can we *look at it?*"

After working at the park for a while, I began to better understand these reactions. Places such as New Salem are largely modern ones, at least from the ground up. Although the interpretive programs go to great lengths to demonstrate the authenticity of the past (and its relationship to the very ground on which visitors stand) the modernity of what is visible to the eye is inescapable. Staff and visitors alike are forced to reconstruct, portray, and imagine an invisible past. Archaeological debris (such as a child's thimble) makes these places and their characters much more real, authentic, and human.

In the immediate vicinity of the large feature 1 storage pit were two smaller basin-shaped pits. One of these actually superimposed feature 1, indicating that the large storage pit had already been abandoned when the small pit was constructed. The two smaller pits were probably excavated at the same time, and appear to have been used in the butchering of hogs.

Slaughtering was usually conducted in late October or November, when the weather "turned cold to stay." The first step in the process was known as scalding, which involved the removal of the bristles from the skin of the hog. Water was poured into an open pit or a large wooden barrel. If in a barrel, the water inside was heated by the immersion of rocks previously heated in a fire. After the water was heated, the hog was pushed from an adjacent sled or platform into the barrel. Once the bristles were loosened, the carcass was removed from the barrel, scraped, and suspended from a pole.[17]

Feature 2 measured about three by five feet and was more irregular in shape than the nearby feature 1, suggesting that less care was taken in its construction. The pit was of the appropriate size and shape to have accommodated a barrel, used in the scalding process. At the base of the feature, adjacent to its northeast wall, we encountered a deep posthole. As there was no evidence that this post had been placed into a hole that cut through the fill of the pit, it appeared to have been intentionally placed at the end of the feature's long axis, and would have been standing while the feature 2 pit was in use. The post may have supported a ramp from which the hog was immersed into a barrel, or it may have been used as part of scaffolding from which the scalded hog was suspended for butchering.

Just three feet away, feature 3 may have also been used in butchering. Found at the bottom of this pit was a pile of heavily burnt limestones. A reddish cast appears on the surfaces of limestones that have been exposed to fire for a long period. The stones were not burned inside the pit itself, however, as the soil around them showed no signs of burning. Instead, these stones may have been heated on a ground surface fire, and were shoveled into a scalding barrel. When they were no longer needed, they were discarded into the open feature 3 pit, the exact function of which is unclear. Also discarded into the pit, however, was a large portion of a hog cranium. This, and a number of bones and teeth found within a thin layer of topsoil surrounding the pits, may have been the remnants of the final butchering process.

The fill of the feature 2 pit contained a small number of early nineteenth century artifacts, most of which appear to have been tossed directly into the open pit after they were no longer needed. Included in this small sample was one of the earliest figural whisky flasks found in Illinois. The flask features the embossed portrait George Washington (with "G. G. Washington" above) on one side, and an American eagle on the reverse (figure 15.11). Below the eagle are the initials "FL" for the manufacturer, Frederick Lorenz of Pittsburgh. This particular de-

FIG. 15.11 A figural whisky flask (decorated with a portrait of George Washington) found in the feature 2 butchering pit.

ONE INCH

sign represents one of the earliest pictorial flasks made in America, first manufactured in 1819 and probably discontinued by the mid 1820s.[18] Close inspection of the surface of the bottle revealed heavy scratching on the flask's most pronounced feature (Washington's cheek), evidently resulting from its shipment or storage in a case with other bottles or abrasive items.

While there are dozens of scenarios that may have led to the tossing of that whisky flask into the pit, it is not difficult to imagine that it played a part of the butchering process as well. Hog butchering was a group effort, and was often considered an excuse for a social occasion. Butchering was also conducted on chilly fall days, and the whisky or brandy contained in the bottle found in feature 3 may have helped keep a few residents of New Salem a little warmer while they prepared for winter.

After we had finished examining the pit features, we expanded our excavations and discovered a series of post holes that described two very clear perpendicular lines, enclosing and meeting near the cluster of pit features. While the reconstructed New Salem is dotted with the quaint and archaic split rail fences (which rest on the ground surface), traditional post-and-rail fences were also used on the frontier. Instead of aligning with the town lot grid, however, this fence line bounded a yard that was oriented a full twenty-five degrees away from the orientation of the town plat. Just outside of the eastern fence line, we found evidence of an undulating rut worn into the subsoil that paralleled the fence line. From its orientation, it was clear that this feature represented the subsurface signature of the roadbed that could be seen in the forest behind the pasture. The built environment of area CC, then, appears to have been oriented with respect to the Spoon River Road instead of the town plat. Further, that road (or the segment that crossed the hill) appears to have been intentionally abandoned as part of the creation of the town itself.

Archaeological evidence of the small house pictured on R. J. Onstot's map was only indirect. Years of erosion had erased the few subsurface traces of what must have been a very ephemeral structure. What remained for us to uncover was a scatter of cut nails, a very small amount of window glass, and burnt clay daub that once lined and fireproofed a log chimney.

The artifact assemblage from area CC is similar to pre-1835 assemblages found elsewhere in the Sangamo. The Queensware sample contains an average ratio of table and teawares, dominated by shell edged plates and painted cups and saucers. Few of the more formal transfer printed vessels are present, and hand painted vessels outnumber printed vessels nearly three to one.

An unusually large percentage of crockery is present within the area CC archaeological sample, and all but one of these vessels are redware. The redware vessels include the typical kitchen bowls and small capacity pots, as well as several undecorated table plates. The plates are identical to those found at the Cotton Hill pottery, and were very probably made there. Also identical to the wares of Cotton Hill is a distinctive redware elbow pipe. As is most often the case in frontier contexts, the single stoneware vessel is a jug. Glass bottles and serving vessels also compose an unusually high percentage of the area CC artifact assemblage. These include liquor and medicine bottles, as well as several tumblers or drinking glasses.

The most surprising aspect of the area CC artifacts assemblage is the lack of whiteware. While the use of pre-1830 pearlware products lingered throughout the 1830s, whiteware products appeared in Illinois in the late 1820s and began entering the archaeological record very shortly afterward. Elsewhere at New Salem, for instance, fragments of whiteware tea and tablewares have been found on a lot believed to have been abandoned by 1833.[19] Other sites in the region known to have been first occupied *after* 1835 usually produce only small amounts of pearlware. Considering that the heyday of New Salem occurred in the mid-1830s (and that most properties were occupied until the late 1830s), whiteware should be found in significant quantities at most sites with the village. No whiteware was recognized at area CC, however. The site seemed older than we expected.

Area CC and New Salem's First Store

The orientation of area CC with respect to the Spoon River Road (rather than the town plat) together with the early nature of the artifacts found there, strongly suggested that the site was abandoned very early in the history of New Salem, and also that at least some of the improvements there were constructed *before* the plat was surveyed in 1829.

Assuming the 1930s resurvey of the village was roughly accurate, the pit features found at area CC were located near the back of lot 5 north. At the front of that lot, the Lincoln League excavated a large stone-lined cellar in 1918, on top of which was later constructed the replica of the Second Berry-Lincoln Store. R. J. Onstot's map also placed a small dwelling in the immediate vicinity of area CC. Clearly, however, the fence line that enclosed the pits at area CC was not oriented with respect to any lot lines. Although area CC may have been only tangentially associated with lot 5, that lot was the only one in the project area that was accompanied by any form of deed record. In fact, the store on this lot was found to have one of the most complex deed records in the village. Further, it was soon discovered that much of the history of the store itself was based on old stories, and not on period documents.

The most well understood era of lot 5 is that associated with its occupation by Lincoln and his business partner William Berry. Sometime in January or February 1833, the two bought out the inventory of Ruben Radford, who had been renting the store building from William Green. The partners moved into the store that winter, and soon purchased more goods on credit. By early 1834 the partnership was struggling under the weight of debt, and the store "winked out" (in Lincoln's words) in 1834. The store building then served as a post office for a time, and may have been moved to Petersburg in the late 1830s. A building iden-

FIG. 15.12 An early nineteenth-century frame building thought by late nineteenth-century historians to have been moved from the site of the Second Berry-Lincoln Store at New Salem to Petersburg during the late 1830s.

tified as the ruins of the historic store was photographed in Petersburg in the 1890s (figure 15.12).[20]

The nature of the archaeology at area CC suggested that we had uncovered features and artifacts that predated the mid-1830s, and so it was necessary to better understand the events in and around the store before its "Lincoln period." After we completed the fieldwork, we returned to the archives. Traditionally, the store on lot 5 was believed to have been constructed by George Warburton, a storekeeper who worked at New Salem between late 1829 and early 1831. A study of the deed records quickly found that there is no record of George Warburton's ownership of this property. Further, it appears that his presence at this particular site is based on second- and third-hand stories that were told long after the village was abandoned. The deeper one looked, the more cracks appeared in the venerable facade of an oft-told history.

It was the correspondence between Lincoln's biographer William Herndon and John McNamar (who in partnership with Sam Hill operated the first store in New Salem) that ultimately provided essential clues regarding the actual origins of this store. In his 1866 letter to Herndon, McNamar presented a detailed description of the earliest days of New Salem. Firstly, he claimed to have been the first "discoverer of Salem as a business point."[21] This fits well with the tradition that he and Hill built the first store in town, which until recently was thought to have been located *next door* to the Second Berry Lincoln Store. McNamar also stated that when he arrived, the place was called Camron's Mill, implying that the sawmill had been completed, but the town had probably yet to be surveyed. This would date McNamar and Hill's arrival sometime in the summer or fall of 1829.

McNamar remembered that upon his arrival (and while his partner Sam Hill was still in St. Louis) he "contracted for the erection of a magnificent store house," paying fifteen dollars for its construction. He also mentioned that George Warburton arrived *later* and built a store at the eastern end of the village. This statement effectively removes Warburton from the history of the Second Berry-Lincoln Store. After a synthesis of the archaeological and archival data, it appears that the store now labeled "Second Berry-Lincoln" was actually the "magnificent store house" for which John McNamar paid fifteen dollars in the summer or fall of 1829. He and Sam Hill ran the first store at New Salem at this site until the fall of 1831, when they moved next door.

Area CC then, may correspond with activities associated with both the early years of the store and the small house situated just to the northeast (as depicted in Onstot's drawing). Several aspects of the artifact assemblage from area CC seem to reflect storekeeping activities. The larger than average number of glass tumblers, similar to those found at the Iles Store site in Springfield, may reflect the serving of liquor at the New Salem store. Like the Brigham-Roll store at Sangamo Town, area CC also produced an unusual quantity of redware, which may somehow reflect its sale and breakage at the store.

The small house illustrated by R. J. Onstot was probably not equipped with a pit cellar (perhaps because the large cellar beneath the store was sufficient), and thus has become largely invisible archaeologically. The building may have served as a short-term residence for New Salem's first storekeepers, who were bachelors at the time. Based on the archaeological evidence, that house was probably abandoned and dismantled after the two moved to the adjacent lot in early 1832. The backyard behind the store building was cleaned up, and travel along the "wet weather road" (that was once the way to the Spoon River) gradually ceased.

As a result of our excavations, the early history of the store building on lot 5 (that would be later occupied by Abraham Lincoln) has been revised. That revision, however, could have been accomplished strictly through a careful reexamination of the archival record. In this case, it was the disconnect between the archaeological remains behind the store and the traditional history of that store that prompted the close reexamination of the history of the site in the first place. In other words, archaeology at area CC inadvertently served to question a documents-based history, rather than providing answers to particular questions. Digging in the ground just pointed the way.

CHAPTER SIXTEEN

Behind Lincoln's New Salem

Archaeology and Revisionism

Based on R. J. Onstot's map, another house once stood at the back of the field near the two ground surface scatters designated as area AA and BB. Here, the dwelling itself once again eluded us—perhaps due to erosion.[1] At area AA we found another cluster of subsurface features that appear to have been located in the "backyard" of the dwelling pictured by Onstot. The age and location of these features soon led us to rethink the old stories regarding the origins of New Salem.

Area AA and the Beginnings of New Salem

The first feature discovered at area AA was a shallow, roughly rectangular depression in the subsoil, measuring about six by six feet.[2] Inside this depression were two deeper, irregular basin-shaped pits that would have extended to a depth of about two feet below the early nineteenth century ground surface. The larger rectangular depression may define the size of a small structure that was used as a privy or outhouse, and the two smaller pits may have served as receptacles for fecal material, deposited below two seats in a bench above (figure 16.1).

As opposed to the deeper, more formal privy shafts used in urban contexts (or later in the nineteenth century in some rural settings), outhouses on early nineteenth century farmsteads in Illinois appear to have been equipped with very shallow vaults, which were frequently cleaned

FIG. 16.1 The feature 1 privy at area AA, prior to and after excavation.

of their contents. The dipping or cleaning of the privy was probably accomplished though a hatch in the back of the building. Such arrangements were still in use during the early twentieth century in the Midwest, although the vaults themselves generally became deeper. The frequent shoveling-out of the facilities scarred the base of the shallow pits,

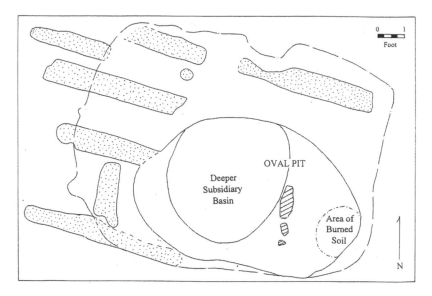

FIG. 16.2 Plan drawing of the still house floor at area AA.

leaving behind a distinctive archaeological signature such as that seen in feature 1 at area AA.

Approximately twelve feet to the west of the privy, our test units encountered a large rectangular stain, well preserved at the base of the old topsoil. In many settings, modern plowing has reached completely through the topsoil, actually disturbing the top of the clay subsoil itself, and virtually destroying any shallow archaeological features. Area AA, was probably never plowed, and much of this unusual feature existed only on the surface of the subsoil itself.

In plan, this feature consisted of a rectangular depression, which was situated on a slight slope and measured approximately twelve by nine feet (figure 16.2). The depression was probably created by foot traffic inside a small, earthen-floored building. The building was too small for a dwelling, and other facets of the feature suggest that it served another function. Firstly, several long, linear depressions were found at the base of the shallow depression. These appeared to have been created by the former presence of planks or puncheon logs placed across this floor during its use. Over time, the weight of foot traffic pressed them into the subsoil, leaving behind distinct impressions. These impressions were remarkably well preserved, marking the exact length and shape of the logs as they had been originally laid on the ground surface. Along the outsides of the impressions were little ridges that had been pushed up from weight applied to the logs when the earth below was soft or damp.

A large, oval-shaped pit (filled with a silty, very fine ash) occupied much of the floor space within this little structure. Behind the pit, in the rear of the structure, was evidence of a crude hearth: a few large limestone slabs surrounding an area of burned earth. At the opposite site of the structure, at its lowest point on the slope, the log impression extended beyond the limits of the rectangular depression itself, suggesting that this end of the building was open, much like a three-sided shed.

Its archaeological remains suggested at least two possible uses of the building. Both smokehouses and still houses were crude outbuildings in which fires were burned, and both types of facilities would have been common in the area. Smokehouses consisted of a simple enclosure in which pork was hung and cured by a continuously smoldering fire. Still houses consisted of shelters for distilling apparatus for making grain alcohol.

If the building had functioned as a smokehouse, however, one would expect the evidence of a hearth to be located closer to the center of the building. In the center of this feature was a large open pit, occupying most of the floor space in the enclosure and suggesting that it may have been the focus of the activity inside. If this building had served as a still house, then the deeper basin adjacent to the small hearth may have held distilling equipment. One distilling device in use during the period was known as a ground hog still, a metal container enclosed in a mound of clay (used to hold the heat) set over a slow burning fire. Such a device may have been built into the rear of this building, and fragments of baked clay were in fact recovered among the limestones here.

The basin-shaped pit in front of the still may have held a container that collected the alcohol from the still itself. That pit may have eventually filled with ash from the adjacent fire. While the fill of the rectangular depression produced few artifacts, fragments of several redware jugs were recovered, and these may have been used for storing, transporting, or serving liquor. While it is certainly possible that the little building served another, undetermined function, the little dirt-floored building was the first of its kind in the archaeological literature of Illinois, and was a delight to behold.

Abraham Lincoln once recalled that, while living at New Salem, he worked "the latter part of one winter in a little still house, up at the head of a hollow."[3] Area AA, however, was probably abandoned before he got to town. The site is located almost completely outside of the limits of the 1829 plat of New Salem, and directly along the remnant of the pre-village Spoon River Road. Like area CC, this site also seems to have had little to do with the New Salem survey.

Artifacts behind the Still House

The artifact assemblage from area AA suggests a slightly earlier and longer occupation than that of area CC—probably first established during the mid-1820s. Also like area CC, no whiteware was recovered here, indicating that the site was abandoned shortly after the platting of New Salem and the rerouting of the Spoon River Road. Area AA also produced the largest and most diverse artifact sample from our three seasons of work at New Salem.

Demonstrating once again the surprising sameness of cupboards on the Illinois frontier, the area AA artifact assemblage fits comfortably within the average patterns for the period, with respect to ratios of Queenswares, crockery, and glass, as well as ratios of table- to teawares. More unusual, however, was a larger than average percentage of painted wares (46 percent of the Queensware assemblage, as opposed to the norm of about 36 percent). These consist almost entirely of broad painted motifs popular during the 1820s (figure 16.3). The occupants of the house at area AA appear to have had little interest in the slightly fancier printed teawares. All of the crockery from the site is redware, and the sample is dominated by jug fragments from the still house. Two finely potted tablewares (a cup and a bowl) may have been made at Cotton Hill. The container glass from the site includes one or two tumblers, a wine bottle, and a few small medicine vials.

Elements of at least three tools were also recovered from feature 1, including the handle and blade portions of at least one pocket knife, a broken whetstone, and a bent iron rod with a flattened end that may have been used as a small gouge. One grooming-related artifact was found in feature 1 as well: a small, double-edged comb made of animal bone. Bone combs and toothbrushes were mass produced in factories in England and the eastern United States, fashioned from cattle bones. This comb, however, was not made for arranging hair, but for removing lice, which would have been a common problem in both the cities and out in the country.

Very near the site of New Salem were outcrops of low grade "bank coal," used during the frontier period by some of the local blacksmiths for fueling their forges. A few small pieces of this coal (which peels apart to form thin, flat sections) were found in feature 1 at area AA. The residents of the site do not appear to have been using the mineral for fuel,

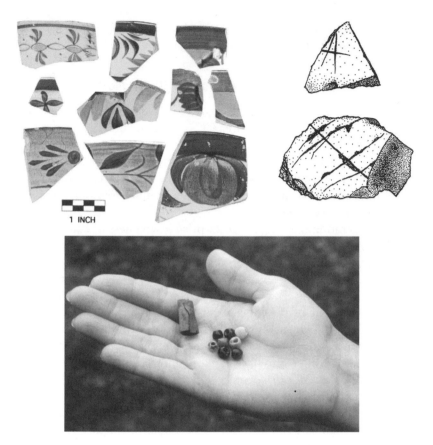

FIG. 16.3 Selected artifacts from area AA: painted pearlwares, an improvised writing slate, and Native American–related artifacts.

though. Instead, the fragments show signs of having been used as improvised writing slates. Factory-cut and polished slate was readily available and affordable at local stores, but in this case, someone on Old Salem Hill decided to make their own.

Small samples of animal remains were recovered at area CC and area AA. At both sites, the remains of domesticated animals far outnumbered wild game. In fact, three years of excavations at New Salem failed to recover a single deer bone. Again, contrasting our old notions of pioneer life, the earliest American settlers of the Sangamon valley ate very well, and did not rely on hunting to survive. At area AA, pork was the most abundant meat in the sample, followed by chicken and small amounts of beef. The chickens were slaughtered while still young, which would have provided better quality meat. Wild game included a few squirrels, and some very large bottom-feeding river fish like the freshwater drum-fish, which would have been nearly six feet long.[4]

One of the most impressive aspects of the artifact assemblage at area AA was the presence of a quantity of items related to the Native American trade. It is reasonably common to encounter the occasional glass seed bead (manufactured specifically for the Indian trade) on frontier-context sites.[5] Beaded items such as belts or bags appear to have been in circulation in frontier communities and were probably inadvertently obtained by some farming families who rarely interacted with Native Americans themselves. The pit features at area AA produced a larger than average number of Indian-related items, however, including a number of small glass trade beads, a rolled brass hair ornament, and a tubular shell, or "wampum" bead. The glass beads themselves do not necessarily place a Native American on site, as they may have been attached to an object obtained by the family second hand. The rolled brass ornament, however, was very likely made by a Native American specifically for wearing on clothing or in the hair, and is more likely to reflect the actual presence of its wearer.

The oral traditions of the lower Sangamon valley often recalled a small Native American population persisting in the area as late as the late 1820s. For instance, tavern keeper James Rutledge's nephew remembered a small group of Potawatomi harvesting pecans in the floodplain north of New Salem. He also remembered Indian women cooking with the wives of American farmers, wearing American dresses, but refusing to give up their moccasins. Associated as they are with an 1820s site along the Sangamon River, the little glass beads found at area AA represent the very last moments of 12,000 years of traditional Native American culture in this particular valley. In less than ten years, that cultural presence would be gone.

The stories told since the first log replicas were built on Old Salem Hill would suggest that town founder John Camron wandered up to an empty hilltop and proclaimed it to be the site of a new town. The archaeological record, however, suggests a more complicated origin of the village. Firstly, the hilltop was crossed by a preexisting trail that connected the new county seat town of Springfield to the Military Tract. The trail was probably a busy one in the 1820s, and thus planning a commercial venture along the road made good sense. Further, Camron was not the first to settle on the hill. Aside from the occasional occupation of the ridge by prehistoric Native Americans for several millennia,[6] the first permanent settlement of the hill by Euro-Americans probably occurred in the mid 1820s, at area AA.

The residents of Area AA probably built a home along the road shortly after the store and tavern opened at nearby Sangamo Town. Near the house, they appear to have constructed a small still house for making grain alcohol. The sale or trade of that whisky may have been the first commercial activity to occur at the site of New Salem. Members of the Potawatomi probably visited the family living here, perhaps during the fall pecan harvest, or during the winter hunt. When John Camron purchased the land in 1828, he may have also purchased the "squatters rights" of those living at area AA, and asked them to leave. Perhaps more likely, however, they were allowed to stay and become part of the new community. Their house stood long enough for R. J. Onstot (or someone he knew) to remember it years later, but it was probably dismantled shortly after the town was platted.

If the residents of area AA were indeed among the families with known New Salem connections, members of the Clary family are perhaps the most likely candidates. William Clary is remembered as one of the early settlers of the immediate area, arriving before New Salem was platted. He opened a "grocery" store in town around 1829, and the store was most often remembered as the scene of much drunken rowdiness. The location of Clary's Grocery, however, is very poorly understood, and only one document (a map drawn by area resident George Spears in the 1860s) places the store in the location of the modern replica—due east of area AA across a ravine. The archaeological feature found by Booton at this site in 1932 might have been a subfloor cellar as he believed, but its shape is also indicative of cellars associated with outbuildings. In fact, it is possible that what is today known as "Clary's Grocery" may have been simply the site of an outbuilding associated with Denton Offutt's store, which was located less than eighty feet away.

While it is little more than an educated guess, area AA may have been the site of an early Clary family residence, and it may have also served as the location of a short-lived grocery store. William Clary left the village around 1832 (fitting well with the artifact assemblage at area AA) and the still house there may have supplied Clary with part of his inventory. The setting of the site is also similar to that of the site marked by Spears nearly thirty years after the abandonment of the village, and he may have confused the road that crossed the hill during the early days of the village with the rerouted road that passed by the mill. We may never know exactly who occupied either site.

Just months before Camron had the town plat surveyed, the store-keepers John McNamar and Sam Hill arrived and probably discussed the new town project with its proprietor. At the time, the place was known as Camron's Mill, a reference to the saw and gristmill completed that spring. The storekeepers were evidently given permission to construct a frame store building on the property, perhaps in exchange for the traffic their business would generate. Following its survey, the town of New Salem would quickly attract more storekeepers and craftsmen. Abraham Lincoln arrived a year and a half later, and like most of his neighbors, left before 1840. Following his death, most recollections of the village focused on its "Lincoln-era" of 1831 to 1837, and few stories were told of its early days as Camron's Mill.

The Saga of the Rutledge Tavern

During the winter of 1994, while I was sifting though the sixty-year-old documents associated with the first archaeological excavations at New Salem, I found two unlabeled black-and-white photographs. These were taken during the summer of 1936, when a Springfield photographer was asked to document some of the proceedings at New Salem. Unlike most of the other images from the investigations, these were not accompanied by any form of correspondence or field drawings.

The photos documented a large cellar, which had been partially emptied of its fill, exposing intact clay walls that extended to a depth of about four feet. At least at the time of the photographs, the excavators had left much of the original fill of the cellar in place. This comes as no surprise, as the early archaeological projects were designed to locate and investigate the cellars themselves, and not to retrieve artifacts. From the two photos, it is clear that this particular feature contained a large quantity of limestone, reflecting a demolished chimney, or perhaps the dismantled walls of the cellar itself.

One of the photos betrayed the location of the mystery site, as the little stone walk leading to the front door of the Second Berry-Lincoln Store can be seen in the background (figure 16.4). This placed the cellar at the southeastern corner of the intersection of the old Spoon River Road and Main Street—or on lot 5 south. According to the villagers' maps and the deed record, this was the location of one of the most legendary Lincoln-related sites at New Salem—the Rutledge Tavern, home of his fabled lost love, Ann Rutledge. For the last sixty years, however, this archaeological site has been the location of a horse pasture, not

FIG. 16.4 Photograph of the partially-excavated Rutledge Tavern cellar, circa 1936.

a replica tavern. That replica was constructed well to the south, on another town lot, and atop a series of old stories and controversies that predated the resurrection of the village.

———

The partners Camron and Rutledge are thought to have built homes for their families in the fall of 1828, shortly after Camron's purchase of the eighty acre parcel on which the town of New Salem would be platted. James Rutledge and his wife Mary Ann had ten children by 1829. There is no record of James Rutledge's lot ownership within the town of New Salem. This is probably due to the fact that he was in partnership with his nephew John Camron, and would not have been required to purchase the lot on which he lived. Shortly after its construction, Rutledge opened his home as a tavern. The family remained at New Salem for less than five years, moving back to a farm north of New Salem in the spring of 1833.

Upon their departure, the Rutledges are said to have sold the tavern to Nelson Alley, and the deed record does indicate that Nelson Alley purchased a portion of lot 5 south (directly across from the Second Berry-Lincoln Store) in November 1832. Alley paid $200 for the western sixty-six feet of the lot, suggesting a substantial (probably commercial) structure was included on that side of the property. Oral traditions remember Alley selling the tavern to Henry Onstot in December 1834. That sale (like many at New Salem) was not recorded in the deed record, however. Onstot is thought to have operated the tavern for one or two years before selling it to Michael Keltner. Again, there is no primary record extant for this transaction. The tavern was probably abandoned sometime during the late 1830s.[7]

Former residents drew several maps of New Salem between 1866 and 1910. Each of these maps placed Rutledge's tavern (referred to as the Log Hotel or the Log Tavern) on the south side of Main Street, directly opposite of the store building now known as the Second Berry-Lincoln Store (figure 16.5). In addition to its depiction on the villagers' maps, there are a few descriptions of the tavern building recorded by families who had visited the tavern or lived nearby during the 1830s. The most detailed is that made by Rachel Clark, whose husband had stayed at the tavern in the winter of 1833–34. Clark remembered the building as having been situated at the intersection of Main Street and the Spoon River Road. She also stated that the building was located directly against these streets, leaving no room on the west or north for a yard. Clark described the building as two stories high, "builded of logs," with four rooms downstairs and one large room upstairs. Harvey Ross, who "put up" at the tavern, described it as "a hewed log house, two stories high, with four rooms above and four below." Ross also remembered that "it had two chimneys with large fireplaces, and not a stove in the house."[8]

The Rutledge Tavern was one of the several buildings first reconstructed by the Lincoln League in 1918, and the State of Illinois rebuilt that replica in the 1930s on the same site. When it was first constructed in 1918, however, the replica Rutledge Tavern was built not on lot 5 south (where deed records and villagers' maps placed the building) but 150 feet to the south, on lot 6 south.

At the site of the league's replica had been the ruins of another log home, which had been the last structure standing at the site of New Salem. The house had been the residence of the Bale family since the mid-1830s, following Jacob Bale's 1832 purchase of the sawmill from John Camron. Abram Bale continued operating the mill long after the abandonment of the village, and remained in the house until sometime around the Civil War.[9] Based on villagers' maps (as well as the deed record), the Bales appear to have moved into John Camron's home, and not the tavern.

The Camron-Bale house was first misidentified as the Rutledge Tav-

FIG. 16.5 Depiction of the Rutledge Tavern from R. J. Onstot's map of New Salem, and the Camron-Bale dwelling misidentified as the tavern in an 1874 Menard County atlas.

ern in the early 1870s, when the house sat as a ruin on Old Salem Hill. These ruins were pictured in an illustrated atlas map of Menard County in 1874. The caption of this drawing labeled the building as the "Salem Hotel, Lincoln's Boarding House." Why the authors of the atlas labeled the Bale home as the ruined tavern is unclear, particularly as elsewhere

in the same publication the last house left standing "amid the eternal soli-
tude that broods over the deserted hamlet" was correctly identified as
the former home of the town's founder, John Camron.[10]

It should be remembered, however, that Old Salem Hill was already
becoming a tourist attraction in the 1870s, and as one local historian be-
moaned, there was little on the hill to look at. Further, Lincoln's biographer William Herndon had begun visiting the area in 1866, and soon
began to focus his research on the supposed love affair between Lincoln
and Ann Rutledge, who lived in the tavern. He presented a lecture on the
topic (called "Abraham Lincoln, Miss Ann Rutledge, New Salem, Pio-
neering and the Poem") in Springfield in 1866. As the ruins of a home
occupied and remodeled by the local miller probably held far less appeal
than those of the home of the lost Ann Rutledge, the identification of
the Bale house as the tavern may have begun with pilgrimages made to
the site in search of Lincoln connections.

In the 1930s, a local resident told those in charge of the New Salem
project that she had been told by a local surveyor that the Bale family
had purchased the old tavern building around 1840, and had subsequently moved the structure to a farm north of the village site, for use
as a corn pen. If the story was correct, then the home of Ann Rutledge
may have met a far less romantic fate than that of the ghostly ruin pictured in 1874.

By the turn of the century, the ruined Camron-Bale house had become
an archaeological site, visible only by the partially filled remains of a well
and a brick lined root cellar that was probably built by the Bales long
after the village was abandoned. The identification of the site as that of
the Rutledge Tavern, however, had become tradition. It was based on
this local tradition (then over thirty years old) that the Lincoln League
erected their replica tavern on lot 6 south, near the old well.

When the state of Illinois began to build the replica village in the
1930s, several individuals (including members of the Bale family) began
to point out the discrepancies between the twentieth-century replica
and the mid nineteenth century deed and oral record regarding the site
of the Rutledge Tavern. In 1931, Ida Bale, who had visited the home of
her great uncle at Old Salem hill as a child, began writing a series of letters to Joseph Booton and the state of Illinois. In her correspondence,
she vehemently stated that the Bale house had never been the Rutledge
Tavern, and that in fact the tavern had stood to the north, on lot 5 south.

Bale also stated that her brother had addressed the archaeological record itself, digging holes into the lot 5 south site and exposing a portion of a stone cellar wall thought to have been associated with the tavern's cellar. According to Booton, Bale had "built up quite a case for her argument and had acquired many supporters."[11]

Perhaps partially in response to Bale's complaints, Booton first conducted excavations at the lot 5 south site sometime prior to 1934. What he found appears to have been the remains of the cellar feature, as well as "stone and brick, ashes, pottery, and bits of implements" which he recognized as early nineteenth century in origin. In a discussion with Thomas Reep (who had been responsible for the placement of the replica tavern sixteen years earlier) Booton expressed his concern about the archaeological evidence (a "sort of cellar . . . or a pit of some kind") that he had encountered on lot 5 south. Booton told Reep that "just what [the feature] is we don't know. It worries me." In his final report made a few months later, he concluded, surprisingly, that his archaeological work had "found nothing definite to show foundations or a former basement."[12]

Based on interviews and his personal correspondence, it is clear that Booton encountered considerable opposition to the notion that the location of the 1918 replica had been in error. In an apparent nod to a then sixty-year-old tradition, Booton left his archaeological findings on lot 5 south unreported, and instead drafted a rather circuitous argument in favor of the lot 6 south site. As a result, the actual site of the tavern was left vacant, and the site of the Camron-Bale house was labeled as that of the Rutledge Tavern, thus excluding the home of New Salem's founder (John Camron) from the reconstructed village.

The unpublished photographs found in the archives in 1994 appear to record a second visit to the tavern site, made during the summer of 1936. At the time, Booton would have had at his disposal the crews from the Civilian Conservation Corps, who had conducted archaeology for him elsewhere in the village, and who were in the process of building the new log replicas. The crews exposed the remains of a large cellar feature and excavated down along its walls to what they believed to have been the clay floor of the feature. At the time the two photographs were taken, the entire fill of the feature had not yet been removed.

Ten years later, Booton wrote an article describing the "many problems" he had encountered while researching and rebuilding New Salem. In his article, he recalled Bale's concerns with the tavern location, and that he had "set about to dig up the facts." He did not mention the revisit to the site that had been recorded in the photographs—or the large, reasonably well preserved cellar feature that he had encountered. Instead, he simply stated that he "found nothing of value," and that the "archaeological work was of no help." [13]

Pulling Back Another Curtain

In 1997, I went before the Lincoln League and hesitantly requested funding to reopen Booton's excavations, in an effort to reestablish the actual location of the Rutledge's 1828 tavern. To their credit and to my great relief, the league responded in a completely positive and enthusiastic manner, wishing, like myself, to better understand the old stories. So in the spring, we returned to the village and began digging again.

Based on the 1930s photographs, we could easily ascertain the location of the cellar feature on lot 5 south. From what was pictured in the photos, we fully expected to find the edges of the cellar below the modern ground surface, surrounded by intact clay subsoil. We also hoped that the excavators had left the bulk of the feature fill intact (as was pictured in 1936), thus providing a sample of artifacts associated with the tavern itself.

We began with a north-south line of shovel tests across the lot. While we found undisturbed clay subsoil at the extreme southern end of the site (well away from the area photographed in the 1930s), the rest of the tests encountered nothing but what appeared to be strangely modern fill soils, in an area much too large for the feature pictured in the photos. We expanded and repeated our tests, finding nothing but a large area of clean fill soil, extending to a depth of over four feet.

We were utterly mystified. The photos clearly depicted a large feature (excavated into intact clay subsoil) at the front of lot 5 south, directly across the street from the replica Second Berry-Lincoln Store. Further, there was absolutely no record of any form of construction or earthmoving activity that may have damaged the site since 1936. We responded to the mysterious soils by opening two deep, perpendicular trenches across the entire area, in hopes of better understanding the stratigraphy of the site.

We found that the fill soils extended across most of the front of the lot. In cross section, we could see that these soils had been deposited into a gently sloping crater, as opposed to a vertically walled cellar. There was no evidence that this disturbance was related to a twentieth century construction project, or to natural erosion. Finally, at fifty-two inches below ground surface, we discovered a thin layer of much earlier soils (containing early nineteenth-century artifacts), as well as the very base of a vertically walled excavation into subsoil. In other words, we found the bottom six inches of the Rutledge Tavern cellar, right where it was supposed to be (figure 16.6). There was not supposed to be, however, a twenty-foot wide crater responsible for removing most of that cellar feature. Worse yet, that crater was directly centered on the remnant of the cellar below, indicating that its excavators had in some way focused on (or targeted) the archaeological feature itself.

There was still a surprising amount of information in that last six inches of soil. From the bottom of our trenches, we learned that the cellar was about ten by twelve feet, and may have been originally lined with two opposing stone walls. Debris from those walls was probably first seen in 1931, when Ida Bale's brother dug into the feature and encountered limestone rubble. On the floor of the cellar (along its eastern wall) was a deep, tapered posthole and an adjacent irregular depression. These may have marked the location of a trap door entrance and small ladder or stair, which had descended into the cellar from above. The post may have supported part of the ladder, while the irregular depression would have been created by footfalls at the base of that ladder—from years of barefooted children sent into the cellar to bring up sacks of potatoes.

On the opposite side of the cellar, excavated into the earthen floor, was a shallow, basin-shaped pit very similar to those often found in the yards of frontier-era farmsteads. This pit probably served a similar function—for the cool and dark storage of vegetable or root crops. If covered by a few planks, the pit may have remained cooler than the rest of the open cellar, and would have still allowed for foot traffic over its covered surface.

From the six-inch remnant of the cellar feature we recovered fragments of a dipt table bowl, a printed plate, a tumbler, and a wine bottle—as well as a small quantity of nails and window glass. These artifacts represent only a small fraction of what would have been encountered in the 1936 excavations. Unfortunately, most of artifacts collected during those excavations appear to have been lost. In 1994, I did find in storage a large envelope marked "Rutledge Tavern," which contained several large fragments of a pearlware transfer printed platter dating to the 1820s. The large size of the fragments suggests that they were probably found in subsurface feature contexts, and may have been saved from the 1936 excavations.

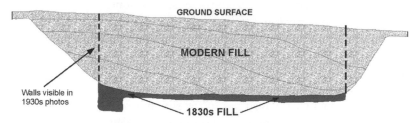

FIG. 16.6 View of the initial test trench at the Rutledge Tavern site in 1997, and a crossectional drawing of original cellar remnant found below modern fill.

Erasing the Past

Based on the stratigraphy recorded in our trenches, Booton's 1936 crew emptied the stone and clay walled feature of all of its post-abandonment fill, including the central portion still present when the two photographs of the feature were taken. It was only a layer of clay wall slump (which the crew evidently mistook for a cellar floor) that protected the actual floor and lower six inches of the feature walls, as well as a very small sample of period artifacts.

The old cellar was not simply filled back in after the pictures were taken in 1936, however. Upon the removal of the feature fill, the intact vertical clay walls of the feature were intentionally cut away, creating a large basin that was centered on the original center of the cellar feature. The shoveling away of undisturbed clay subsoil surrounding the feature would have been no small feat, and may have been accomplished mechanically. In doing so, all traces of the original feature (down to fifty-two inches below ground surface) were completely erased. The resulting crater was then filled with clean imported soil, leaving no traces of nineteenth century activity on the site.

This activity was completely unnecessary to backfill and regrade the site. The only apparent reason to remove the clay walls of the cellar (which could only be appreciated by a controlled, archaeological re-excavation of the site) would have been to create a large, irregular basin that could not be mistaken for an old cellar. All artifacts and old soils were removed, and clean soil was brought from somewhere else. The gouge was filled and seeded.

There will always be a struggle between memory, storytelling, written records, and the interpretation of archaeological footprints. There can never be one authority. In this case, however, more arrows pointed to the tavern location on lot 5 south. Oral traditions, archival records, and archaeology agreed in a reasonably straightforward manner. After reading our excavation report, one historian proclaimed that the archaeologists' actions reflected a "tyranny of the system" over the truth about the location of the Rutledge Tavern.

I'm not sure that what happened in 1936 was that simple. The historiographic drama that played out in the summer of 1936 demonstrates the high stakes that were in play for the new custodians of this venerated site. The replica tavern had become a living place, occupying the landscape much longer than had its namesake. Joseph Booton made a choice. It was not, however, the "tyranny" of his new scientific principals or of governmental control that led to his decision—it was the tyranny of local memory.

I personally find Booton's later remarks the most disappointing. The replica village had always been a compromise, but his remarks about the site that he uncovered in 1936 are not consistent with his obvious ability to interpret archaeological evidence. While he stated that archaeology had been "of no use," his excavations had plainly encountered the evidence that he had been looking for. He apparently found that evidence too complicated and poorly timed, however. Not only did he finally look away from the archaeological record, but someone on the hill had that record nearly destroyed. The crater that had been left on lot 5 south was meant to appear as nature, not history. Imagine pages 1 through 95 of a 100-page book torn from their bindings, and a cover blackened. In the summer of 1997, we were not supposed to see.

CHAPTER SEVENTEEN

The End of the Trail

Old Peoria Rediscovered

North of Sangamo and at the end of Edwards' Trace, most of the French character of Peoria quickly dissolved into the soil after Captain Craig's fires died out in the fall of 1812. The villagers did not return to the ruins, although a few families resettled down river on the opposite shore. Animals moved into the abandoned Fort Clark, and for a short time, Peoria was a very quiet place. After a few years of silence, the Americans began to visit, following the trace from the south. At first, they came to hunt or fish, but soon they began building their log houses. By the mid-1820s, Peoria—the last stand for the old ways of the eighteenth century—had become an American place.

In less than a generation, the residents of Peoria began looking for the archaeological traces of its French heritage. As early as the 1840s, local historians searched for the location of La Salle's 1680 Fort Crevecoeur. Tell-tale "heart-shaped" springs, suspicious rises in the floodplain, and hints of charcoal or iron implements have been credited as evidence of this very historic place, but the short lived fort itself has yet to be found.

The forts of the seventeenth century had paved the way for the villages of the eighteenth century, and two French towns came and went on the west bank of the river. By the early twentieth century, Peoria residents wished to find these as well. Now and then, construction projects would accidentally unearth bits and pieces of the previous lives of Peoria. A cache of gun barrels and silver ornaments—probably buried in the grave of a member of the Potawatomi—were found while digging up a plum tree. Another grave, encountered while building a marina, was found to contain a brass kettle, a *Turlington's Balsam of Life* medicine bottle, and a pair of trade silver ear bobs. The landowner "soldered a new base" on the decayed kettle, and had the earbobs melted down for use in a walking cane.[1]

Our contemporary understanding of the locations of these two villages is based on land claims made to the United States government by descendants of the original villagers, years after the abandonment of French Peoria. In the 1930s, the old land claims and the resulting surveys were overlaid onto modern city maps by historian Percival Rennick.[2] Modern archaeology came to town in the early 1980s, when Illinois State University investigated the site of the first (or "Old") French village. Based on Rennick's village plat overlay, archaeologists tested ten modern lots using a backhoe and hand excavation. No eighteenth-century features or artifacts were identified. The French past of Peoria remained elusive.

In the summer of 2001, the Department of Transportation began plans for the relocation of a principal city street at the northern end of modern downtown Peoria. I was given a map of the proposed construction area and was asked to assess the nature of the potential archaeological resources that might be impacted by the project. There was little excitement in the early phase of the project, as the neighborhood in which the construction was to take place was not subdivided until well after the Civil War. Looking at the map, however, several names of the side streets immediately rang a bell. Indeed, our project area had been visited by archaeologists once before, and the construction was headed right for the center of what had been identified by Percival Rennick as the location of the Old French Village, established during the mid-eighteenth century.

Our testing brought us to the very same lot investigated in the 1980s. The previous researchers had devised an excavation strategy based on the hopes of encountering intact, buried ground surfaces and French period artifacts. In much of this part of the city, however, there has been little broad filling of the landscape, and the surface on which we stand today is largely the same surface stood upon in 1800. When no obvious eighteenth century artifacts were encountered in the trenches, the backhoe was directed elsewhere, and nothing was found.

In 2001, our crews approached the site somewhat differently.[3] We made no assumptions about the nature of the potential eighteenth century deposits, and we opened broad excavations designed to look for any and all forms of subsurface disturbances. Aside from the obvious late nineteenth century carriage house foundations and twentieth century sewer lines, we also found what we (and many researchers before us) had been looking for. Just below the modern surface, we encountered the archaeological footprint of the first French structure to be identified in the Peoria region (figure 17.1).

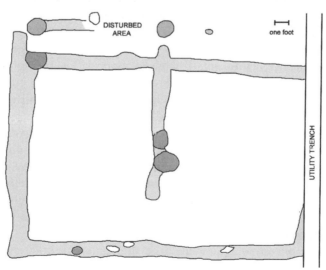

FIG. 17.1 The small post-in-earth French dwelling found at the Old French Village locale of downtown Peoria, 2001.

Most of the dwellings built by the French during the eighteenth century in Illinois are far more visible archaeologically than the log houses built by the Americans during the nineteenth century. While the French also used logs in the construction of their homes, these logs were placed upright, usually seated in narrow trenches excavated into the subsoil. This resulted in exact footprints of the structures, often including partition walls and exterior porches, which are visible archaeologically in the subsoil.

Located in the front yard of a house built in the 1870s, and crossed by modern utility lines (and even a previous archaeologist's backhoe trench) were the subsurface wall trenches of a small post-in-earth dwelling. The building was rectangular, measuring roughly thirteen by twenty feet. The structure was divided into two nearly equal sized rooms. Evidence of a small addition, and perhaps a gallery (or open exterior porch) was found on the west side of the building. Finally, after so many years of looking, Peoria could point to a French archaeological feature.

As most of the old topsoil had been lost to urban development, very few eighteenth-century artifacts were found in our excavations around the house. We recovered a single hand forged nail, a fragment of a wine bottle, a few pieces of dried mud chinking (or *bousillage*), as well as a small quantity of animal bone. Included in the sample of bone was a heel bone of a bison—one of the last such animals to have roamed Illinois.

From the early nineteenth century land claims surveys, it appears that the small structure was situated on land once owned by Louis Chatellereau, a farmer and fur trader. Chatellereau lived at the old village from the 1770s until his death in 1795. At the time of his death, his estate included three horses, twenty-five head of cattle and oxen, and seven hogs. He had fifty-six bushels of wheat and five hundred pounds of flour on hand. His estate also included one "Negro fellow." Chatellereau also owed wages to nine men for their work as *engages*, or hired fur traders.

Based on our understanding of the limits of his property and the location of the original street that one passed through the village, our excavations were conducted in what would have been the rear of his residential lot. With this in mind, the main house on the property was probably located closer to the river, and may have been destroyed by modern construction. The small structure discovered archaeologically probably served as a dwelling, but it was small for houses in French colonial Illinois. Its location away from the main street suggests that it may have functioned as a dwelling for a farm hand, a fur trader, or perhaps the slave mentioned in the estate papers.

Given the lack of dramatic artifacts and the subtlety of the feature itself, I was very pleasantly surprised by the reaction to our work by the general public and the press. The significance of the French heritage of Peoria was immediately recognized, and the excavations were soon in the national news—for the right reasons. More importantly, the local citizenry were elated with the overdue appearance of their French history in the ground. There was never any question that the village had been here, but that unassuming impression in the subsoil gave the stories an inescapable and haunting authenticity.

———

I returned to Peoria in 2004, this time to conduct casual research rather than state-funded salvage archaeology. While the Old French village was eventually covered over by a residential neighborhood, the later La Ville de Maillet or New Village (settled in 1778) became the site of the commercial heart of downtown Peoria and was probably largely destroyed by modern development. Just to be sure there was nothing left, however, I overlaid the land claims surveys on to a modern street map, as well as the Sanborn fire insurance maps of the late nineteenth century. This allowed me to see the extent of the neighborhood's development across the entire plat of the New Village.

It soon became obvious that late nineteenth century industrial buildings had heavily damaged much of the eighteenth century village. One area, however, near the south end of the village, had been used primarily as a coal storage yard during the second half of the nineteenth century, and seemed to have escaped major development. By 2004, the site was completely unobstructed by standing architecture. So in the spring of 2004, using a small amount of private funding, crews from the Sangamo Archaeological Center began looking for a piece of La Ville de Maillet.

The site was much different than the one tested in 2001. In that project, the ground surface had actually been lowered slightly by urban development. At this site, we encountered the opposite—five feet of fill soil deposited during the second half of the nineteenth century. At the base of our fifth deep trench, however, we found something very exciting: a layer of well preserved but deeply buried topsoil. Essentially, at five feet below the 2004 ground surface, we struck the ground surface of 1800 (figure 17.2).

In that buried topsoil were the first glimpses of the second French village at Peoria. Although a lack of time and funding limited the area we could investigate, our trenches encountered a light midden dating to the late eighteenth and early nineteenth century, as well as another French

ONE INCH

FIG. 17.2 View of the 2004 excavations at La Ville de Maillet, with artifacts recovered from the buried pre-1820 topsoils: gunflint, burnt creamware, redware, and a carbonized corn cob.

feature: a fragment of large wall trench that would have been used to support a fence line made of vertical posts. Scattered on both sides of that fence line were very small quantities of creamware, redware, animal bone, eighteenth-century gunflints, and even a small burnt corncob.

The bits of plain redware and creamware buried beneath five feet of fill and mixed with deer, beaver, and bison bones were remarkably powerful for such unassuming debris. Most of the creamware was fire shattered, and from our archival research we learned that this particular lot (once owned by Antoine Leclaire) had been burned by Captain Craig during his 1812 attack on the village. While there was plenty of burned household debris on the early nineteenth century frontier, it is possible that the tiny pieces of burned creamware found in our trenches were reverberations of Craig's malicious fires.

Our View from the Twenty-First Century

Down the trail, Americans began to colonize the Sangamon River valley while the fire-shattered creamware was still lying on the ground at Peoria. Some of the first changes noticed by the new settlers occurred in the natural world. The legendary numbers of flies and snakes that had plagued the first settlers were quickly reduced, as were the honeybees that drew some of the first Americans to the area. The forests began to thin in the face of so much firewood, but this was probably not noticed by most. Within five years of the first remembered cabin to be built in the valley, two new towns had been platted and many new plans were hatched. Twenty years later, the place had become the state capital of Illinois. The frontier had moved further north, leaving yet another new American community in its wake.

A lot of things changed at Sangamo after the summer of the Black Hawk War. The Royal brothers moved on, one sick with lead poisoning and one following the church. One of their last kiln loads would be discovered in the 1990s, in a big pit labeled feature 1. John McNamar and Sam Hill abandoned the little dwelling behind their "magnificent store house," and nearby an old still house was dismantled. Elijah Iles became more and more wealthy, and the location of his historic store (once the center of the community) was eclipsed by the new public square. The little addition in the rear of the store was soon torn down, sealing up a small sample of the debris from Iles's storekeeping days. At Elkhart Hill, Richard and Margaret Latham probably opened their tavern around this time, remodeling their house and filling in an old cistern. The widowed Mary Latham prepared to leave the family home that would be remembered as the first such house in the region. Along the river, Sangamo Town lost its tavern, its two stores, and its original mill, leaving Charles Broadwell nearly alone in what was supposed to be a thriving downtown. Rainstorms washed mud into open cellars.

Across the nation, new products and technologies quickly changed life at its most prosaic levels, and the gulf between 1820 and 1850 was seen as incredible even then. Steel plows effectively cut through the ancient prairies of the Midwest, and "Lucifer matches" made fire without striking a stone. Packaged foods made mealtime more interesting, and better stoneware made leftovers safer. Railroads began to appear on some parts of the landscape, forecasting the future. Gaslight began to illuminate city streets, and cooking stoves pulled us away from the hearth for the first time in human history.

And then the stories started—of pioneer hardships, forests filled with savages, and of making do without:

> Oh! What changes have swept over these people in the swift flight of time since that day. . . . The mental anguish that I suffered, tongue cannot tell or pen describe. . . . Ye of Sangamon of 1879 who prate of hard times, prithee, would you think, if you had to remain at home alone, a stranger, in this vast wilderness.
>
> Mrs. John Lock, July 30, 1879[4]

Archaeological sites of the period betray another reality to the life described by Mrs. Lock. The frontier left behind surprising items given their original context. As an archaeologist specializing in the period, I soon found myself learning much about English teacups, and little about gun hardware. The log houses may have been neomedieval dwellings at the edge of the wilderness, but they were well stocked with fine, nonessential goods. This contrast must have been remarkable.

The archaeological history of this particular American frontier seems to speak of behavior that actively attempted to disprove the warnings made by La Salle's men 150 years earlier as they looted Fort Crevecoeur. We are *not* savages. Yes, the phantoms on these sites seem to say, we are living in the forests inside homes made of logs and mud, but we do so by choice. The little worlds that we carve out of the wilderness are altogether different than the huts occupied by the neighboring Potawatomi and Kickapoo "savages."

Hence, the single most common artifact type from such archaeological sites, not counting nails or brick fragments, are English teacup or saucer fragments. On the early nineteenth century American frontier, the stocking of the cupboard with goods that were not really practical or necessary for survival was clearly part of an appropriate practice— as elemental as the surveying of village lot lines or replacing fords with bridges.

Many decades later, long after the passing of the frontier and the deaths of its pioneer participants, the objects plowed up at their home sites can be easily mistaken for what they are to us today: a broken plate, a bottle, or a button. Particularly because these items were mass-produced, such assumptions are natural. The meanings of objects, however, are not fixed. They can be manipulated or renamed by their users in different ways and in different settings. Within the early nineteenth century log cabin, a shell-edged plate was probably an all-too-common comfort item—something most families had always purchased, nearly invisible to them unless it was missing. A printed tea cup imported from England was an appropriate formality at the table set by the store-keeper's wife, but glass stemware may have been regarded by most as excessive or unnecessary.

The apparent plainness of a coarse redware pitcher found on an archaeological site is misleading. It was not purchased out of necessity, or for a lack of something better. It was a choice, the meaning of which is not readily apparent today. Such was the strength of the tradition of redware crockery in certain households that potters such as the Royal brothers and John Ebey managed to find a market for old fashioned plates and plain redware table bowls in the face of the thousands of fancier, inexpensive Queenswares stocked at the local stores. Yes, brass buttons kept vests closed, teacups served warm liquids, and figural brandy flasks stored and dispensed liquor. Each of these, however, could have been replaced by cheaper, more practical, bone buttons, tin cups, and wooden kegs. They weren't replaced, however, perhaps because they *meant* something beyond their obvious utilitarian function. And that meaning was probably different in the time and place we call the frontier.

It is often virtually impossible to picture the rich complexity of someone's little domestic universe while standing on its plowed-up, partially-excavated archaeological remains. One hundred and seventy five years ago stood a log house and some small buildings just behind. A garden, some fences, some paths. Four log piles and three wood piles. A rope strung between two trees, with an ugly shirt blowing in the wind. A horse and some cows in a pen. Hogs wandering in the distance. Three barrels lying in some weeds and dozens of things we do not think to imagine. One hundred and seventy-five years later, a stripped clay surface rapidly dries out in the summer sun. What was once "home" is now occupied by several pick up trucks, a backhoe, and five or six archaeologists on their hands and knees, troweling away next to lunch boxes and a radio.

Slowly, archaeology creeps across the landscape, occasionally rescuing a site from something new and modern. Most are not rescued, however, and surprisingly little is done with those that are. I would like to think that someday, an archaeologist will recover that single andiron that Christiana Tillson watched tossed from a hot fire by a stubborn pioneer nearly 200 years ago. I doubt that will happen, but somewhere, that andiron still exists. Its peculiar past does as well.

And what if that andiron is recovered? Many of the details presented in the preceding pages are not revelatory observations on the history of the human occupation of Illinois. We should not be surprised to find whisky bottles at a tavern site, or scissors and thimbles from a farmstead. These artifacts, however, are very real shadows of the habits and desires of the people who actually composed that remarkable time that was the frontier.

Few of us can really fully accept the authenticity of the past, or of the places that were once part of that past. Old documents and recollections often become like parables, obscuring the humanity of the characters that sparked these tales. At New Salem, the public is aware that the log houses are replicas, and the staff is aware that they are dressed in period costumes. A tiny thimble is pulled from the ground, and suddenly the old phantoms fill with flesh.

Archaeological remains, at their most basic, are connections, windows, fossils, or reverberations of a reality that would otherwise exist only on paper. The difference between a story and the perceived authenticity of that story is tangibility. An archaeological excavation is the tactile touch that keeps a past event, an abandoned place, or a distant lifetime from becoming yet another tale to be accepted or dismissed. As invisible or intangible as the past becomes, its connection to us remains. The things in the ground are the paths.

Notes

Chapter 1

1. Solon Buck, *Illinois in 1818* (Illinois Centennial Commission, Springfield, 1917), 58.
2. William Faux, *Memorable Days in America* (Simpkin and Marshall, London 1823), 309.
3. Clarissa Emely Gear Hobbs, "Autobiography of Clarissa Emely Gear Hobbs," *Journal of the Illinois State Historical Society* 17, 4 (1925): 612–14.
4. Letter from William Greene to William Herndon in Wilson and Davis, *Herndon's Informants* (University of Illinois Press, Urbana, 1998), 408.
5. Inter-State Publishing, *History of Sangamon County Illinois* (Chicago 1881), 60.
6. The site of Eliza's fiancé's rural Tazewell County home was recently discovered as part of Illinois Transportation Archaeological Research Program surveys. Unfortunately, it was found to have been largely destroyed by early twentieth century road construction.
7. Charles Hoffman, *A Winter in the West* (Harper, New York 1835), 33; Thomas Hamilton *Men and Manners in America* (A. M. Kelly, New York 1833), 173.
8. Christiana Tillson, *A Woman's Story of Pioneer Illinois* (Southern Illinois University Press, Carbondale, 1995), 58.
9. Edmund Flagg, *The Far West* (Harper, New York 1838), 5.
10. Rebecca Burlend and Edmund Burlend, *A True Picture of Immigration* (Citadel Press, New York, 1968), 42–43.
11. O. E. Rolvagg, *Giants in the Earth* (Harper and Row, New York, 1927), 32.
12. Charles Boewe, *Prairie Albion: An Early Settlement in Pioneer Illinois* (Southern Illinois University Press, Carbondale, 1962); Grady McWhiney, *Cracker Cul-*

ture: Celtic Ways in the Old South (University of Alabama Press, Tuscaloosa, 1988).
13. Boewe, *Prairie Albion*, 46.

Chapter 2

1. John Francis McDermott, *Old Cahokia* (St. Louis Historical Documents Foundation, St. Louis, 1949), 234.
2. William McAdams, *Records of Ancient Races* (C. R. Barns, St. Louis 1887).
3. It has generally been assumed that the first controlled excavations conduced by the Dickson family occurred as part of the opening of their burial exhibits in 1927. Recently, I examined several Dickson family photo albums, and discovered a series of photographs that include a carefully excavated burial, dated October 1915 and attributed to Marion Dickson.
4. Kenneth Farnsworth, *Early Hopewell Mound Explorations* (Illinois Transportation Archaeological Research Program, University of Illinois, Urbana 2004).
5. Our work at New Salem State Historic Site was partially funded by the Illinois Historic Preservation Agency, in cooperation with the New Salem Lincoln League, which is a private organization.
6. A recently discovered county document reveals Lincoln may have ultimately acquired a half interest in the store property. See Robert Mazrim, *Magnificent Storehouses and Forgotten Lot Lines* (Sangamo Archaeological Center, Elkhart, Illinois 2005).
7. Joseph Booton, transcribed interview with Thomas Reep (1934 manuscript, on file Illinois Historic Preservation Agency, Springfield).

Chapter 3

1. The Peoria, Kaskaskia, Cahokia, Tamaroa, and Michigamea were the five principal tribes present in the eighteenth century.
2. Duane Esarey, *The Illinois Indians Before 1673*, paper presented at the 68th Annual Meeting of the Society for American Archaeology, Milwaukee, Wisconsin 2003.
3. Larry Grantham, "The Illini Village of the Marquette and Jolliet Voyage of 1673," *The Missouri Archaeologist* 54 1993: 1 20; Kathleen Ehrhardt, "Linking History and Prehistory in the Midcontinent: Archaeological Investigations at Marquette and Jolliet's 'Peouarea'" *Aboriginal Ritual and Economy in the Eastern Woodlands: Essays in Memory of Howard Dalton Winters* (Illinois State Museum, Springfield 2004).
4. Robert E. Warren and John A. Walthall, "Illini Indians and the Illinois Country 1673–1832," *The Living Museum* 60, 11 (1998): 4–8; Wayne Temple *Indian Villages of the Illinois Country* (Illinois State Museum, Springfield, 1966).
5. Clarence Walworth Alvord, *The Illinois Country 1673–1818* (Illinois Centennial Commission, Springfield, 1920); Floyd Mulkey, "Fort St. Louis at Peoria," *Journal of Illinois State Historical Society* 37 (1998): 301–16.
6. Carl Ekberg, *French Roots in the Illinois Country* (University of Illinois Press, Urbana 2000).

7. Margaret Kimball Brown and Lawrie Cena Dean, *The French Colony in the Mid-Mississippi Valley* (American Kestrel Books, Carbondale, Illinois, 1995), 21.

8. Large-scale construction projects, technically eligible for state and federally funded archaeology, continue to destroy the remains of antebellum St. Louis to this day. The construction of a new football stadium in the early 1990s and a new baseball stadium in 2004 destroyed vast areas of archaeological deposits.

9. N. D. Mereness, *Travels in the American Colonies* (Macmillan, New York, 1916), 363; Clarence W. Alvord and Clarence E. Carter, *The Critical Period: 1763–1765* (Illinois Centennial Commission, Springfield, 1915), 293; E. G. Mason, *Phillippe de Rocheblave and Rocheblave Papers: Historical Sketch and Notes* (Fergus Historical Series, Chicago 1890), 262; Robert Mazrim, *New Light on the Old French Village of Peoria* (Sangamo Archaeological Center, Elkhart 2002).

10. Judith Franke, *French Peoria and the Illinois Country* (Illinois State Museum, Springfield, 1995).

11. Gales and Seaton, *American State Papers: Public Lands* (Washington 1834), 3:476.

12. Zimri Enos, "The Old Indian Trail, Sangamon County, Illinois," *Journal of the Illinois State Historical Society* 4, 2 (1911): 218–22; John Mack Faragher, *Sugar Creek, Life on the Illinois Prairie* (Yale University Press, New Haven, Connecticut, 1986).

13. This research is summarized in Robert Mazrim, *"Now Quite Out of Society": Archaeology and Frontier Illinois* (Illinois Transportation Archaeological Research Program, University of Illinois, Urbana 2002), 23–50.

14. C. E. Carter, *The Territorial Papers of the United States*, vol. 16, *The Territory of Illinois 1809–1814* (Washington, D.C., 1948), 288.

15. Seymour Feiler, *Jean-Bernard Bossu's Travels in the Interior of North America, 1751–1762* (University of Oklahoma Press, Norman, 1962), 107; Charles Balesi, *The Time of the French in the Heart of North America* (Alliance Française, Chicago, 1992), 161.

16. Duane Esarey, "Seasonal Occupation Patterns in Illinois History: A Case Study in the Lower Illinois River Valley" *Illinois Archaeology* 9, 1 and 2 (1997): 164–219.

17. Early Woodland pottery has been found by the author on Elkhart Hill, and recovered by collectors from other nearby upland sites along the route of Edwards' Trace. The unique Middle Woodland site is known as the Yellow Bluffs site, and is located just east of Elkhart Hill. A Mississippian component is present at that site, as well as the nearby Shire site. In Macoupin County (and also located directly along the trail) is the Bunker Hill site, which produced a large cache of ceremonial blades from Late Archaic mortuary contexts.

Chapter 4

1. Clarence Alvord, *Kaskaskia Records* (Collections of the Illinois State Historical Library, Springfield, 1909), 421.

2. Edmond Flagg, *The Far West*, cited in Belting, *Kaskaskia Under the French Regime* (Southern Illinois University Press, Carbondale 2003), 27; Carter, *The Territorial Papers of the United States*, vol. 16, *The Territory of Illinois 1809–1814*, 93.

3. Thomas Ashe *Travels in America* (New York 1811), 290; Frederick Bates 1807

cited in James Neal Primm, *Lion of the Valley: St. Louis, Missouri* (Pruett Publishing, Boulder, Colorado, 1990), 88.

4. Buck, *Illinois in 1818;* McWhiney, *Cracker Culture: Celtic Ways in the Old South;* Henry Glassie, *Pattern in Material Folk Culture of the Eastern United States* (University of Pennsylvania Press, Philadelphia, 1968); Nicole Etcheson, *The Emerging Midwest* (Indiana University Press, Bloomington, 1996); Samuel Hilliard "Pork in the Antebellum South," *Annals of the Association of American Geographers* 59, 3 (1969): 461–80.

5. Selwyn Troen and Glen Holt, *St. Louis* (New Viewpoints, New York, 1977), 25; Robert Kirkpatrick, "History of St. Louis 1804–1816" (masters thesis, Washington University, St. Louis, 1947), 16.

6. Troen and Holt, *St. Louis,* 211; Primm, *Lion of the Valley: St. Louis, Missouri.*

7. Boewe, *Prairie Albion,* 119.

8. Eliza Farnham, *Life in Prairie Land* (University of Illinois Press, Urbana, 1988), 242.

9. Robert Mazrim, *"Now Quite Out of Society": Archaeology and Frontier Illinois* (Illinois Transportation Archaeological Research Program, University of Illinois, Urbana 2002), 173–89; Mazrim and John A. Walthall, *Queensware by the Crate* (Sangamo Archaeological Center, Elkhart, Illinois 2002).

10. Such barter was based on fixed market prices for produce at the nearest entrepot, such as St. Louis.

11. Farnham, *Life in Prairie Land,* 114.

12. Barbara Lawrence and Nedra Branz, *The Flagg Correspondence: Selected Letters 1816–1854* (Southern Illinois University Press, Carbondale, 1986), 24.

Chapter 5

1. Lawrence and Branz, *The Flagg Correspondence,* 16; Hoffman, *A Winter in the West,* 41.

2. Lawrence and Branz, *The Flagg Correspondence,* 26.

3. Lawrence and Branz, *The Flagg Correspondence,* 32.

4. Curtis Mann, "Beer on the Frontier," *Illinois Heritage* 7, 2(2004): 9.

5. Mrs. Perry Smith "Reminiscences of an Old Settler," *Illinois State Genealogical Society Quarterly* 10, 4 (1978): 217–19.

6. Lawrence and Branz, *The Flagg Correspondence,* 19.

7. Farnham, *Life in Prairie Land,* 191.

8. Tillson, *A Woman's Story of Pioneer Illinois,* 74, Robert Mazrim, *Abandoned Cellars and Community Memory: An Examination of the Archaeology and Interpretations of the New Salem Site* (report submitted to the Illinois Historic Preservation Agency, Springfield, 1995), 48.

9. Burlend and Burlend, *A True Picture of Immigration,* 50.

10. Tillson, *A Woman's Story of Pioneer Illinois,* 81; Peter Cartwright, *Autobiography of Peter Cartwright* (Cranston and Curtis, Cincinnati 1856), 330; Burlend and Burlend, *A True Picture of Immigration,* 49; Farnham, *Life in Prairie Land,* 39; Tillson, *A Woman's Story of Pioneer Illinois,* 66.

11. Farnham, *Life in Prairie Land,* 127.

12. Farnham, *Life in Prairie Land,* 127.

13. Farnham, *Life in Prairie Land*, 38.

Chapter 6

1. George Holley et al., *Historic Archaeology of the Scott Joint-Use Archaeological Project* (report submitted to the Illinois Department of Transportation, Springfield, 1996); Mazrim, *"Now Quite Out of Society,"* 102–55.
2. Charles Faulkner, "The Pit Cellar: A Nineteenth Century Storage Facility," *Proceedings of the Symposium on Ohio Valley Urban and Historic Archaeology* (Archaeological Survey, University of Louisville, Louisville Kentucky, 1986), 54–65; Mazrim, *"Now Quite Out of Society,"* 162–63; Joseph Phillippe and William Walters, "Rats, Damp and Fowl Miasma: Some Thoughts on the Literature and Archaeology of Pioneer Cellars," *Wisconsin Archaeologist* 67, 1 (1986): 37–46.
3. William Oliver, *Eight Months in Illinois* (Southern Illinois University Press, Carbondale 2002), 141.
4. The effort of digging a substantial hole near the house for burying garbage was hardly necessary on the rural Illinois frontier. Farms of this period were situated on 40 to 160 acre tracts of land, most of which included a variety of ravines or overgrown areas where garbage could have been disposed. Further, an early nineteenth century rural household would have been troubled with little bulky garbage to dispose of in the first place. Free ranging hogs, dogs or raccoons would have devoured butchered carcasses and food remains shortly after they were deposited on the ground. Wood scrap was probably burned in the fireplace for heat. Durable materials (such as window glass, iron scrap or broken ceramic and glass vessels) seem to have been first left in rubbish piles or scattered about in certain areas of the farmyard ground surface.
5. Edith Longbons, who was born in Wabash County in 1920, remembered shallow pits dug into the garden during the fall, filed with potatoes, apples, or cabbages, and covered with straw, heavy paper, and soil. Curtis Mann, personal communication, 2003.
6. The exception to this may have been in the floodplains, where shallow, sometimes-flooded wells could have been occasionally replaced. The Losch Farms site in Madison County included several wells and cisterns that do not appear to have been contemporary with one another. See Mazrim, *"Now Quite Out of Society,"* 67–82.

Chapter 7

1. *Louisiana Gazette*, November 9, 1808, 3:3.
2. Holley et al., *Historic Archaeology of the Scott Joint-Use Archaeological Project*; Joseph Phillippe, "The Robert Watts Site: Archaeological Excavation of a Late Eighteenth / Early Nineteenth Century Euroamerican Farmstead," *Illinois Archaeology* 5, 1 and 2 (1993): 512–36; Mazrim, *"Now Quite Out of Society,"* 53–157; Mazrim, *The Historic Component of the Lillie Site: An Incidental Glimpse of Robert Pulliam's Territorial Period Homestead* (report submitted to the Illinois Transportation Archaeological Research Program, Urbana 2003). Mazrim, *The*

Perrackson Site (report submitted to the Illinois Transportation Archaeological Research Program, Urbana 2004).

3. This assumption is probably based on expectations learned from prehistoric sites, which often include special function features such a roasting or smudge pits that do produce artifacts directly associated with their use.

4. Stanley South, *Method and Theory in Historical Archaeology* (Acedemic Press, New York, 1977), 95.

5. Neil Ewins, *"Supplying the Present Wants of Our Yankee Cousins . . . ": Staffordshire Ceramics and the American Market 1775–1880* (City Museum and Art Gallery, Stoke-on-Trent, 1998).

6. For discussions of these ware types see Ivor Noel-Hume, *Guide to Colonial Artifacts of North America* (Knopf, New York, 1969); Noel-Hume, "Creamware to Pearlware: A Williamsburg Perspective" in *Ceramics in America*, ed. Ian Quimby (Winterthur Museum, Deleware, 1973); Ted Lofstrom, Jeffrey Tordoff, and Douglas George, "A Seriation of Historic Earthenwares in the Midwest, 1780–1870," *Minnesota Archaeologist* 4, 1 (1982): 3–12; George Miller, "A Revised Set of CC Index Values for Classification and Economic Scaling of English Ceramics from 1787 to 1880," *Historical Archaeology* 25, 1 (1991): 1–25; George Miller, "A User's Guide to Ceramic Assemblages, Part Four," *Council for Northeast Historical Archaeology Newsletter* 26 (1993); George Miller and Robert Hunter, "How Creamware Got the Blues: The Origins of China Glaze and Pearlware" in *Ceramics in America*, ed. Ian Quimby (Winterthur Museum, Deleware, 1973).

7. Potter John Ebey did use the term *redware* in an 1882 recollection, however. See chapter 11.

8. Galena-area potteries in northern Illinois, which continued to make redware well into the last quarter of the nineteenth century, are an exception. See Wayne Horney, *Pottery of the Galena Area* (Telegraph-Herald, East Dubuque, Illinois, 1965); Floyd Mansberger, *Nineteenth Century Redware Production in Northwestern Illinois: Archaeological Investigations at the Elizabeth Pottery Site, Jo Daviess County, Illinois* (report submitted to the Illinois Department of Transportation, Springfield, 1994).

9. Mazrim, *"Now Quite Out of Society,"* 274.

10. Robert Mazrim and Dennis Naglich, *Further Archaeological Investigations at Lincoln's New Salem State Historic Site: Evidence for the First Joshua Miller Residence and Blacksmith Shop* (report submitted to the Illinois Historic Preservation Agency, Springfield, 1996), 53.

11. Mazrim and Naglich, *Further Archaeological Investigations at Lincoln's New Salem State Historic Site*, 50.

12. Nineteenth-century archaeological sites have been excavated as part of cultural resource management programs in Illinois since the late 1970s. Given the deadline driven, increasingly competitive nature of contract archaeology, however, "big picture" synthesis of findings has usually suffered. The cumulative effect has been a stack of hard to find descriptive reports, full of artifact inventories, but lacking in the kind of databased summary that allows for the next report to build on the findings of the last. This is particularly true with the mass produced material culture of any given era in the nineteenth century. Often, archaeological reports describe artifacts as if they have not been seen be-

fore. While a few token artifacts from a site might be compared or contrasted with those from one or two other sites, there have been few attempts to crunch numbers from a series of sites to begin to see the larger patterns responsible for the debris in the first place.

13. The initial study, published in 2002, included data from seventeen short-term sites dating from ca. 1810 to ca. 1835. The database has since expanded to include over thirty frontier-context sites across Illinois, comprising over 1500 ceramic and glass vessels.

14. Unfortunately, sherd counts are still far more common than vessel counts in the archeological literature of the Midwest, although this is beginning to change. Prior to 1995 in Illinois, fewer than 10 percent of the technical reports of excavations at historic sites included vessel counts. Simple inventories of fragments are not reliable indicators of practices or behavior at a particular site; they are simply catalogs of destruction. As an example, a site bearing sixty fragments of five pearlware plates and forty fragments of fifteen whiteware plates does not produce an assemblage composed of 60 percent pearlware. The site is actually dominated by whiteware vessels by a margin of 3 to 1. The description of how badly damaged objects became after they were no longer in use does not provide a picture of the behavior of their original owners.

15. Mazrim, *The Old Greene County Courthouse and the Riddle of Buried Eden* (Sangamo Research Services, Athens, Illinois, 1997).

16. While many residents of the frontier would have added to their collection at local estate sales, those estates had also been breaking and buying new vessels as well.

17. With the exception of chamber pots, which are found in urban contexts into the early 1840s.

18. Mazrim and Naglich, *Further Archaeological Investigations at Lincoln's New Salem State Historic Site,* 44.

19. Part of this dominance based on the fact that, by counting each vessel individually, saucers and cups are inventoried separately. Cups and saucers were usually sold as a pair, and were intended to be sold in sets of six. So, by counting saucers and cups separately, we may be elevating the teaware count. The counts were kept separate, however due to the fact that we rarely find matching cups and saucers. A red cup and a blue saucer, then probably reflect *two* cup and saucer sets, or four vessels. For this reason, we keep the counts separate, and also for this reason, they are probably a reasonably accurate picture of the ratio of each vessel type in the household over time.

Chapter 8

1. *Report of the Sangamon River Basin in Illinois* (Illinois State Planning Commission, Springfield, 1938).

2. Bellin Map 1755, in Tucker and Temple, *Atlas and Supplement of Indian Villages of the Illinois Country,* plate 24 (Illinois State Museum, Springfield, 1975).

3. Alice Berksen, "Cultural Resistance of the Prairie Kickapoo at the Grand Village, McLean County, Illinois" *Illinois Archaeology* 4, 2 (1992): 107–205.

4. The excavations at the site, conducted by the Illinois State Museum in the early 1970s, have yet to be fully reported.

5. John Walthall, F. Terry Norris, and Barbara Stafford, "Woman Chief's Village: An Illini Winter Hunting Camp," in *Calumet and Fleur-de-Lys*, ed. John Walthall (Smithsonian Press, Washington D.C., 1992).

6. Esarey, "Seasonal Occupation Patterns in Illinois History: A Case Study in the Lower Illinois River Valley," 25.

7. The frontier era town site of Exeter, located in the central Mauvaise Terre valley, is thought to have first been the site of fur-trade related activity as late as 1819. Private artifact collections from the area include a few potentially associated with late eighteenth or early nineteenth century fur-trading activity.

8. Brink, McDonough & Co., *History of Madison County Illinois* (Edwardsville, Illinois 1882), 72.

9. James Davis, *Frontier Illinois* (Indiana University Press, Bloomington, 1998); Theodore Calvin Pease, *The Frontier State 1818–1848* (University of Illinois Press, Urbana, 1919); Frank Stevens, *The Black Hawk War including a Review of Black Hawk's Life* (Chicago, 1903).

10. Carter, *The Territorial Papers of the United States*, vol. 16, *The Territory of Illinois 1809–1814*, 290.

11. Carter, *The Territorial Papers of the United States*, vol. 16, *The Territory of Illinois 1809–1814*, 197.

12. Ninian Edwards, *History of Illinois from 1778 to 1833 and Life and Times of Ninian Edwards* (Illinois State Journal Company, Springfield 1870), 314.

13. Edwards, *History of Illinois*, 313.

14. That honor may go to a small trading post said to have been established by the Lorton (or Lartonaire) brothers on the Sangamon River near the modern city of Decatur in or before 1816. While an archaeological site dating to the early nineteenth century has been found at the traditional location of the post, the exact year of its construction and the nature of its occupation is still very poorly understood. See Hall et. al. *The Search for the Lortons' Trading Post* (Illinois State Museum, Springfield, 1969); Curtis Mann "The Laughton Brothers: First Settlers of the Sangamon River Valley?" *The Feature* 1, 2 (2005): 1.

15. John Reynolds, *My Own Times* (University Microfilms, Ann Arbor, 1968), 82; Carter, *The Territorial Papers of the United States*, vol. 16, *The Territory of Illinois 1809–1814*, 363.

16. Reynolds, *My Own Times*, 87.

17. That village was probably what is known today as the Rhodes site.

18. Carter, *The Territorial Papers of the United States*, vol. 16, *The Territory of Illinois 1809–1814*, 269; Reynolds *My Own Times*, 86–90.

19. Tucker and Temple, *Atlas and Supplement of Indian Villages of the Illinois Country*, plate 29.

20. Lucien Campeau, "Les Cartes Relatives a la Decouverte du Mississippi: par le P. Jacques Marquette et Louis Jolliet" *Les Cahiers des Dix* 47 (1992): 41–90.

21. Much of this brief summary of the Long map comes from an unpublished paper by the author and Duane Esarey.

Chapter 9

1. C. E. Carter, *The Territorial Papers of the United States: Volume XVII The Territory of Illinois 1814–1818* (Washington, D.C., 1950), 432.

2. Carter, *The Territorial Papers of the United States*, 482–85.

3. Carter, *The Territorial Papers of the United States*, 487, 503.
4. In 2002, Illinois Transportation Archaeological Research Program (ITARP) excavated part of what is believed to have been Pulliam's farm in Madison County. Only a single pit feature associated with the early nineteenth century occupation of the site was encountered (the remaining features were prehistoric). That pit, probably used as an exterior food storage facility, contained a small sample of artifacts dating to the 1810s. See Robert Mazrim, *The Historic Component of the Lillie Site: An Incidental Glimpse of Robert Pulliam's Territorial Period Homestead* (report submitted to the Illinois Transportation Archaeological Research Program, Urbana 2003).
5. One of the earliest accounts of Pulliam's journey appeared in John Carroll Power, *History of Early Settlers of Sangamon County Illinois* (Wilson and Company, Springfield 1876). John Mack Faragher has written an extensive history of the settlement established by Pulliam (*Sugar Creek, Life on the Illinois Prairie*), and more recently, David Brady has provided a more detailed look at Pulliam's sometimes-troubled life in Madison County during the 1810s (David Brady and Bill Furry, "Hero or Hellion? *Illinois Times* 29, 45 [2004]: 9–14). The site of Pulliam's home on Sugar Creek has yet to be identified archaeologically, but may have been destroyed by suburban residential development as recently as the late 1980s.
6. Inter-State Publishing, *History of Sangamon County Illinois*, 46.
7. Lawrence and Branz, *The Flagg Correspondence*, 17.
8. Lawrence and Branz, *The Flagg Correspondence*, 24.
9. E. P. Baker, "Travels in Illinois in 1819 Ferdinand Ernst," *Transactions of the Illinois State Historical Society for the Year 1903* (Illinois State Historical Library, Springfield, 1903), 150–65.
10. That number is drawn from the tax records dating to 1821, and the assumption that there were also a number of people had moved on prior to the making of the tax lists, or who were missed by county officials. See Curtis Mann, *The First Citizens of Sangamon County* (Sangamo Archaeological Center, Elkhart 2003).
11. Curtis Mann and David Brady, "Sangamo Township," *Historico* (Newsletter of the Sangamon County Historical Society, November 2003).
12. Mann and Brady, "Sangamo Township."
13. Sangamon County Commissioners minutes, April 10, 1821.
14. Buck, *Illinois in 1818*, 95.
15. Mann, *The First Citizens of Sangamon County*, 62.
16. *Edwardsville Spectator*, February 22, 1825, 3:2.
17. Curtis Mann, personal communication 2005.
18. Informal census published in the *Sangamo Journal*, December 12, 1835.
19. Davis, *Frontier Illinois*, 205.
20. Cartwright, *Autobiography of Peter Cartwright*, 249, Inter-State Publishing, *History of Sangamon County Illinois*, 173; Fern Nance Pond, "The Memoirs of James McGrady Rutledge, *Journal of the Illinois State Historical Society* 29, 1 (1936): 76–88.

Chapter 10

1. Latham family papers, Abraham Lincoln Presidential Library Manuscripts Collection, Springfield.

2. Baker, "Travels in Illinois in 1819 Ferdinand Ernst," 150–65.
3. James Rice, *Peoria City and Peoria County Illinois: A Record of Settlement, Organization, Progress, and Achievement* (S. J. Clark, Chicago, 1912), 131.
4. Latham family papers, Abraham Lincoln Presidential Library Manuscripts Collection, Springfield.
5. James Latham probate papers, Peoria County.
6. Simeon Shaw, *History of Staffordshire Potters; and the Rise and Progress of the Manufacture of Pottery and Porcelain; with Reference to Genuine Specimens* (Praeger, New York, 1970), 234.
7. Several have been found at Fort Michilimackinac in northern Michigan, which was abandoned in 1781. See Lyle Stone, *Fort Michilimackinac: An Archaeological Perspective on the Revolutionary Frontier* (Michigan State University, East Lansing, 1974), 177.
8. It is possibly the mark of William Christie of Leith.
9. Dennis Naglich and Mary Jo Cramer, *Davenport House Site: 2003 Archaeological Investigations* (unpublished manuscript, Archaeological Research Center, St. Louis, 2004); Robert Mazrim, *Archaeological Testing at the Upper Village of Prairie du Chien, Wisconsin* (1999–2001 manuscript and notes, on file Sangamo Archaeological Center, Elkhart).
10. Oscar Schilke and Raphael Solomon, *America's Foreign Coins* (Coin and Currency Institute, New York, 1964).
11. Inter-State Publishing, *History of Sangamon County Illinois*, 177.
12. A courthouse fire destroyed most of the court and deed records relating to Logan County from 1837 to 1857.

Chapter 11

1. The principal citation for this chapter is the author's report on our excavations at Cotton Hill. See Robert Mazrim, *The Earthenware of Cotton Hill: An Archaeological Study of Redware from the Ebey-Brunk Kiln Site in Sangamon County, Illinois* (Sangamo Archaeological Center, Elkhart 2003).
2. Steven Ahler et al., *Cultural Inventory of the Hunter Lake Area: A Proposed Reservoir Impoundment in Sangamon County, Illinois* (Illinois State Museum, Springfield, 1994).
3. It is also possible that the kiln in 1860 was in a different location that that of the mid-1830s kiln.
4. Royal family papers, Abraham Lincoln Presidential Library Manuscript Collection, and Richard Hart, *Genealogy of the Descendants of Thomas Royal* (manuscript on file, Sangamo Archaeological Center, Elkhart).
5. Royal family papers, Abraham Lincoln Presidential Library Manuscript Collection, Springfield.
6. Power, *History of Early Settlers of Sangamon County Illinois*, 631.
7. Fred Lockley, *Impressions and Observations of the Journal Man* (undated manuscript on file, Sangamo Archaeological Center, Elkhart).
8. John Ebey "The Beginnings of the Clay Business" *White Hall Republican* 1/7/1882 1:5.
9. Power, *History of Early Settlers of Sangamon County Illinois*, 125.
10. Sangamon County Census of Industry, 1850.

11. Bonnie Gums, "Yellow Ware in Illinois: The Wilhelms' Kiln," *Ohio Valley Historical Archaeology* 11 (1996): 175–93; Robert Mazrim, "An Overview of Redware Vessels Recovered from Quincy, Illinois" (manuscript on file, Sangamo Archaeological Center, Elkhart, 1995).

12. "William Carpenter Grocery Account Book," December 11, 1830–March 16, 1831, Abraham Lincoln Presidential Library Manuscript Collection.

13. In Vermilion County, the Kirkpatrick family established a stoneware kiln during the late 1830s, which produced alongside the typical utilitarian wares a number of more fancifully decorated items, as well as anthropomorphic smoking pipes. See Bonnie Gums et al., *The Kirkpatricks' Potteries in Illinois: A Family Tradition* (Illinois Transportation Archaeological Research Program, Urbana, 1997).

14. Mazrim, *"Now Quite Out of Society,"* 245–48, Mazrim and Walthall, *Queensware by the Crate.*

15. Mazrim, *"Now Quite Out of Society,"* 209, 265–68.

16. Leslie Haskins "Three Early Oregon Potteries of Barnett Ramsey," *Oregon Historical Quarterly* 43, 3 (1942): 175–93.

17. The feature 1 samples appear to date circa 1826–32, while the samples from units 1 and 2 date ca. 1830–50.

18. For example, Steven Pendery, "Changing Redware Production in Southern New Hampshire," *Domestic Pottery of the Northeastern United States*, ed. Sarah Peabody (Academic Press, Orlando, 1985).

Chapter 12

1. The principal citation for this chapter is our report of excavations at the Iles Store site. See Mazrim and Curtis Mann, *The Beginnings of a State Capital* (Sangamo Archaeological Center, Elkhart 2005).

2. Sangamon County Commissioners' Court Minutes, June 5, 1821.

3. Elijah Iles, *Sketches of Early Life in Kentucky, Missouri, and Illinois* (Springfield Printing Company, Springfield, 1883), 28; Inter-State Publishing, *History of Sangamon County Illinois*, 582; *Illinois State Journal*, August 15, 1859.

4. Chapman and Company, *History of Tazewell County, Illinois* (Chapman and Company, Chicago 1879) 206–7.

5. Iles, *Sketches of Early Life in Kentucky, Missouri, and Illinois*, 31; Inter-State Publishing, *History of Sangamon County Illinois*, 514; *Illinois State Journal* August, 15, 1859.

6. Paul Angle, *Here I Have Lived: A History of Lincoln's Springfield* (Abraham Lincoln Bookshop, Petersburg, Illinois, 1971), 11.

7. Mazrim, *"Now Quite Out of Society,"* 25–28, Malcolm Rohrbough, *The Land Office Business* (Oxford Press, New York, 1968).

8. Angle, *Here I Have Lived: A History of Lincoln's Springfield*, 12n.

9. Cartwright, *Autobiography of Peter Cartwright*, 246.

10. *Edwardsville Spectator*, February 22, 1825.

11. *Sangamo Journal*, April 27, 1933.

12. *Sangamo Journal*, September 28, 1833.

13. Farnham, *Life in Prairie Land*, 92.

14. The artifact assemblages associated with three additional store sites were com-

pared to the Iles assemblage. These include Area CC at the New Salem Site in Menard County (1829–32); the Davenport House at Rock Island (1818–34); and lots 25 and 32 at Hutsonville, Illinois (ca. 1832–49). Mazrim and Naglich, *Archaeological Investigations of Two "Forgotten" Households at Lincoln's New Salem State Historic Site;* Naglich and Cramer, *Davenport House Site: 2003 Archaeological Investigations;* Robert Mazrim, *Ceramics and Glass from the Davenport Site* (manuscript on file at Sangamo Archaeological Center 2005), Robert Mazrim, *Keeping Accounts: Archaeology and Retail Activity at the Town of Hutsonville, Illinois 1832–1849* (report submitted to the Illinois Transportation Archaeological Research Center, Urbana, 1999). Each site functioned both as a dry goods store as well as a residence for its proprietor.

15. Mazrim, *"Now Quite Out of Society,"* 256–62; Robert Mazrim, *Bladeless Knives Without Handles: A Plea for Definition of Terms and Quantification of Data Sets in Historical Archaeology in Illinois,* paper presented at the Society for Historical Archaeology 37th Annual Conference on Historical and Underwater Archaeology, St. Louis, Missouri 2004.

16. Dr. Terrence Martin of the Illinois State Museum examined the animal remains from the Iles Store site.

Chapter 13

1. Inter-State Publishing, *History of Sangamon County Illinois,* 914.

2. Extensive archival research into the Broadwell family's many activities and land holdings was also conducted by Sangamon State University students and staff during the 1980s as part of the background research for the Clayville interpretive center. Most of this material was never published.

3. Tarbell, *The Early Life of Abraham Lincoln* (S.S. McClure, New York 1895), 104.

4. Farnham, *Life in Prairie Land.*

5. Tillson, *A Woman's Story of Pioneer Illinois,* 26.

6. Recently, some unusual white clay stub stemmed pipes have been recovered from 1830s–40s contexts in Illinois. The origin of these pipes is unknown. See Mazrim, *The Hinsey Site in Tazewell County* (Sangamo Archaeological Center, Elkhart 2003).

7. The earliest date of pipe making in the Point Pleasant community is poorly understood, and is based solely on changes in property ownership, as opposed to well-dated archaeological contexts or more specific genealogical information. While the distinctive Point Pleasant motifs are generally thought to postdate 1838, a few have been recovered from pre-1840 assemblages in Illinois, suggesting that they were being manufactured by the mid-1830s. See B. B. Thomas and Richard Burnett, "A Study of Clay Smoking Pipes Produced at a Nineteenth Century Kiln at Point Pleasant, Ohio," *The Conference on Historic Site Archaeology Papers 1971* 6 (1972): 1–31. James Murphy, "Clay Tobacco Pipes from the Tom Peterson Site, Clermont County, Ohio," *Proceedings of the Symposium on Ohio Valley Urban and Historic Archaeology* (University of Louisville, Louisville Kentucky), 3:61–71.

8. Sangamon County Court Records, Moses Broadwell.

9. The property was sold to a private owner in the early 1990s.

10. Broadwell family papers, Abraham Lincoln Presidential Library manuscript collection, Springfield.
11. Broadwell family papers, Abraham Lincoln Presidential Library manuscript collection, Springfield.
12. Eugene Gross, "A Sketch of Springfield," *Springfield City Directory and Business Mirror for 1866* (Bronson and Nixon, Springfield 1866).

Chapter 14

1. Faux, *Memorable Days in America,* 137.
2. Mazrim, *"Now Quite Out of Society,"* 211.
3. McWhiney, *Cracker Culture: Celtic Ways in the Old South,* 233.
4. Mark Wagner and Mary McCorvie, *The Archaeology of the Old Landmark: Nineteenth Century Taverns Along the St. Louis—Vincennes Trace in Southern Illinois* (Center for American Archeology, Kampsville, Illinois, 1992).
5. John Burrison, "Alkaline-Glazed Stoneware: A Deep South Pottery Tradition," *Southern Folklore Quarterly* 39 (1975): 377–403.
6. As this book goes to press, the author has identified what is believed to be the site of William Holland's ca. 1819–22 blacksmith shop, at Indian Point in Menard County. Holland was appointed by the United States government to serve as blacksmith for the Kickapoo tribe, then residing in the prairies to the northeast. Perhaps not coincidentally, the site lies due west of Elkhart on what was the northern periphery of the Sangamo Country in 1819, and very near the line patrolled by rangers seven years earlier. Initial testing indicates that the site is largely intact, and promises to yield a significant sample of blacksmithing debris from the early years of settlement in the region.
7. Power, *History of Early Settlers of Sangamon County Illinois,* 627.
8. *Sangamo Journal,* December 29, 1831, 3.
9. Farnham, *Life in Prairie Land,* 92.
10. Inter-State Publishing, *History of Sangamon County Illinois,* 49.
11. Clark was issued a tavern license to sell liquor by the serving at the store building. There is no evidence that he operated a traditional tavern that offered room and board.
12. George Miller, "Origins of Josiah Wedgwood's 'Pearlware,'" *Northeast Historical Archaeology* 16 (1987): 83–95; George Miller, "A User's Guide to Ceramic Assemblages, Part Four," *Council for Northeast Historical Archaeology Newsletter* 26 (1993).
13. Noel-Hume, *Guide to Colonial Artifacts of North America,* 129.
14. No broad painted blue motifs are present in the refined assemblage from Fort Massac (in southern Illinois), which was abandoned in 1814, suggesting that they may not have appeared in any quantity until after the war (John Walthall, *Minimum Vessel Count for Refined Earthenwares at Fort Massac: American Component 1794–1814,* manuscript on file, Sangamo Archaeological Center, Elkhart, 1996).
15. Only a portion of the cellar was excavated—the rest was left in preservation.
16. Mazrim, *"Now Quite Out of Society,"* 280.
17. The wares from the Athens kiln are poorly understood, but those found in nearby late 1830s and 1840s domestic contexts are coated in a heavy, usually

underfired manganese glaze, resulting in a metallic-brown surface finish. The later products from that pottery also appear to have often suffered from a poor "fit" between the clay body of the vessels and the slip glazes applied to their surfaces. Fragments found archaeologically are often missing their exterior surfaces, or are very friable.

Chapter 15

1. This does not include the failed plat of Centerville along the Sangamon River northeast of Springfield. There is no evidence that this town site was actually improved.
2. There is new evidence that Lincoln somehow acquired a partial ownership in the property on which Offutt's store was located, and that a building stood on this property at least as late as 1835. See Thomas Schwartz, "Find the Missing Link: A Promissory Note and the Lost Town of Pappsville," Bulletin of the 55th Meeting of the Lincoln Fellowship of Wisconsin, *Historical Bulletin*, no. 51 (1995); Robert Mazrim, *Magnificent Storehouses and Forgotten Lot Lines* (Sangamo Archaeological Center, Elkhart 2005).
3. Springfield did not become the state capital until 1839.
4. For instance, Henry Onstot's log home was moved to Petersburg, and was ultimately surrounded by later nineteenth-century frame additions. Portions of the original log walls, which once stood on Salem Hill, are still intact inside the house.
5. Ida Bale, "New Salem as I Knew It" (manuscript, on file at Illinois Historic Preservation Agency, Springfield, 1944).
6. R. D. Miller, *Past and Present of Menard County, Illinois* (S. J. Clarke, Chicago, 1905), 18.
7. T. G. Onstot, *Pioneers of Menard and Mason Counties* (Forest City, Illinois, 1902), 81.
8. Josephine Chandler, "New Salem: Early Chapter in Lincoln's Life," *Journal of the Illinois State Historical society* 22, 4 (1930): 501–58.
9. Joseph Booton briefly summarized his archaeological work in his *Record of Restoration of New Salem* (State of Illinois, Springfield, 1948). Hagan's 1948 season was the subject of a brief, unpublished summary. In 1979, Melinda Kwedar assembled some of this material for an unpublished historical summary of the New Salem properties. See Kwedar, *A Comparative Analysis of Land Ownership, Archaeology and Structures* (report submitted to Illinois Department of Conservation, Springfield, 1979).
10. Robert Mazrim, *Abandoned Cellars and Community Memory: An Examination of the Archaeology and Interpretations of the New Salem Site* (report submitted to the Illinois Historic Preservation Agency, Springfield, 1995); Mazrim and Dennis Naglich, *Archaeological Investigations of Two "Forgotten" Households at Lincoln's New Salem State Historic Site* (report submitted to the Illinois Historic Preservation Agency, Springfield, 1996); Mazrim and Naglich, *Further Archaeological Investigations at Lincoln's New Salem State Historic Site: Evidence for the First Joshua Miller Residence and Blacksmith Shop* (report submitted to the Illinois Historic Preservation Agency, Springfield, 1996); Mazrim and Naglich, *New Salem's Lost Tavern: Archaeological Investigations on Lot 5 South First Survey, at*

Lincoln's New Salem State Historic Site (report submitted to the Illinois Historic Preservation Agency, Springfield, 1998); Mazrim, *Magnificent Storehouses and Forgotten Lot Lines* (Sangamo Archaeological Center, Elkhart 2005).

11. For a modern overview of the reconstruction of the historic village and its social and political contexts, see Richard Taylor and Mark Johnson, "The Spirit of the Place: Origins of the Movement to Reconstruct Lincoln's New Salem," *Journal of Illinois History* 7, 4 (2004): 174–200, and "A Fragile Illusion: The reconstruction of Lincoln's New Salem" *Journal of Illinois History* 7, 4 (2004): 254–80.

12. *Illinois Tourist Guide* (Illinois Chamber of Commerce, 1932).

13. Mazrim, *Abandoned Cellars and Community Memory*, 16–24.

14. Hagen also addressed the problem of the western half of the resurvey, which he basically solved by identifying the actual archaeological signature of Main Street, well to the south of the replica street. His findings were not incorporated into the reconstructed village.

15. Joseph Booton, transcribed interview with Thomas Reep (manuscript on file Illinois Historic Preservation Agency, Springfield, 1934).

16. Half of feature was left in preservation.

17. John Allen, *Legends and Lore of Southern Illinois* (Southern Illinois University, Carbondale, 1963), 160.

18. George McKearin and Helen McKearin, *American Glass* (Crown Publishers, New York, 1948), 495.

19. Mazrim and Naglich, *Further Archaeological Investigations at Lincoln's New Salem State Historic Site*, 43–44.

20. Ida Tarbell, *The Early Life of Abraham Lincoln* (S.S. McClure, New York 1895), 175.

21. Letter from John McNamar to William Herndon in Wilson and Davis, *Herndon's Informants* (University of Illinois Press, Urbana, 1998), 258–59.

Chapter 16

1. The house site may have been damaged by erosion at Area BB, or may have been located in a forested area not tested in 1995.

2. These are the dimensions of the feature at the first point of definition.

3. David Donald, *Lincoln* (Simon and Schuster, New York, 1995), 50.

4. Dr. Terrance Martin of the Illinois State Museum analyzed the faunal remains from our work at New Salem.

5. Mazrim, *"Now Quite Out of Society,"* 221–23.

6. Evidence of at least one prehistoric burial mound can be seen in the tree-covered bluffcrest over looking the replica sawmill.

7. Onstot, *Pioneers of Menard and Mason Counties*, 150; Benjamin Thomas, *Lincoln's New Salem* (Southern Illinois University Press, Carbondale, 1954), 20–21.

8. Bale "New Salem as I Knew It," 29, Joseph Booton, *Record of the Reconstruction of New Salem* (State of Illinois, Springfield, 1934), 63.

9. In 1995, our crew conducted salvage excavations in front of the replica tavern in advance of construction of a wheelchair ramp. The midden found on the site reflected an occupation that extended until at least 1850.

10. Brink & Company, *Illustrated Atlas Map of Menard County Illinois* (Philadelphia 1874), 15.
11. Joseph Booton, "New Salem Restoration Involved Many Problems," *Illinois Public Works* (Summer 1946): 10.
12. Booton, *Record of the Reconstruction of New Salem.* Transcribed interview with Thomas Reep.
13. Booton, "New Salem Restoration Involved Many Problems," 10.

Chapter 17

1. *Peoria Journal Transcript*, May 7, 1933, 7.
2. Percival Rennick, "The Peoria and Galena Trail and Coach Road and the Peoria Neighborhood," *Journal of the Illinois State Historical Society* 27 (1935): 351–63.
3. The 2001 excavations were conducted by the Illinois Transportation Archaeological Research Program under the supervision of the author and David Nolan. See Robert Mazrim, *New Light on the Old French Village of Peoria* (Sangamo Archaeological Center, Elkhart 2002).
4. Inter-State Publishing, *History of Sangamon County Illinois*, 192.

Index